°Climate
# Design

Design and planning
for the age of climate change

ORO editions

# Contents

Foreword

# Design and planning for the age of climate change: context and assumptions

Peter Droege

This book brings together powerful new practices and innovative thinking in urban planning and landscape design, soils and water engineering, energy and transport infrastructure, and socio-economic change. These disciplines are transformed and merge at a rapid pace, interacting and converging. The process is driven by two major energy challenges at the very foundation of the world we have created. One is global warming: three-quarters of the climate destabilising carbon waste dispatched by humans into the atmosphere are generated through the burning of coal, gas and oil, and the use of cement; the remainder is released by agriculture, the management of soils, and disturbance of the global forest cover. A simultaneous challenge is delivered by mounting fossil fuel supply risks: the feared oil peak is likely to be already with us. The related financial upheaval of recent years added to the urgency to rethink unsustainable development practices—and the response has been swift. Speculative, short-term thinking is giving way to a far sharper focus on enduring investment assets: those capable of securing, not undermining the resilience of place, community, and regions. Enlightened government policy and future-minded private investment alike support this momentous shift.

Uninformed planning and urban design choices contribute to the climate conundrum in direct ways: primarily through inefficiency and dependence on fossil fuel. Given this energy source and current building, use, and management practices, 40 to 50 per cent of emissions are typically attributed to the build environment. Poor design results in monocultural, non-productive parks, excessive asphalt surfaces, and generally low albedo levels on hard surfaces: the preponderance of dark colours in warm climates traps heat and builds up local temperatures. Uninformed water use, lack of efficiency, and wasteful urban systems raises the energy demand for pumping alone.

Low-quality, speculative projects quickly fail in economic downturns and can even contribute to the erosion of social stability. Buildings and urban areas that are not free of fossil energy content in their making nor entirely powered by renewable sources, developments that reinforce unsustainable consumption habits, and settlements encroaching on forests, wetlands, grasslands, or fragile dunal landscapes carry the greatest threat since they directly add to resource depletion and climate destabilisation.

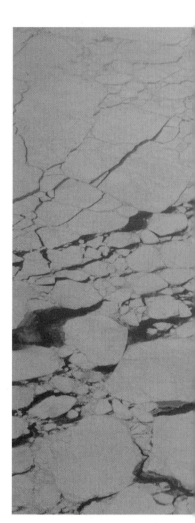

Poor design results in monocultural, non-productive parks, excessive asphalt surfaces, and generally low albedo levels on hard surfaces...

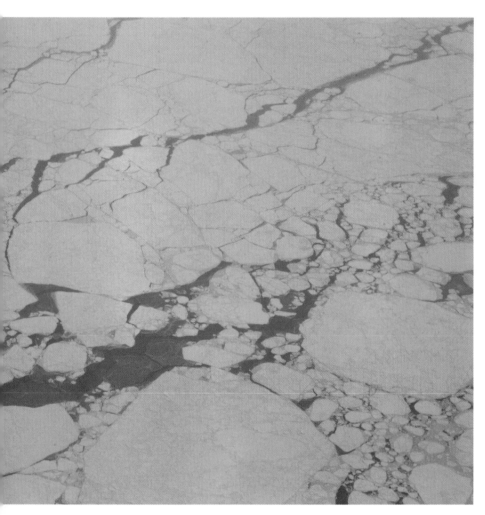

Concentrations of global warming inducing gases are now a full third *above* historically sustainable levels of 280 parts of carbon dioxide gas per million of atmospheric volume (ppm). Concentrations are projected to reach 390 ppm in 2009 to 2010, rising nearly two per cent annually. Many engaged in international climate negotiations still describe 450 or even 550 ppm $CO_2$ as 'safe'. Yet planetary systems already approach out-of-control status at 380 ppm and at the comparably small 0.7 degree temperature rise that was experienced in the twentieth century. The rising acidification of carbon-flush, warming oceans, and their reduced capacity to absorb airborne $CO_2$ at this seemingly early stage create a more profound threat than even sea level rises. Sane voices call therefore for a lowering to 350 ppm (Hansen 2008)—or, better yet, to 280 ppm. This can be a very long-term aim at best, and yet, in order for it to have any chance of being ever achieved, requires immediate action.

The measures most capable of lowering emissions also limit the exposure of the world economy to non-renewable production capacity declines. A staggering 88 per cent of world primary (commercial) energy consumption was of fossil fuel in 2003, with 95 per cent of all motorised transport on road, rail, sea, and in the air depending on oil (BP 2004, Lenzen et al 2003). Global oil production capacity is most likely to have peaked in 2006, precipitating a global decline of three per cent or more from here on (Schindler and Zittel 2007). A steeply rising global energy demand curve requires bold substitution action in efficiency, demand management, and the rapid phasing in of renewable energy.

To attempt a serious shift towards biosphere stability, greenhouse active gas has to be removed from the atmosphere and sequestered. A great agricultural transformation, an entirely fresh look at biomass management, and, at the very least, a global forest and wetland regeneration campaign are needed, going far beyond what is being pursued today. How to achieve this in a fractioned, resource depleting, under-regulated world is the challenge of this time. Some pin their hopes on a perfect, if elusive, carbon trade regime; some bank on enlightened self-interest or local regulations; others wait for global agreements on tackling the root causes of deforestation. Whatever paths are ultimately chosen and successful, it requires a fundamental rethinking of land planning and management professions, and their foci and methods.

While United Nations Framework Convention on Climate Change thinking holds that a global agreement must be reached before reasonable action is likely to occur, the evidence does not support this, giving rise to great hope. This book shows a dramatic shift across a wide range of professional fields, intelligently and swiftly responding to the global emergency. The professions sense, amplify, and respond to demand from private and public clients who are mindful of a dramatic demand for fossil fuel substitution, land and water body regeneration, primary resource reuse, and a host of other measures, collectively approaching intelligent, practical approaches to geo-design.

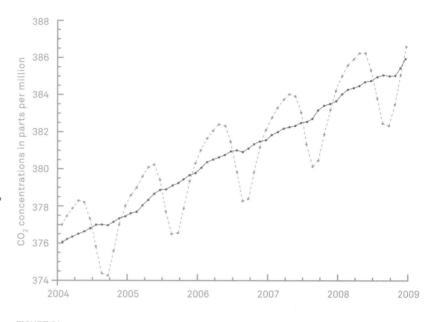

**FIGURE 01**

Steady march into oblivion or landmark triggering change? Global monthly mean $CO_2$ concentration to February 2009, measured by the National Oceanic & Atmospheric Administration (2009). The green line indicates the monthly mean values of atmospheric $CO_2$ concentrations, centred on the middle of each month.

A great agricultural transformation, an entirely fresh look at biomass management, and, at the very least, a global forest and wetland regeneration campaign are needed, going far beyond what is being pursued today.

The water sensitive projects in this book are but one example for this principle. These are not simply means of responding to changing water regimes. They also serve to lower the carbon intensity of the host economies and cities and battle climate change: healthy wetlands and water bodies are powerful $CO_2$ sinks. Water efficiency and sensitivity can be an even more effective greenhouse gas abatement tool than changing light bulbs and other energy saving efforts. From China westward to California, countries increasingly face the prospect of 'peak water' (WWI 2009). One fifth of California's electricity is used for the pumping, storing, and treatment of water and in some cities the relative figure becomes half. And throughout much of the twentieth century about half the country's freshwater uptake in the United States has served the cooling of coal-, oil- and uranium-fired power plants (Gleick 1994).

This book is filled with living projects by a wide range of professionals and their personal readings, beliefs, and experiences. It carries the styles and characteristics of its contributors and we are proud to present them in their personal diversity. The book is also testimony to a fundamental realisation: comprehensively conceived, integrated projects carry the day. The designs and programs in this volume do not make a false distinction between adaptation efforts and mitigation practice. They testify to the fact that the best form of adaptation is to mitigate—and that the very best efforts indeed deliver both greater resilience in responding to change and a firm and fundamental determination to eliminate fossil fuel combustion and help absorb more carbon from the air. Adaptation efforts, while critical, will not suffice alone.

This rich source book for ideas and practice delivers an urgent call to global, national, state, and local governments and to all investors and clients to focus on the enduring, constructive transformation of energy and transport infrastructures and on making our urban and rural support systems climate-stable and renewable source-based, strengthening global prospects. It is time to concentrate both investment and imagination on building on the finest traditions of urban planning, landscape architecture, land and water resource management, and infrastructure development. Above all, this is also a challenge of lifestyle transformations, supported by well-conceived environments (Lenzen 2008). The physical planning and design profession has a great role in enabling individual choices that shrink our collective carbon footprint to a negative size and eliminate the scourge of non-renewable energy dependency.

# The emerging direction

# Revolution of practice

## Joe Brown

Ancient civilisations had no doubt that natural forces held sway over the lives of humans. Early societies lived in close rhythm with the ebb and flow of the natural world, knowing they would face nature's ferocity if they dared cross it. Only in modern times, when we had steered rivers, levelled wilderness, moved mountains, and erected vast cities, did it become possible to believe that we alone designed our destiny. The twentieth century saw such feats of science and technology—splitting the atom, walking on the moon—as to make us believe that any increase of the dominion of human will was positive progress.

Fifty years ago, a few thinkers knew this was not the case. Witnessing the wanton attitude with which twentieth century society consumed land and resources, they foresaw a time of reckoning. In 1960, Garrett Eckbo warned, 'the most important issue that faces all landscape architects, environmental planners, and designers in the twenty-first century will be precisely the integration, perhaps by shotgun, of current economic and political thinking with ecological reality'.

Fifty years later, we need look no further than a devastated New Orleans to know that we have not conquered nature. It would no longer be sufficient to heed the warnings of Eckbo and others; the time when we might have averted climate consequences has passed. We now face a world thrown out of balance by our actions. Sprawling development consumes land, energy, and water at unsustainable rates. Buildings and cars spew carbon into the atmosphere. Open space and biodiversity dwindle before the onslaught. Temperatures and sea levels rise. In the first decade of the twenty-first century, we have begun to see the violent consequences of our disregard, as the sea begins to devastate coastal cities without warning.

**Sprawling development consumes land, energy, and water at unsustainable rates. Buildings and cars spew carbon into the atmosphere.**

The climate crisis stems from a crisis in our built environments, which are suffering from a lack of holistic thinking. Many perspectives shape the built environment, but all too often, each one looks to its own goals and methods; the collective system is the focus of no one. The only way we can make a real difference in our impact on the global environment and climate is through a holistic approach to policy, planning, engineering, and design, wherein all work collaboratively toward the common goal. That goal must be the functional integration of built and natural environments. Built environments should be viewed as the extension of natural environments, allowing natural systems to function and working with these systems in high-performance buildings and landscapes. At the same time, we must not lose sight of our goals of economic productivity and social equity.

Infrastructure refers to the technical solutions that aid the flow and movement of society, granting water, energy, and mobility to large populations. When we think of infrastructure, we think of roads, bridges, transit lines, airports, power lines, and wastewater systems. We think of hard, built things—the things we can thank for the lifestyle to which we are accustomed. We have great respect for this realm. Nature is an afterthought by comparison. We might rather gaze upon a forest than a maze of power lines, but we know what the power lines grant us. We don't quite know what the forest is doing for us.

But we should—because we know that long before we conceived electrical grids, life on Earth was drawing all of its power from the light of the sun. Long before we built wastewater systems, the natural hydrological cycle was functioning. Every moment, we breathe oxygen that is produced by trees. Nature works. It can work with us, and it can work for us, as long as we make room for it and design built systems that cooperate with it. It's time to think of natural systems as green infrastructure.

A hundred years ago, when we decided to develop a tract of land that included a creek, we would have taken pride in our ability to encase that creek in pipes, bury them, and build on top of it. It's time for a new kind of pride—in our ability to think functionally about natural features and creatively about their incorporation within built environments. A creek running through the midst of a city is a sought-after experience for people; it's a habitat for species, and it's green infrastructure.

Not only must we design a future in which our built environments are not at odds with nature: we must introduce immediate interventions that protect our cities from the consequences we have already incurred. As Victor Olgyay wrote in 1963, creatures must, if they cannot physiologically adapt to changes in the natural environment, prepare what defence they can. In some cases this will mean built structures that will resist the sea. In most cases this will mean new planning strategies that regenerate our settlements so they are not in contention with changing natural forces.

**The only way we can make a real difference in our impact on the global environment and climate is through a holistic approach to policy, planning, engineering, and design, wherein all work collaboratively toward the common goal.**

Climate infrastructure will be the systems that enable this regeneration. Imagine a waterfront park. It is a place for people, a place of attractions, a place of economic activity, as well as social inclusion and cohesion. It includes wetlands and naturally processes water. It includes solar panels and harnesses energy. It is highly walkable and encourages a healthy, zero-carbon lifestyle. And at the same time, its design features double as defences against a rising sea level.

Something as complex as climate infrastructure—integrated systems that deliver a variety of functions while having a net positive effect on our environmental footprint—requires an interdisciplinary approach. Environmental and ecological professionals must determine performance targets; planners must form a strategy for meeting those targets while meeting the demands of conventional infrastructure; and designers must realise this strategy in built form, knitting it within social fabric.

These types of interventions require more than crossing the boundaries of disciplines. We must also cross the boundary of public and private, and we must cross boundaries between agencies. Government must learn to address all of the issues that intersect in the land and community in a manner that promotes holistic solutions. The design and planning profession has the responsibility to raise awareness of this need and demonstrate ideas that will spur the concerted response that is necessary.

We must accelerate the response. It's time for the most innovative techniques in design, planning, and engineering to come together with forward-thinking policy. Without this paradigm shift, we face a planet that will become unliveable. With this shift, we can create cities that will be organs of environmental equilibrium, mitigators against climate change, and healthy places for people to live.

Our path of progress has led us back to the knowledge we once possessed. As modern humans, armed with the scientific understanding to forge great cities, we stand alongside our ancient ancestors in knowing that our lives are inseparably linked to the oceans, the forests, the skies and stars.

# Principles, concepts, and visions

Professor Peter Droege posed six questions to respected professionals from around the world. Here they respond and share their thoughts on carbon-sensitive design and planning and its role in mitigating and adapting to climate change.

**Professor Peter Droege**, Sydney, is an authority on renewable energy, urban design, development, and infrastructure. He serves as Expert Commissioner on Cities and Climate Change to the World Future Council and as a Steering Committee Member of the Urban Climate Change Research Network, and he is Asia Pacific Chair of the World Council for Renewable Energy.

**Curtis Alling**, Sacramento, is an environmental planner and a recognised authority on US environmental legislation and regulations and an experienced manager of complex environmental impact assessment, climate change policy, and conservation planning programs.

**Christopher Benosky**, New York, specialises in wetland and stream restoration, hydrologic and hydraulic analyses, stormwater management, dam and geotechnical engineering, and construction management. He has been involved in the restoration of more than 10,000 acres of wetlands throughout the Atlantic coast of North America.

**David Blau**, San Francisco, is an environmental planner and landscape architect who specialises in river corridor and greenway systems and integrating design thinking with ecological restoration principles.

**Claire Bonham-Carter**, San Francisco, has extensive experience in sustainable design and construction and is working on climate action plans for northern Californian cities and sustainability design guidelines for plans ranging in scale from a downtown area in San Francisco to large new communities in Saskatoon, Canada and Santiago, Chile.

**Roger Courtenay**, Alexandria, is a landscape architect whose project experience throughout North America has made for innumerable lessons of place-making, urban design, and landscape architecture that serve people, habitat, and environment.

**Richard W. John**, London, has advised British Government on climate change policy, particularly how to include sustainability and energy efficiency in planning requirements and building regulations.

**Jon Shinkfield**, Melbourne, is a landscape architect and urban designer who focuses on design frameworks for energy generation, consumption reduction, waste minimisation, and the integration of production-based gardens in an urban context.

**Nathalie Ward**, Brisbane, is a landscape architect who strives to create sustainable and meaningful places in her work in the realms of high-density residential design, park design, urban design, infrastructure, site rehabilitation, and visual impact assessment.

The panel

**FROM LEFT TO RIGHT**
Professor Peter Droege, Curtis Alling, Christopher Benosky,
David Blau, Claire Bonham-Carter, Roger Courtenay,
Richard W. John, Jon Shinkfield, Nathalie Ward.

**Claire Bonham-Carter:**
Competition to achieve
environmental goals. In many
ways it's driving the sustainability
agenda in new development:
competition between countries,
states, cities, counties, and towns;
between global companies and
across sectors; and between
schools and colleges. Clients
in our industry are reconsidering
their standard view, redefining
what they see as high performance
as the competition grows even
within the building sector.

**David Blau:** Environmental
sustainability is moving from
just being planning jargon to the
mainstream population. Concerns
over energy, transportation,
and water are now in the forefront
of everyone's mind.

**Richard W. John:** Climate change
and issues of security of energy
supplies, remain at, or near, the
top of government's development
agenda. This important focus has
now filtered through the planning
system, to government agencies
that fund development, and to
developers and their supply chain.

**Nathalie Ward:** It's no longer
acceptable for sustainability
not to be part of the conversation.
The bar has been raised for the
design industry and we need to be
smarter in our thinking to maintain
our competitive edge, with
increasingly creative results.

**Curtis Alling:** Young professionals
and students in college and
high school clearly grasp the
imperative—they will have to live
with climate changes. This bodes
well for continuing the momentum
of progress towards more climate-
friendly planning.

Roger Courtenay: There's an emerging recognition that economic theory must change to address human and environmental sustainability. Ultimately, economic theory and practice, the motors of human activity and initiative, must provide a more viable alternative to the linear growth-dependent economic theories which have brought us to the brink. Theory and practice more aligned with how environmental processes unfold—cyclically, without waste and with great efficiency, and without negative impacts to the system as a whole—will be the basis for building a roadmap to human survival.

Chistopher Benosky: By rethinking traditional hard engineering solutions and using nature as our guide, we are able, in many cases, to provide the same level of service in our designs, while reducing our carbon footprint and helping fight climate change.

David Blau: With the dramatic increase in the price of energy and fuel, people are quickly responding by changing their habits and preferences.

Claire Bonham-Carter: More people are thinking about the environment for the first time or in a new light. If it gets technical words into common parlance, then we are at the beginning of the paradigm shift we need to get people to live in a more climate friendly way.

Chistopher Benosky: We're also seeing a 'back to nature' approach to design and planning. More and more designers and planners are focusing on ecologically-sensitive approaches.

## What's the most hopeful development in design and planning?

Roger Courtenay: Developments in design and planning in the last few years have been more or less technology-based. Larger and much more significant influences shaping the built and physical environment offer the most hope for the future.

Nathalie Ward: It's a positive, renewed trend—looking to the successes of natural systems as the basis for the processes and structures we design into our living environments. Our design solutions must be flexible and able to adapt to the pressures of population growth and climate change, ensuring robustness in the ecological, economic, and social structures of our urban and landscape environments.

Chistopher Benosky: As a profession, we're slowly learning how to use nature in our built environments to not only benefit the local flora and fauna, but also provide a better quality of life for residents and entire communities.

David Blau: More emphasis is being placed on transit-oriented development than ever before, increased densities, walking, or biking to work.

Jon Shinkfield: Creation of carbon-neutral environments is being implemented and tested in the harshest of global climates, such as at MASDAR in Abu Dhabi. The thinking on transport systems, heating and cooling, food and forestry production, and recycling will and have already informed the thinking of many other developments throughout the world. Changes in world climate will see numerous areas of the world dealing with these same extremities.

**Roger Courtenay**: Resistance to change and ignorance are major barriers: the belief that the status quo is always somehow better than 'what might be' and wilful resistance to knowledge-based, rational decision making and maturity. We need worldwide standards of education and democratic process on a thoroughly secular basis to overcome these barriers and to give the changes my colleagues are spelling out any chance of systemic success.

**Chistopher Benosky**: People need to understand the basic causes and detrimental effects climate change will have on their lives and the lives of their children and believe this is a real threat to our way of existence.

**David Blau**: The Hurricane Katrina disaster is comparatively small relative to what may happen to most of Florida or the Central Valley of California with sea-level rise and massive Delta levee failure.

**Chistopher Benosky**: Even if people are aware of the issues, they may not be willing to do anything about it if their personal costs are too high. Economic viability is another major barrier.

**David Blau**: Let's remember that climate change has been happening since the origins of planet Earth. I guess we mean 'serious global warming' when we say 'climate change'. I think the greatest barriers are two-fold: the year-to-year climate variations mask the longer-term urgency, and the sheer magnitude and scale of the problem makes it difficult to comprehend.

**Chistopher Benosky**: The design community is beginning to understand these issues, but I don't believe an overall majority of people consider climate change will affect their lives in the near future.

**Jon Shinkfield**: Prevailing economic conditions are a great obstacle, and this is represented by cheap fossil fuel and low water costs. As fuel prices have increased, we've seen a corresponding and steady growth in bicycle usage in Melbourne: bicycle sales outstripped that of motor vehicles in Melbourne in 2008. If we project this reaction further, we'll be forced to implement dedicated cycle infrastructure, not only reducing carbon uptake but improving the health of our residents. If the price of fuel escalates so transporting fruit and vegetables becomes prohibitive, then people will look to cheaper locally-grown goods they can access without a car: we'll also see a rise in local growing and trading, both formal and informal.

**Jon Shinkfield**: Politically, interdepartmental barriers continue to prevent the flow of carbon reduction initiatives and infrastructure. Where we have a main roads system not solely focussed on traffic flows and congestion, the result will be few immediate, safe, and convenient alternatives to the private car.

**Curtis Alling**: The tremendously strong existing linkage between fossil fuel use and prosperity is deeply embedded in global industry, power generation, and transport. Replacing this linkage with one between renewable sources and prosperity is necessary to achieve long-term greenhouse gas reduction.

**Claire Bonham-Carter**: I agree, take the building sector for example. It's relatively easy to tackle individual new buildings as self contained units through regulating building regulations and energy codes, but we all know a collection of individual sustainable buildings does not necessarily make for a sustainable development.

**Claire Bonham-Carter**: When new development happens piecemeal in a neighbourhood, or adjacent parcels of land are being developed by different companies at different timescales, how do you put in place the costly infrastructure upfront so later development can take advantage of it? This is the challenge for our governments.

**Nathalie Ward**: Lack of leadership at a government policy level is a huge barrier. Leadership is often about making unpopular decisions for the greater good and governments need to lead the way through policy and incentives. New technologies and initiatives often come at a financial price and in a competitive market it is difficult for private entities to take the lead when it may price them out of their market.

## What's the greatest barrier to fighting climate change?

**Claire Bonham-Carter**: The lack of big picture planning and long-range thinking nationally and internationally makes it difficult to project beyond the timescale of standard government tenures. For a really sustainable community or town or city, we need to be thinking on a much larger scale and this requires a huge amount of coordination and visioning between multiple agencies and stakeholders to plan for new transit systems or efficient large scale water and energy infrastructure.

**Richard W. John**: Limited capability exists to calculate true overall carbon emissions from particular development approaches. Politicians, planners, and developers don't necessarily understand the wider sustainability issues or act in a sensible way on what is usually a complex situation.

**Richard W. John**: There are limited experts, supply chain, and product availability to provide the necessary solutions. The requirement for rapid change also means there is a dearth of recognised 'best practice' on how aspects of low-carbon developments actually work in practice.

**Chistopher Benosky**: Our design solutions need to not only be carbon friendly, but economically viable for us to be successful in fighting climate change.

**Jon Shinkfield:** It's been fascinating to watch the advances in thinking in the United Kingdom as a result of aggressive targets and then to capture the flow on effect of that thinking. Without that tool we rely on an enlightened development industry and this clearly is not the solution.

**Jon Shinkfield:** Legislation is the key driver in achieving change. Aggressive rather than passive targets for carbon consumption reduction are required to stimulate thinking, technology, and cost reduction.

**Nathalie Ward:** Advisory panels, task forces, and workshops are successful mechanisms to bring key thinkers together to tackle issues across professional boundaries.

**Roger Courtenay:** Commitment to change is a rite of personal self realisation and self actualisation. Professionals need to realise that just building sustainably isn't enough. Personal responsibility for a sustainable globe starts at home and flows from there into all facets of daily life.

**Richard W. John:** We also need to embrace a rapid learning curve on the wide range of solutions becoming available.

**Richard W. John:** Greater links between universities, professionals, and policy makers would cut short the process. Universities can support the profession by adapting to provide the new skill sets needed and through researching new ideas and technologies.

## What needs to change in your profession to achieve necessary change?

**Richard W. John:** We need to act as advocates for low-carbon and climate-adaptive development, as well as meeting minimum standards.

**Nathalie Ward:** Designers need access to the policy makers to help inform decision making. There are some great examples of innovative outcomes through government involvement of professionals and academics in tackling key problems.

**David Blau:** We need to be much more outspoken on the topic and to always link economic progress with environmental quality and make sure our clients realise the two are inseparable. We should hold our clients accountable for sound environmental planning and use of sustainable principles.

**Curtis Alling:** We need to create early successes in defining comprehensive solutions that accomplish environmental and economic goals, demonstrate how quality of life can be maintained, and then broadcast these achievements to demonstrate their possibility.

**David Blau:** More analytical tools would help us demonstrate the potential effects of global climate change. Most models are regional in nature and don't scale down well to individual watersheds or communities.

**Chistopher Benosky:** Education for design professionals is essential. At this point in time I don't believe typical engineers, architects, and planners in our profession have a comprehensive enough understanding of climate change issues and the best design solutions.

Jon Shinkfield: Regardless of prevailing global economic conditions, it's imperative we have agreed and legislated global carbon targets. This will spawn new products, technology, and monitoring and management programs. As advancement breeds new advancement, a developed industry in carbon reduction technology will be firmly established.

Richard W. John: More widely accepted mechanisms would help evaluate and advance low-carbon and climate-adaptive development approaches at all scales.

Claire Bonham-Carter: There needs to be an understanding that we have to change the way we do things, even if it is easier and cheaper to carry on in the same old way. It can be hard to do this, when our clients believe their projects are already sustainable, or are simply not yet persuaded either of the existence or the urgency of climate change. We need everyone to consider the most sustainable solution as the only solution for their project— even if they don't happen to have the sustainability consultant on their team.

Nathalie Ward: A shift is needed to put the global good before that of the individual entity, which will require strong leadership from government and corporate organisations, as well as strategic partnerships.

Curtis Alling: We need to vigorously require environmental expertise and thinking be infused into all planning and development projects, to discover and maximise every opportunity to respond to the challenges of climate change. Environment, planning, and design professionals, working together, must lead the way.

Jon Shinkfield: Are we satisfied that our urban stormwater, laden with suspended solids (many toxic) and with high levels of nitrogen, is disposed of directly into our urban streams and rivers and the ecosystem associated with those streams is all but completely wiped out? Can we think of a new paradigm where we understand the dynamics of consumption, depletion, renewal, and restoration? The severity of climate change, not the concept but the reality, is helping us to achieve this view, albeit too late!

## What's the most important change to accomplish in the next few years?

Nathalie Ward: A willingness to invest in and test new methodologies and technologies is necessary. This requires methods of project procurement and delivery that encourage innovation over 'safe' or budget driven outcomes. Our profession has the opportunity to lead the way in terms of new thinking and design forms that respond to the need for change.

Claire Bonham-Carter: We need to be willing to suggest to clients new solutions and approaches that might differ to their standard. Saying the client didn't ask for it should no longer be an acceptable excuse.

Chistopher Benosky: Education is needed within our profession, as well as education of the public and our clients on how to approach design projects in the context of global climate change.

Claire Bonham-Carter: There needs to be a stronger element of practical sustainable design skills taught in schools and universities, so basic concepts of functionality and sustainability are the standard foundations of any new design, not aesthetics.

Roger Courtenay: The most important change will involve commitment to and development of standards that work towards 'net negative growth' (where new endeavours are offset by a net reduction in overall footprint) and population control, and their weaving into the infrastructure of everyday life, including design and planning. How will we best plan and design for a future in which the demographics of the globe will be significantly altered?

Claire Bonham-Carter: Whoever said, 'the requirement for mechanical services is a failure of architecture' highlighted the need for architects and engineers to work together from early concept stages of a design to minimise mechanical heating or cooling services. Similarly, landscape architects who have not consulted water sensitive design or ecological water engineers during their layout and design and before selecting their plant palette is unlikely to be delivering a sustainable solution to their client. These connections between different experts need to be made early and made often to get a low impact solution designed and delivered.

**David Blau:** Let me give a specific client example. The largest water provider in Northern California, serving nearly 1.5 million people, commissioned us to prepare their long-range water supply plan out to year 2040. Their water supply originates in the Californian Sierra over 100 miles away and is a snow-fed watershed. We were asked to look at all the modelling that has been done by the state on reductions in Sierra snowpack, earlier spring runoff, changes in flood hydrology, and the like and predict how this might affect planning for 2040. Supply is likely to be diminished while demand will increase due to longer, hotter summers when peak demand occurs—a double whammy. Our sensitivity analysis convinced the client that a robust and flexible solution was called for. This would not have been the approach even two years ago, but is now the prudent way to plan for future unknowns.

**Claire Bonham-Carter:** For years, practitioners in the sustainable design and construction field have relied on sustainable building competitions or a particularly interested client or a sponsored project to allow them to practice their skills. With the policy competition now hotting up, we now get the opportunity more often; indeed, increasingly companies are more likely to be asked to demonstrate their track record in sustainability in order to get the plum job.

**Jon Shinkfield:** They're sympathetic to environmental issues, but only as legislation tightens. Without legislation requirements, and because higher environmental benefit most often comes at higher cost, clients often opt for the less expensive alternative, which is generally the least environmentally acceptable.

**Claire Bonham-Carter:** Clients react to the market. The market reacts to legislation and trends. There is growing evidence that people would like to walk down the street to buy essentials rather than get in their car; that companies would like to operate out of buildings with some sort of environmental rating; that green office buildings are achieving rental premiums.

**Claire Bonham-Carter:** I've heard increasingly from colleagues across the industry about clients coming back to their design team, well down the project timescale, to ask retrospectively if they can go for LEED certification, having firmly ruled it out before. It's a wise design team that goes ahead and designs the most sustainable project they can even if their client has shown initial reluctance.

## How have client attitudes changed?

**Richard W. John:** In the United Kingdom, client attitudes have changed hugely, in response to shifts in environmental policy and public awareness.

**Chistopher Benosky:** In the United States, more clients are seeing the value of carbon friendly projects and as the public becomes educated and aware, demand will increase as well.

**Nathalie Ward:** In Australia, our clients are increasingly sophisticated in their understanding of the need to respond to the impacts of climate change; their own clients and markets are demanding that of them.

**Nathalie Ward:** New thinking and technologies could be sold to clients on the basis of reputation building, marketing edge, or financial return; ultimately the best results can only be achieved through a strong partnership.

**Curtis Alling:** Green projects are gaining the advantage in attracting marketplace appeal and financing for development. This trend is pushing even the more reluctant clients. Forward-looking developers have asked for help to re-plan already approved projects to respond to the new regulatory context or green-priority financing.

**Roger Courtenay:** Sustainability is becoming ingrained and the outlook there is good. The larger idea of change in valuation and the growth curve have not arrived anywhere near consciousness in most clients, public and private. On the other hand one can sense, around the edges perhaps, the tiniest smell of fear—fear that the status quo may become untethered, and new metrics and new bases for decision-making are flowing in (and are necessary) as a result of environmental awareness.

Chistopher Benosky: It's refocused my professional life. For most of my professional engineering career I've focused on ecological restoration, stormwater management, and flood control. In the past, however, ecological restoration was done for impact mitigations, stormwater management was focused on efficiently transporting water off a site, and flood control meant simply creating barriers to protect our built environment. These issues are now looked at as ways to combat global climate change.

David Blau: I'm enjoying the fact that more people are finally getting it. I like to work with progressive, enlightened clients and seek them out. I cycle between being very depressed by the topic (several environmental groups have calculated that we need between two and three Planet Earths to sustain the current world population) to being very charged up about the challenge. I try to stay in the latter mode.

Curtis Alling: The topic of climate change is the most quickly emerging and evolving environmental issue I've experienced in my 30-year career. Never before has thought leadership been more crucial to our profession. I've devoted considerable energy to advancing the dialogue among clients, colleagues, and peers.

Nathalie Ward: I'm seeking to influence real decisions that shape the way people live and interface with the environment.

Roger Courtenay: I'm concerned that many professionals believe we can continue the status quo just by building sustainably —that no other aspects of life need change. I'm trying to move my practice away from building all but the most necessary, most precious, and most defensible kinds of projects. I search—so far not so successfully—for projects that achieve permanent net reduction in the human footprint.

## How's climate change altering your outlook on your professional life?

Claire Bonham-Carter: It hasn't necessarily changed my outlook, just made it easier to practice what I have believed for many years. The growing evidence of climate change in our daily lives just makes my professional ambitions all the more urgent. It also makes it more competitive and more interesting. Sustainability is no longer the niche market it once was; every company is trying to establish expertise in how to tackle climate change. This makes it harder to keep or gain a reputation. Competition again, driving us forward.

Richard W. John: Climate change has become one of the major issues affecting development, so I've seen a huge growth in work on low-carbon and climate-adaptive developments. And we are considering a range of approaches and technologies once thought of as inappropriate or unacceptable, such as using small scale water treatment schemes to reduce overall energy use.

Jon Shinkfield: I'm acting to save what's being lost: not because of impending global doom, but because we need the balance of our ecological systems to live well and to be healthy.

Chistopher Benosky: We have an obligation and duty to educate the public and our clients and develop design solutions that help offset the effects of climate change. We no longer can design a site without thinking of its global implications.

# Flux

## Professor Richard Weller

*Climate change* suggests an anomaly, but the climate has never *not* been changing. As 'the weeping philosopher' Heraclitus (ca. 535–475 BC) famously said, 'all is flux'. The contemporary paradigm of chaos (the mapping of states far from equilibrium) confirms this notion. Chaos theory explains that nature works by way of constant flux because there is a fundamental asymmetry written into the fabric of the universe. It is this gap between the two forces of stability and instability (order and disorder) that begets life. Too much of either is deadly. The weather—a process seeking balance but never reaching stasis—is but one expression of the flux.

That one particular species, in this case humans, has become ubiquitous across the surface of the Earth and is causally connected to climatic fluctuations is also not anomalous. For two billion years cyanobacteria consumed hydrogen and released oxygen, unwittingly creating the conditions of their own demise: the very conditions we would come much later to enjoy as *fresh air*. Not unlike the cyanobacteria, we have, at least since the industrial revolution, earnestly set about creating the conditions of *our* demise. And from a non-anthropomorphic perspective, perhaps that is now exactly what the Earth needs to rebalance its systems. But history shows humans can survive almost anything: we are, for want of a more ennobling expression, rat-cunning.

Citing the truism that all species, particularly rats, would take over the world if they could, one might condone our ubiquity as the natural course of things. But this is self-ingratiating sophistry. It is also incorrect as such because firstly, a complex, healthy ecosystem generally does not allow any one species to dominate and secondly, because the difference between us and other species that have multiplied to excessive proportions in evolutionary history is that we know the consequences of what we are doing. We know that by excessively exploiting our environment we are making life harder for many of our own kind in the future. We also know that we are extinguishing many other forms of life in the process.

For a species that prides itself on knowledge, our wanton destruction of life's diversity is all the more remarkable because we do it with no idea of the real value, the real meaning of what we are destroying. Ignorance in this instance is not a case of paradisiacal bliss; on the contrary, all the feedback about climate change is telling us we have to change our ways. To truly change we need new values.

Apart from the philosophical and spiritual problems associated with the ecological crisis, the obvious thing to do about climate change when it comes your way is simply move to higher ground, preferably to areas with good soil and predictable rainfall. But this is also problematic.

Because science largely avoids explicitly addressing questions of meaning, we must—if we are to find some values upon which to base our actions—turn to theology or philosophy; sacred and profane sides of the same talisman. Even though the world's main religions must at some point value all life forms as evidence of God's omnipotence, theological interpretations always tend to weigh too conspicuously in humanity's favour. Alternatively, try as it might, philosophy cannot find God (or anything) with any certainty, so it can hardly be expected to confer unique importance upon either humanity or the Earth and then guide us through the ecological crisis. Consequently, despite the fundamental problem of its incompatibility with capitalism, many turn to environmentalism.

In its deeper ecological form, environmentalism believes everything that is alive is important irrespective of (other) human values. Deep ecology argues that we have neither the divine right nor the philosophical luxury of destroying any of evolution's work in progress. But deep ecology's moral veracity in this regard only works when you do not subject it to the very same evolutionary logic that is otherwise its own foundation. For evolution shows that, among other things, life can pick up from any point in time with any old shred of DNA and proceed, randomly, to build extraordinary kingdoms. That life will do this over millennia only to then be periodically decimated and then start all over again is confounding to say the least. Even less helpful is the fact that life will continue to do this for the next four billion years only for the sun to then explode and incinerate everything within reach of that cataclysmic event in our home star's life cycle. And yet, life's absolute determination to keep going in any form whatsoever is also surely testament to the possibility that *it* is, in the cosmological scheme of things, profoundly meaningful.

Apart from the philosophical and spiritual problems associated with the ecological crisis, the obvious thing to do about climate change when it comes your way is simply move to higher ground, preferably to areas with good soil and predictable rainfall. But this is also problematic. Since 10,000 BC when we started making food come to us instead of us going to it, the *raison d'être* of the city has been, and remains, *not* to move. If you play the history of urbanism backwards you see that cities rise and fall with great frequency but they do not move; they have tap roots. Those roots are not only certain resources, but stories.

The fundamental dynamic of cities over time, their catch-22, is that as their populations increase so too does the amount of food and energy they must extract from their peripheral landscape. Unlike the light-footed nomad who ranges across terrain more or less in tune with the landscape's biorhythms, culling and being culled, cities incubate more people than the surroundings can sustain. Only technological innovation and territorial acquisition can then satisfy the city's hunger, not to mention its desires. In order to transcend local environmental limitations the city has rhizomatically flourished into a global network of cities warring and trading to stay alive.

The world's population is now essentially stuck in the mechanics of cities and these systems are cumbersome to change. As *the flux* gathers momentum and forces the issue, cities will stubbornly resist environmental change. Cities with money will reengineer their levels to temporarily resist the flux, but as the waters rise and the deserts grow, the poor of the world-city will become nomadic, again. But things are now different for the nomad: there is no new territory to move into. You can go to the ends of the Earth in the twenty-first century only to find that the world-city has been there before you and already sucked out all its nutrients. Not only that, you will be intruding upon other scavengers, one of the main reason cities started in the first place.

**That one particular species, in this case humans, has become ubiquitous across the surface of the Earth and is causally connected to climatic fluctuations is also not anomalous.**

Not only has the global city no more land to exploit; the advent of climate change also reminds us that we cannot simply engineer the world in a manner that is incongruous with natural processes. This is hubris. Because they are phantasmagorical theatres of human imagination disconnected from and desensitised to local environmental feedback, cities encourage hubris. In spite of paradisiacal taboos, this is also their brilliance. Now, however, it is the chemical composition of the atmosphere, not God, telling us we have unleashed chaos upon the world.

Chaos in this sense is not a new aesthetic order. Chaos means having to desperately move our farms, rebuild our cities, and absorb a global diaspora of millions of environmental refugees. The world-city will, for the first time in its history, now have to adapt to the environmental limitations of the chaotic de-natured world we have created. It also means that we will have to learn how to reconstruct the subtle complexity of ecosystems. The entire metabolism of the city will need to be reimagined and redesigned if we are to evolve it from a machine to an organism; one responsive to conditions of flux. And this need not be couched in terms of deprivation and punishment; rather, this can be a new creative phase in the evolution of the city—a more sophisticated form of eco-engineering than anything before.

Because landscape architecture is right at the interface of how the hardware of the city is reconciled with landscape systems, it would seem to be a profession with an important role to play. However, in a carbon saturated world, much of the actual work landscape architects will be called upon to do will be banal. It will be back to Mesopotamian basics—a landscape architecture of food and water, though this time without the naive poetry of paradise.

If there is to be a great philosophical work of landscape architecture in this century, it will still have to do what all the classics have done. It will have to look to the sky and speak of something more than the agricultural mechanics of survival. But rather than fantasise about perfect geometric orders in the heavens and then simply re-project these ideal forms on to the Earth, a landscape architecture of the twenty-first century will be about reconciling the sky with the ground. This will be a landscape architecture of asymmetrical flux.

Productive places

# Reconnecting living and consumption

## Jon Shinkfield

It is no longer adequate to consider the provision of open space in our cities in the absence of embedded thinking in natural systems and without those systems being part of a cycle for the production of energy, water, and food. We have somehow lost our way in our urban and rural environments, misunderstanding the relationships between living and consumption and our expectation surrounding these two factors. We plunder our resources in search of an artificially constructed aesthetic in the complete absence of a holistic approach to energy and production, and we continue to fail to understand the immediacy of the impact this has on our local, regional, and global ecologies.

Absent is the idea of climate mitigation, water management, reclaimed biodiversity, social engagement and exchange, learning, production, and activation. Too often we settle for space rather than place, for the benign in preference to the productive, and for an aesthetic rather than a core social agenda of engagement, interaction, and carbon consumption reduction. It is rather the consideration of a path toward mitigating the effects of environmental degradation, unstable economies, poorly developed social structure, and unmanageable costs associated with high energy-based upkeep and maintenance and intensive and non-productive irrigation and fertilisation.

**ABOVE**
It is no longer adequate to consider the provision of open space in our cities in the absence of embedded thinking in natural systems and without those systems being part of a cycle for the production of energy, water, and food.

Historically, communities have bought and sold, laboured and produced, and had their being in their trade and trading relationships. Their key was in localised production, trade, and exchange, resulting in a corresponding developed social structure; where there was a need to know a neighbour as part of daily life and sustenance; where spaces were established as a framework for life's gathering, selling, socialising, and communicating. Can we again capture the qualities so lacking in our contemporary urban environments, not just because of the impending issues of climate change but because we need to do this for reasons of true sustainability and survival?

**Too often we settle for space rather than place, for the benign in preference to the productive, and for an aesthetic rather than a core social agenda of engagement, interaction, and carbon consumption reduction.**

I am immediately inspired by the idea of a locally-available productive place where produce can be grown, purchased and exchanged and where the community can chose an alternative to the tasteless, coloured-down food from the supermarket. Where I can take a short walk to peruse what is in season or catch a train for one or two stops to arrive and emerge into a productive, cool, and therapeutic landscape of organic value.

Or where, as an alternative, I can ride my bicycle only a short distance to a place of production, trading, and selling; where power for pumping and production is produced through local photovoltaic arrays; where water is harvested and stormwater treated; where overland flow from production areas is cleansed via wetlands prior to capture and reuse or stormwater discharge; and where native frogs, fish, dragonflies, and tortoises are part of the wetland systems.

Instead, the regularised experience is one where we are confronted with an urban retail centre; a hostile and vacuous urban transit-oriented development; a dense urban environment bereft of anything other than transport orientation, most often completely unrelated to community interaction and exchange.

It would seem we misunderstand and misappropriate the true meaning and opportunity of our public realm. Is it not to be investing personally and publicly in places of re-localisation; where food is produced and sold in-situ; where water systems contribute to a productive landscape of forestry and food; where private space and public spaces are coordinated and available; and where energy is produced and managed as part of the open space network at both block and neighbourhood levels? Can we consider a landscape whose aesthetic is in fact cyclic, based on the systems and timings of the production cycle?

Urban forestry as an essential part of our streetscapes, and particularly our freeway environments, is a viable consideration; where a financial return is achieved on what would otherwise be a cost on cost landscape—cost of installation and cost of management with no return. In the case of roadways, access to and transport of the renewable timber product is always available, minimising the transport costs of the 'raw' material. To further this example, water from the roadways can be used to passively or structurally irrigate trees: irrigation with the purpose of production and productivity as distinct from a purely aesthetically motivated solution. If power is required as part of the functioning irrigation system, then photovoltaics can be installed to cover the energy uptake. This type of forestry system harvests carbon from the air, produces a viable product in the longer term, and can be repeated for multiple crops.

In these current and impending times of climate change and environmental degradation, our consideration of integrated and holistic approaches to localised production of energy, water, and food within the public urban realm is critical. In a very practical way, this decentralisation and relocalisation reduces and minimises vehicle transport movements, increases physical activity and therefore the healthiness of a neighbourhood, draws down on what is otherwise wasted stormwater from our streetscapes and aids urban water management, assists with the reclaiming of lost biodiversity (particularly that associated with creek lines and wetlands), encourages and develops social engagement and exchange, provides a place for intergenerational learning, provides an activation, surveillance and safety to open space, and, most of all, yields productive land as part of the urban fabric of place.

**In these current and impending times of climate change and environmental degradation, our consideration of integrated and holistic approaches to localised production of energy, water, and food within the public urban realm is critical.**

# The story of apples and fish: designing for urban productivity

## Ichsani Wheeler

The concept of a productive place summons to mind images of bucolic apple orchards and wild harvests from pristine nature. The only problem is that there are likely few other people around. It's just like that perfect fishing spot no one knows about; securely abundant and peacefully awaiting harvest. It's safe to say that such a spot would be far removed from the nearest city. Similarly, idyllic apple orchards are generally found a good distance from our urban lives. However, such division and physical separation between where the majority of us live and our current productive places is quite common (Mazoyer and Roudart 2006). Post industrial countries such as Britain and the United States, for instance, have in less than four generations gone from 60 per cent of their workforce employed in food production to less than one per cent today (Tudge 2007).

How then can we get a sense of a possible future city with productive places woven into its fabric? Can we imagine what kind of city could provide not only modern amenities, but deliver them in such a way as to stitch together energy efficiency with those ecosystem services found in functioning, living habitats: clean water, food, and air? Can people really grow healthy, self-organising, and resilient living skins, layer upon layer on the bare bones of a concrete jungle?

To be able to eat that fish or pluck that apple with confidence (while still creating beneficial microclimates, cycling nutrients, and managing water supplies) we must learn how to grow these city skins and systems to take the function of a city towards natural ecosystems capable of perpetuation through self organisation. The case for reformulating cities along the lines of natural systems was expressed long before climate change hit the public lexicon. The approach of designing with nature is not new, yet it has a remarkably consistent goal. Even the numerous justifications for such an approach, expressed in differing language and with differing examples (Mollison 1988), have an essential common theme—cultural sustainability modelled on natural resilience.

## How then can we get a sense of a possible future city with productive places woven into its fabric?

In a fully functioning and healthy natural ecosystem there is no waste, only tightly woven cycles of matter that reflect the abundance of the elements involved and the energy driving the process (Volk 1997). Less available elements (like phosphorus) are captured and cycled at far higher ratios than more abundant ones (such as calcium). Energy from photosynthesis cascades through the intricately convoluted web of life, self-organising and building the resilience that is thought to be the key to perpetuating an environment (Walker and Salt 2006). Nature wastes nothing and makes much from little.

When cities are perceived from this ecosystem position, they become abundant with unrealised resources just waiting to be cycled into more beneficial forms. Where matter goes, energy is right there with it. It seems simple enough, but inability to see uses in place of wastes has led many cities (where potable water is used for everything from irrigation to toilet flushing) into water shortages, while their stormwater systems efficiently whisk away great volumes of rain. Similarly, agricultural lands are suffering declining health, as food arriving in our present day cities carries into our refrigerators embodied costs in water, fossil energy (Trivedi 2008), loss of soil carbon, and ecological decline (Russel 2000). Meanwhile, our city's 'waste' organics are sent for a pit stop in landfill on their way to atmospheric methane; or pass through sewage systems on their way to becoming an algal bloom destined for a natural water body near you.

All that matter, harnessed at great energetic cost, is used only once before being discarded. This represents a considerable loss of energy to our food production systems, while simultaneously degrading the wider planetary ecosystem. This makes our current cities ecologically weak—organisms that slowly degrade their wider environment rate poorly in the sustainability stakes and come in with a low likelihood of perpetuation. With such urban rapaciousness, we must inevitably go further and further away to find our fish and apples. On top of these external costs, most current urban ecosystems provide only limited capacity to buffer fluctuations in environmental parameters before a crisis is induced. This means a heat wave can challenge electricity systems by spiking demand for air conditioning as easily as droughts highlight the weaknesses of a simplified water supply.

Our cities can approach a state of ecosystem resilience by using design informed by nature, making long-term cultural sustainability a realistically achievable goal (Walker and Salt 2006). This means we may have a constructive way forward through such ecological weaknesses and methods to assure supplies of apples and fish in perpetuity. How can we use what is currently wasted to help where we live become ecologically productive, manage our water supplies, buffer our microclimates, and reduce our dependence on fossil energy?

To illustrate this complex goal we can consider a high-rise building (with commercial and residential tenants and an adjoining multi-level parking complex) and where we could fit our hypothetical apple orchard and abundant fishing spot. The roof top could house the orchard, but we find only the car park can take the weight of the soil, the water it holds, as well as the biomass it grows—so this is where our productive garden will be situated. Organic residues from residents are recycled through worm farms before enriching the soil of the productive gardens, decreasing residential garbage. Some of these nutrients come back as produce shared among the residents, increasing vegetable and fruit consumption. Water for the garden is harvested from the residential roof to supplement rainfall, reducing stormwater coming off the site to that of a rural environment. The health of the local stream improves. As small children frequent the garden, all gardening is done organically. Insects and birds appear and take up residence. Plants are healthier and show more verdant growth and newly arrived bees help the orchard yield abundant harvests. The garden assumes more of a social role, bringing people together and perpetuating not only the knowledge of food growing, but rare heirloom varieties as well.

A decision is made that vertical surfaces of the car park and the building are ideal places for low maintenance plantings—green skins to serve as biodiverse, air cleaning, and water purifying temperature regulators. Greywater from the building is recycled onto these surfaces and as they grow electricity use of residential and commercial tenants declines. People stop to look at the building. They take photos and bring their friends. Businesses on the ground floor start to pick up. By now energy prices are increasing and the businesses on the ground floor start to show interest in the residential roof, until now only harvesting water. The roof gets a thin green skin of grasses and an array of solar panels goes up. Heating and cooling costs decline again and the building now produces most of its own energy. The amount of water harvested from this roof declines, but there was already more than enough for the garden so makes little difference.

Over time, car use declines so a resident leases a level of the near-empty car park and the unused roof of the next building along. In the car park, large tanks are installed and filled with fish. These tanks are connected to hydroponic tubes spread over the leased roof, where leafy greens and herbs grow and are fertilised by fish waste, returning clean oxygenated water to the tanks. The fish are fed from insect larvae raised on vegetable scraps and the fresh produce is sold to residents and the cafe downstairs. More people visit. Some come to the cafe because the building is cool and peaceful; word also spreads that the fish is the best dish on the menu. Others come to learn. Whole blocks begin to follow suit and soon the city becomes more green than grey. People are surprised—it wasn't long ago there was talk of abandoning the city.

**Our cities can approach a state of ecosystem resilience by using design informed by nature, making long-term cultural sustainability a realistically achievable goal.**

At the whole-city scale, changes are also afoot. A petition emerges to support redirection of city-wide sewage flows, to be fed to a giant system of biomass beds to strip the sewage of its nutrients. Water coming out of the beds then passes through extensive wetlands before eventually heading back to the river. The petition says the biomass is to be regularly harvested and pyrolysed, taking those few extra steps to turn waste into a source of renewable, carbon-neutral fuel. The charcoal by-product is to be returned back to the agricultural landscapes outside the city limits, improving their degraded soils.

The petition also says residents will soon be able to swim in the river again and maybe sometime in the future, the shellfish will be good to eat and the prawns and big fish will return—if the plan goes ahead. One of the residents is particularly happy at this prospect, since fishing in a tank was missing the character of the old days next to the river.

# Energy: creating an energy efficient landscape with green roofs

## Gary Grant

A preponderance of hard and impermeable surfaces ensures cities are hotter and drier than their rural hinterland. Take a typical roof as an example: a roof constructed in a traditional way with an exposed waterproof material, especially if it is dark in colour, will absorb solar radiation and heat up quickly during the day. Solid building materials may store heat and re-radiate that heat into the atmosphere at night. Multiply this effect across a whole city and that causes an urban heat island effect, where the city centre is warmer than the surrounding countryside.

For example, even in London, which has a fairly mild climate, the urban heat island causes summer night time temperatures in the centre to increase by five to six degrees Celsius in comparison to suburban districts. In many North American and Asian cities, where summers can be much warmer, the problem is even more serious and urban heat islands are predicted to become worse with climate change, especially in regions where summer temperatures are set to increase.

People in buildings with conventional roofs which heat up quickly in the sun are often heavily reliant on air conditioning. Without cooling, buildings can become very uncomfortable and during heat waves lives can be lost. The Paris heat wave of August 2003, for example, killed at least 100 people and episodes of that kind are predicted to increase in frequency with global warming. As cities get hotter energy consumption increases. If that energy is supplied by burning fossil fuels, that extra consumption increases atmospheric carbon dioxide levels and hence global warming.

Green roofs and living walls (together known as building-integrated vegetation) can be used to tackle these problems, improving the thermal performance of the buildings on which they are installed and benefiting the wider urban environment. A green roof insulates the building fabric from solar radiation. Even in temperate climates, a conventional roof may heat up to 50 degrees Celsius in direct sunlight. However, with a green roof the vegetation and growing medium shields the building fabric from direct sunlight so extreme temperature fluctuations do not occur. A study in Ottawa by the National Research Council of Canada found the temperature variation on a conventional roof surface was as high as 45 degrees Celsius, while under a green roof the fluctuation at the waterproof membrane did not exceed six degrees Celsius (Liu 2002).

**As cities get hotter energy consumption increases. If that energy is supplied by burning fossil fuels, that extra consumption increases atmospheric carbon dioxide levels and hence global warming.**

Factors other than the ability of a green roof to insulate a building from the sun come into play. The transpiration of water from the vegetation on a green roof causes evaporative cooling. In addition, green roofs have a greater reflectivity (or albedo) than most conventional roofing materials. These factors combine to improve comfort levels within the building, reduce demand for air conditioning, and help to counteract the urban heat island effect. The ability of green roofs to provide evaporative cooling depends on the amount of water stored in the substrate, which in turn is influenced by the type of substrate and its depth.

Even the most lightweight green roofs shade and protect and provide some evaporative cooling. It is possible to use recycled waste water to deliberately boost evaporative cooling on a green roof. The Possman cider cooling and storage facility in Frankfurt, Germany has gone further than this—water is cooled on a wetland roof and recycled, reducing water demand and saving money in the cooling costs of both the water and the building.

The cooling effect of green roofs has been elegantly demonstrated by the City of Chicago, where temperatures have been monitored on two similar government buildings; one with a green roof and one without. On one hot summer day in 2001, the conventional roof was 28 degrees Celsius hotter than the green roof. The practical effect of roof greening is to delay by several hours the time that people on upper floors feel the need to switch on their air conditioning. It has been estimated that whole scale greening of the city's rooftops in this way could reduce peak electricity demand by 720 megawatts (equivalent to the power output from 240 diesel locomotives) and save more than US$100 million per annum (City of Chicago n.d.).

Modelling by the New York Heat Island Initiative has indicated that the greening of 50 per cent of the roofs within the metropolitan area would reduce temperatures by up to 0.8 degrees Celsius (Rosenzweig, Gaffin and Parshall 2006). The same study also looked at various mitigation strategies other than green roofs, including white (reflective) roofs, and noted that green roofs provided greater benefits. The study recommended that a combination of strategies is adopted to tackle the urban heat island effect, including roof greening and urban forestry (Slosberg, Rosenzweig and Solecki 2007).

**The practical effect of roof greening is to delay by several hours the time that people on upper floors feel the need to switch on their air conditioning.**

Very similar predictions have been produced for Tokyo, which has a severe urban heat island problem. The city has now introduced policies that require green roofs to be installed on a significant proportion of new buildings. In Toronto, it has been estimated that more than fifty million square metres of roof space could be greened. Sophisticated computer modelling has indicated that greening these rooftops would reduce the urban heat island effect by up to two degrees Celsius, saving millions of dollars in electricity (Ryerson University 2004).

**ABOVE**
Even in temperate climates, a conventional roof may heat up to 50 degrees Celsius in direct sunlight. However, with a green roof the vegetation and growing medium shields the building fabric from direct sunlight so extreme temperature fluctuations do not occur.

**ABOVE and RIGHT**
Even the most lightweight green roofs shade and
protect and provide some evaporative cooling.

Green roofs can also save energy during cold weather. The extra insulation provided by air trapped in the growing medium and drainage layers of a green roof reduces heat losses. The precise insulation value of a green roof varies according to the water content of the substrate, which in turn is dependent on how rainy the weather is; however in Germany people living in domestic buildings with green roofs have reported winter fuel bills savings of between three and ten per cent.

It is often suggested that a choice needs to be made between greening roofs and covering them with photovoltaic (PV) panels, however in Germany and Switzerland PVs have been erected on frames above green roofs in a way that increases the efficiency of the PVs. This happens because evapo-transpiration from the green roof creates a cooler microclimate. Photovoltaic panels lose efficiency as temperatures soar and green roofs tend to keep temperatures down—a genuine synergetic effect. Roofs treated in this way produce electricity while still cooling the building and providing wildlife habitat—a true example of multi-functional design.

Roofs are also a valuable component of sustainable drainage systems, intercepting rainfall and reducing the speed and volume of runoff. Studies over a number of years have shown an extensive green roof with 100 millimetres of substrate retains 50 per cent of the annual rainfall it receives. A roof garden with more than 500 millimetres of growing medium retains more than 90 per cent of its annual rainfall (Roth-Kleyer 2009). This characteristic may become even more important in regions where climate change is predicted to increase the intensity and frequency of rainstorms. The retention and evaporation of rainwater from green roofs also reduces the pressure on drainage infrastructure and when used in combination with other water sensitive design features reduces the likelihood of flash flooding in urban catchments.

As well as reducing heat transfer into the building, green roofs also prolong the life of the waterproof membrane. For example, the waterproofing layer on the green roofs of the waterworks in Wollishofen, Zurich, installed in 1914 and protected from harmful ultra violet rays and frost by soil, are still in good condition after more than 90 years. Manufacturers suggest that covering a waterproof layer with a green roof system will double its life. Extensive roofs require little maintenance: two visits a year are recommended to check drainage outlets and remove any debris, but many green roofs receive no maintenance without any reported problems. In Germany and Switzerland, experience of installing and managing green roofs for the past 30 years has shown these features to be practical and money-saving.

**Studies over a number of years have shown an extensive green roof with 100 millimetres of substrate retains 50 per cent of the annual rainfall it receives.**

Worldwide, energy efficiency in the built environment, reduction of the urban heat island effect, and dealing with heat waves and rainstorms will become even more of a concern as climate changes. There is now a growing body of evidence to demonstrate how green roofs and living walls can play an important role in addressing these issues. Thermal performance improvements alone are a good enough reason to adopt building-integrated vegetation, however the other benefits of improved water management, the provision of wildlife habitat, longevity of building fabric, and amenity make this approach a winner.

# Food: integrating agriculture into landscapes

## Gary Grant, with a case study by Isaac Brown

Agriculture is a relatively new invention. For most of our history (the human species is at least 100,000 years old) we have been hunter gatherers and the first farmers did not appear until after the end of the last ice age, around 10,000 years ago, somewhere in the Middle East. The first towns were probably established as fortified granaries. Certainly agriculture made the first towns possible and is the foundation of civilisation. The archaeological record reveals how civilisations rose and fell, with decline more often than not caused by drought, deforestation, loss of soil, and crop failure.

Throughout the world there are lands which were once clothed with natural vegetation now denuded of soil. Agriculture has usually begun with a brutal clearance of the wilderness followed by a few decades of ploughing or grazing until the Earth is exhausted. Until now people have been able to move onto new lands, however the world's population of 6.7 billion (expected to peak at 9 billion at least) has now cultivated most of the suitable land (and some which is unsuitable). And the failure of agricultural landscapes continues still. For example, Jared Diamond (2005) argues that much of Australia's rangelands are in terminal decline.

**Modern industrial-scale farming is reliant on cheap oil and gas for the production of fertilisers, the fuelling of machinery, and the transportation of produce.**

New approaches are needed. Examples of sustainable agriculture do already exist. Perhaps the best known and most widespread example is that of the rice paddies of East Asia, some of which date back thousands of years. In 1911 Franklin Hiram King published *Farmers of Forty Centuries: Or Permanent Agriculture in China, Korea and Japan*. He was able to describe how carefully rice farmers fertilise the soil with manure; how they learnt to grow nitrogen fixing legumes centuries before the practice was adopted in the West; and how they combine rice growing with the raising of fish, silk worms, and livestock in an elegant agricultural ecosystem. The book is also interesting because it is the first reference to permanent agriculture and the basis of the portmanteau word permaculture coined by Mollison and Holmgren in the 1970s.

Permaculturalists advocate an ecological approach to designing agriculture and human settlements, with the aim of creating long-term stability and self sufficiency, as opposed to the now usual reliance on geographically-scattered, industrial, oil-fuelled food production systems. Permaculture is usually small in scale and relies on a thorough understanding of a site's local environment. Borrowing from organic farming, polycultural agricultural systems, agro-forestry and knowledge of traditional farming methods proven by indigenous peoples over centuries, permaculturalists look to minimise waste and maximise diversity.

Interest in such systems is increasing as modern city dwellers contemplate rising oil and food prices and their disconnection with the natural environment. Modern industrial-scale farming is reliant on cheap oil and gas for the production of fertilisers, the fuelling of machinery, and the transportation of produce. It is sometimes said that modern farming is a process for turning oil into food. Farming schemes that reduce reliance on oil are becoming increasingly attractive to people as prices rise and as climate change bites.

Permaculture is now an inspiration for those seeking to integrate agriculture into new landscapes and the built environment. Large-scale industrial farming, with its monocultures and heavy pesticide use, is unsuitable for small sites and can be dangerous for the public. There is now much interest in integrating small-scale agriculture into new communities, not only because local low-carbon food production is being driven by oil price rises and environmental concerns but also because such projects are expected to make settlements more pleasant places to live.

Al Sila is an arid, unvegetated peninsula with virtually no freshwater, lapped by the beautiful, clear waters of the Arabian Gulf. The conventional way of operating a resort in a remote desert location is to ship in all food, but in their early concept planning the designers wanted to consider the possibility that a substantial proportion of this could be grown locally using methods in tune with the local ecology. The designers first asked, what can be grown with seawater?

One answer was provided by Carl Hodges, founder of the Seawater Foundation, who has pioneered agriculture based on channelling seawater onto arid, unproductive land to grow Salicornia, an edible salt marsh plant that can also be used to produce biofuels. At his test site in the desert state of Sonora on the Mexican Pacific coast, Hodges has excavated channels to irrigate fields of Salicornia, which contains high levels of oil and protein and has similar productivity to freshwater crops like alfalfa. Researchers have also identified other salt loving (or halophytic) plants that have the potential to be cultivated. Hodges (1993) argues that seawater farming can provide food, fuel, and income to people living in otherwise unproductive areas. By creating mangrove forests, which grow in shallow seawater, it is also possible to create carbon sinks. Now others are following his lead.

The Indian state of Tamil Nadu has more than 100,000 hectares of hypersaline coastal land rendered useless for conventional crops by poor past farming practices. It may be possible to bring these lands into cultivation by using seawater farming techniques, growing mangrove forests and Salicornia and raising prawns in specially-built coastal ponds. A pilot project is already underway in Tamil Nadu's Tiruvarur District. There has also been an attempt to establish experimental seawater farms on the Red Sea coast on the Horn of Africa, an area frequently threatened by drought and famine (Hodges et al. 1993).

There is now much interest in integrating small-scale agriculture into new communities, not only because local low-carbon food production is being driven by oil price rises and environmental concerns but also because such projects are expected to make settlements more pleasant places to live.

**LEFT**
In this draft concept for Al Sila, ecotourism is taken to a new level—not just reducing the impact of a resort but creating new marine and intertidal habitat and developing new farming, energy production, and water management techniques. This design exploration advanced to early concept stage in 2008, however further development of the scheme is subject to feasibility analysis and government planning directions.

At Al Sila, the designers were also keen to adopt these ideas. In their early concept scheme from 2008, the first component of an integrated seawater farming system would be a newly-created mangrove forest and lagoons; a natural habitat elsewhere on this coast. New mangroves and lagoons would provide valuable nurseries for wild fish that would spend their adult life out in the Gulf; however the mangroves would also be a location for the collection of prawn larvae which could be fattened in nearby ponds. As well as being a source of prawn larvae, the mangroves would also be valuable wetland habitats, attracting resident and migratory waterbirds. The upper salt marsh would also provide a useful buffer between the farms and the open waters of the Gulf, filtering and cleaning runoff. Water would also be taken from the new mangrove creeks to create ponds for fish like Tilapia, which would also be raised for food.

Waste saltwater from fish and prawn farming could then be used to grow Salicornia, which, as demonstrated by the Seawater Foundation, can be eaten, fed to livestock, or used to produce biofuels. Livestock would be a local source of meat and their dung could be used to fertilise more conventional fields nearby. These more conventional fields, growing a much wider range of fruits and vegetables that the saltwater farm, would be irrigated using greywater and treated wastewater from the resort. It would be possible to cultivate dates, olives, citrus fruits, legumes, capers, melons, and tomatoes, among many other crops.

Water for the resort would be supplied by a large array of solar stills. Power for the resort and the associated farms would be provided by photovoltaic arrays in the hinterland. The whole system could become carbon neutral, with any modest inputs of fossil fuel compensated for by the sequestration of carbon in the newly-created mangrove forest.

The ultimate test for all these interrelated agricultural installations is this: could they survive and support a small community of people if (for the sake of argument) the resort component of the development were ever to close? Of course changes would be needed, because the population would fall, however a system would have been created with the potential to support a self-sufficient community. Another benefit of this scheme is that it could become a model for communities elsewhere, including some in underdeveloped countries with similar climates and seaside locations where people live in real poverty and deprivation.

Further development of the scheme is subject to feasibility analysis and government planning directions, however the concept does represent ecotourism taken to a new level—not just reducing the impact of a resort but creating new marine and intertidal habitat and developing new farming, energy production, and water management techniques that have the potential to be adopted by millions of vulnerable people living in similar environments elsewhere.

# Case study: integrating organic farming with community development at Prairie Crossing

## Isaac Brown

Many new masterplanned communities across the United States are enjoying the benefits of local, small-scale organic agriculture. From providing a secure and healthy source of food, to stimulating vibrant social interaction, community farms are quickly surpassing golf courses as the preferred community open space amenity. Cost-benefit analysis of these programs shows the carbon footprint associated with food supply may be greatly lowered by reducing the emissions from long distance food delivery which commonly exceeds 1,500 miles from field to table in the United States.

One of the most successful of these communities is Prairie Crossing just outside Chicago, which was developed by Vicky and George Ranney with masterplanners William Johnson and Associates and broke ground in 1993. Prairie Crossing features a regional commuter rail stop, a mixed-use village centre with 36 condominiums and 359 single-family homes designed following local vernacular styles, learning centres, a charter school, and many other leading edge sustainability strategies. Prairie Crossing's buildings were constructed using the highest energy efficiency standards at the time, including a Gold LEED school building.

The development's 678 acres were originally dedicated to conventional corn and soybean farming. Now, nearly 70 per cent of the land is protected from development and more than 40 per cent has been converted back to native prairie, wetlands, and lakes. An organic farm now occupies 100 acres, with community-supported agriculture, farmer training programs, a learning farm, and small livestock operations. The working organic farm was central to the Ranney's vision of a healthy and community-oriented development and it has attracted many home buyers.

Prairie Crossing's farm operations increase local food production and public support for it. A commercial organic family farm leases over 40 acres and sells its produce at farmers markets and to the 300 families who are members of the community-supported agriculture program. Each week, member families from Prairie Crossing and surrounding communities collect their weekly share of freshly harvested fruit and vegetables. Their annual membership payments bring an influx of capital each spring, which sustains farm operations for the entire year and resolves seasonal revenue fluctuations.

**RIGHT**
At Prairie Crossing, an organic farm now occupies 100 acres, with community-supported agriculture, farmer training programs, a learning farm, and small livestock operations.

Prairie Crossing's business development centre leases certified organic land to beginner farmers and offers them practical and commercial training. The centre aims to counteract the steep decline in the American farm population brought by industrial agriculture and to increase the number of new farmers growing local produce without pesticides and herbicides and without dependence on petroleum.

The learning farm runs an educational program for students from the local charter school, along with a summer day camp for children and a summer job program for teenagers, which teaches them how to grow and harvest produce and sell it at farmers markets. Local people can also lease garden plots and learn sustainable practices at classes on growing, cooking, and preserving foods.

Prairie Crossing embodies perhaps the most holistic approach to sustainability within the current mainstream development movement. It addresses multi-modal transit and regenerative design and has fostered a community deeply engaged with its local ecology—perhaps one of the best ways to help mitigate and adapt to climate change.

# Water: urban landscapes and water management

## Stephane Asselin

The pace of construction and development, particularly in Asia, is transforming the landscape so much that urban areas are increasingly divorced from the natural environment. Water availability and use is a particular challenge. Water is not only essential to biological life; it plays a vital role in our cities, commerce, industry, and agriculture. It also provides tremendous recreation and tourism value.

Urbanisation often results in covering previously vegetated or porous areas with roadways, parking lots, houses, and other developments. The corresponding increase in impervious surfaces decreases rainfall infiltration, often bringing warmer and more polluted runoff and amplifying flood risks. These harmful effects can be mitigated through intelligent design that mimics and works with natural processes. This involves respecting natural constraints, making space for water, and recreating functional floodplains and ecosystems.

Designing projects that use land to collect, treat, and reuse water helps protect and conserve one of the world's most precious resources. As well as providing water for human use and consumption, design that incorporates water management helps preserve aquatic ecosystems and biodiversity. Using natural processes to store water mitigates flooding risks, increases infiltration, and reduces energy required to store and treat water. Water features in urban areas also provide cooling effects to mitigate heat island problems. One of the key benchmarks of sustainable urban planning is to assess carefully the availability of water resources to influence plant selection.

### Climate change driving demand for multi-functional and adaptable spaces

New climate models project that sea levels may potentially rise by upwards of one metre in the coming century, which could have severe consequences on coastal areas (International Scientific Congress on Climate Change 2009). Melting glaciers in Greenland and Antarctica will increase flood risk in some areas; reduced mountain snow levels will reduce runoff and potable water availability in others. An average temperature increase of two degrees Celsius or more will change rainfall patterns, which will add further stress in areas already suffering from floods and droughts.

An integrated approach that respects the water cycle is necessary to mitigate the potential impacts of climate change on water supply and flooding. This is increasingly evident as populations, economics, and water supplies are mismatched in various parts of the world. Changing weather conditions will further exacerbate water stress in some areas.

*Climate change and flooding*
Climate change is expected to increase the frequency of heavy rainfall events in mid and high latitudes (Intergovernmental Panel on Climate Change 2007). Urbanising land use usually increases the amount of impervious surface area, which in turn alters local hydrology by impacting runoff, evaporation, and recharge rates. There are many opportunities at the catchment level to develop and use land for more than just its intended use, including for mitigating the impact of higher incidences of heavy rainfall.

Design can provide a short-term adaptive response to avoid significant increases in flooding risk. In addition, integrated design can provide long-term benefits by increasing infiltration and recharge. Once fully implemented, the Beijing Urban Stormwater Runoff Management System, for example, will improve stormwater resources utilisation and manage stormwater into natural detention and treatment facilities.

Multifunctional parkland and channel design along Alameda Creek in California provides another example of integrated design. Originally designed to contain a 500-year flood, the creek was severely under capacity due to heavy siltation. Instead of directly desilting the creek (and disrupting the established marsh and associated ecosystem), an integrated approach was taken where researchers analysed alternatives to restore the creek's capacity and habitat value (Asselin, Demgen and Johnson 2005). The proposed alternative restored 4000 acres of salt ponds and provides valuable habitat. Not only does this integrated approach provide flood control and ecological benefits—the projected total cost of the project was less than the original desilting option.

**LEFT**
Urbanisation often results
in covering previously
vegetated or porous
areas with roadways,
parking lots, houses and
other development. The
corresponding increase
in impervious surfaces
decreases rainfall infiltration,
often bringing warmer and
more polluted runoff and
amplifying flood risks.

*Climate change and water scarcity*
Climate change is expected to exacerbate water
supply problems in already semi-arid areas.
Large regional increases in demand for irrigated
water are projected, exposing hundreds of millions
of people to water stress. Designing to increase
infiltration and recharge groundwater supply is
essential to adapt to and mitigate the water stress
caused by climate change. New developments
should be planned and designed to ensure
adequate water supply and lessen storm damage.

Working with China's Ministry of Water Resources,
a feasibility study was developed to analyse the
need, requirements, and design of a National
Flood Control and Drought Relief Decision Support
System. This system interfaces with real-time
flood forecasting systems on the Huai River and
provides management tools to minimise human and
economic losses from floods and droughts. It is
designed to use offline space to store stormwater,
encouraging infiltration and providing a robust
decision making tool that modernises China's
drought and flood management capabilities.

*Interconnection between energy and water*
Urbanisation and high consumption contribute to the scarcity of water and energy resources and increase the importance of their sustainable use. Climate change will intensify pressures on these resources, with more of both required as populations and temperatures continue to rise (Colombo and Karney 2003, p. 240, cited in eds Cabrera and Cabrera 2003). Efficient operation of water distribution systems will become increasingly important as energy is required to distribute and treat water. Likewise, large volumes of water are required to produce most forms of fossil fuel-based energy.

Natural solutions to water conveyance, storage, and treatment can reduce energy usage significantly. Single-pass water use results in minimal resource recovery and compounded energy usage (Lawrence Berkeley National Laboratory 2008). Reclaimed and reused water increases water's utility and reduces the energy intensity associated with water collection, treatment, and distribution.

The use of natural systems such as wetlands to detain and treat water can provide a viable alternative to traditional wastewater treatment technologies that are fossil fuel dependent. While raw sewage still requires some level of conventional wastewater treatment facilities, combining them with natural systems can greatly reduce their size. Wetland ecosystems are robust and can withstand volume changes while maintaining consistent quality of discharge, in addition to neutralising or transforming pollutants into nutrients.

Aside from providing habitat value and public amenity, wetlands are also one of the least expensive treatment systems to operate and maintain. Minimal fossil fuel energy or chemicals are required to maintain wetlands and their treatment processes (Kadlec and Knight 1995, p.31). In addition to their water, habitat, and energy benefits, wetlands also serve a critical role in mitigating the effects of climate change by acting as carbon sinks. The Shanghai Chemical Industry Park Natural Treatment System, for example, was designed to purify industrial wastewater effluent for recycling within the park and for discharge into the Hangzhou Bay.

**Design not just for aesthetics, but for function**
The growing challenges and impacts of climate change require an immediate integration of functionality into design and planning. Growing global demand for water resources will necessitate increasing attention to multi-functional design. Designing purely for aesthetics will be eclipsed by design that simultaneously creates environmental, economic, social, and aesthetic value. Projects that use land to collect, treat, and reuse water will minimise flooding risk, help manage and prevent droughts, promote ecological productivity, provide public amenity, sequester carbon, and save energy. This integrated approach provides manifold benefits without increasing costs, and proves that functionality can compliment, not supplant, aesthetic value.

# Case study: improving stormwater resource utilisation and water quality in Greater Beijing

Beijing faces a water crisis that affects the quality of ground and surface water, as well as access to clean freshwater resources, due to growing development and environmental pressures. Beijing also faces frequent small-scale flooding, which results in economic losses and traffic congestion. In response, the Beijing Urban Stormwater Runoff Management System (or BUSWRMS) was developed: a comprehensive plan to improve stormwater resource utilisation and water quality in Greater Beijing.

Cross-cutting technical analysis, financial analysis, implementation and investment planning, and a pilot study were all undertaken during the project, which aimed to develop a real-time monitoring system to decrease the impacts of heavy and sudden storms, to manage and maintain an undersized, outdated, and damaged stormwater pipe network, and to overcome the difficulties of coordinating numerous government agencies responsible for different aspects of the city's stormwater management.

An integrated GIS planning tool was developed to interface with hydrologic and hydraulic models and real-time data collection networks. These models predict and monitor rainfall volume in the Beijing metropolitan area, incorporating real-time weather gauges and data from water sensors throughout the city to forecast stormwater runoff volumes. This unique city-wide program accurately predicts stormwater runoff volumes and manages diversion into natural overflow detention and treatment facilities, such as stormwater wetlands, swales, and detention facilities.

Yi Zhuang, a subdistrict of Beijing, served as a pilot site, where simulations of the existing condition were performed for different storm events to establish the baseline condition. Flooding under the baseline condition was then compared with flooding after the construction of best practice stormwater facilities. The proposed facility, a detention basin, was designed to attenuate the stormwater flow in the pipeline, thereby mitigating surface flooding while treating stormwater for reuse or discharge.

The BUSWRMS has the potential to improve urban planning by optimising growth strategies based on water supply for the various districts around Beijing: new developments can be planned according to their proximity to existing water supplies and infrastructure. The project enables planners to determine how new and planned developments would affect river hydrology, base flow, and groundwater infiltration. It identifies the impacts of new development on water supplies and sets a baseline for the types and amount of mitigation measures required for a new facility. It may also bring significant cost benefits. Stormwater recovery benefits and savings from retrofitting existing combined sewer pipes and constructing new stormwater pipes could total approximately US$46.3 million. Annualised risk of financial losses could decrease by approximately US$2.3 million.

The BUSWRMS provides an innovative and cost-effective solution to stormwater flooding, a serious problem that confronts many urban areas. The traditional approach would have been to upgrade stormwater pipelines to more rapidly transport stormwater downstream to prevent flooding, which would preclude the reuse of a great deal of water. Instead, this design solution fuses sustainable stormwater management, stakeholder collaboration and coordination, advanced technologies, and modelling to enhance Beijing's capacity to manage its ongoing water crisis.

# Case study: improving water quality and creating habitat within a chemical industry park in Shanghai

An innovative natural wastewater treatment system has been constructed among the dozen or so modern petrochemical industrial facilities located within the 3000-hectare Shanghai Chemical Industrial Park near Hangzhou Bay.

The Shanghai Chemical Industry Park Natural Treatment System uses a rigorous, engineered approach to water quality improvement to purify industrial wastewater effluent for recycling within the industrial park and for discharge into the Hangzhou Bay. Most of the 30-hectare site was formerly abandoned aquaculture, which was hydraulically isolated from the drainage and irrigation canals throughout the site.

The primary objective of the system is to improve water quality of treatment plant effluent to meet the Level IV National Standard of Surface Water Quality. A range of alternatives to pre-wetland treatment were analysed, such as aerated lagoons, a nitrifying trickling filter or bio-tower, and modifying the treatment plant's operations. These were assessed for their ability to achieve water quality performance measures, the space and capital they require, operations and maintenance costs, visual impacts, their capacity for wetland treatment, and their acceptability to the operator. Based on these criteria, a trickling filter mechanism was adopted to achieve project goals.

**ABOVE**
While improving water quality is its primary goal, the treatment system also incorporates aesthetic features and wildlife habitat in its design to create a recreational hub for the park's employees and visitors.

The natural treatment system was designed to process over 22,000 cubic metres of partially-treated industrial wastewater a day, with innovative components such as:

- A trickling filter mechanism to remove ammonia;
- A shallow-water oxidizing pond to reduce chemical oxygen demand (or COD);
- Two parallel free surface wetland systems to remove nitrates and heavy metals and to reduce COD and biological oxygen demand (or BOD); and
- Plant species selected to withstand highly saline conditions and with proven treatment capability.

While improving water quality is its primary goal, the treatment system also incorporates aesthetic features and wildlife habitat in its design to create a recreational hub for the park's employees and visitors. The visitor centre includes a unique water observation room sunken into the ground where the soil, water, wetland plants, and water column can be observed simultaneously.

The treatment system also offers a wetland research centre for academic groups in the Greater Shanghai area. It features a bird observation tower to view wildlife and provides opportunities to better understand the characteristics and removal efficiencies for specific constituents of wastewater treatment plant effluent and various vegetation types.

Shanghai Chemical Industry Park Natural Treatment System is unique within China, marking the onset of an expanding interest in creating natural water treatment systems. The project is an example of a truly integrated approach to water and land management, which achieves the goals of cost-effective water quality improvement, habitat creation, public amenity, and improved research opportunities.

Applications

# Design and natural systems: design with nature

**James Rosenwax, Celeste Morgan, Dr Courtney Henderson**

Climate change is a complex process. It is non-discriminatory in its outreach and to best understand its implications and our potential response we must appreciate it as an evolutionary challenge. So how do designers, planners, and engineers meet this challenge? How can we design and manage new and existing communities to combat rapid climate change and cope with life on a warming planet? What tools do we have to mitigate temperature extremes, water scarcity, reduced agricultural productivity, and floods and to protect precious biodiversity? Answers to these questions are challenging, yet surprisingly they surround us in the biosphere in which we live.

Before we begin to craft our design response, we must understand the effects climate change will have on the places we influence through design. These effects are not consistent in type or magnitude, so as with any good design solution, context and place must direct and inspire. Climate change presents challenges to the elemental basis of our world, affecting every facet of our understanding of natural systems. Ancient alchemy simplified life through the four elements of earth, air, water, and fire. Similarly, climate change can be better understood through its effect on each: changes in climate will change the productivity and stability of land (earth), change wind and air pollution patterns (air), simultaneously create flooding, sea level rises, and water shortages (water), and change the temperatures and weather we experience (fire).

Just as the alchemic elements only have meaning as a complete set, when we plan and design to respond to changes to natural systems, we must take a comprehensive approach which understands the complexity of nature. The term biomimicry was conceptualised as recently as 1997, but humans have always learned from nature over our evolution.

Biomimicry maintains that the greatest and most efficient responses to environmental conditions are those that come through imitation of nature, where systems have evolved and refined themselves over millennia. Learning from biomimicry, we can only benefit from bringing a greater understanding and sensitivity to the flexibility and responsiveness of natural systems to the challenges of our cities' futures. Trusted techniques and innovation are sure to play a role in our response, but in the face of change, our only mentor can be the Earth itself. After all, it has experienced this level of change many times before.

Biomimicry maintains that the greatest and most efficient responses to environmental conditions are those that come through imitation of nature, where systems have evolved and refined themselves over millennia.

In many of the environments we design, natural templates exist which enable us to provide passive responses to reduce energy requirements and biologically heal the land. For example, wetlands can filter pollutants from water and tree canopies can modify humidity, lower temperatures, and reduce dust. In the spirit of biomimicry, we can use our knowledge of natural systems gained through science, research, and analysis to design communities that support and heal, rather than counteract, our environment.

So how does this affect our design approach to open space and the establishment of new communities? We now need to consider the wider value of landscape and open space to ensure it serves more purpose than just amenity. It will have to become a productive place where the requirements of sustainable human habitat and supportive ecologies are all met by functions such as filtering water and air, storing carbon, producing food, generating microclimate energy, stabilising and buffering against storm surges, and storing flood waters. This fusion of ecosystem services is best achieved through an integrated design approach, drawing on inputs from many disciplines, including engineering, architecture, science, and planning and grounding these on a strong foundation of an active, engaged, and informed community.

Ecosystems evolve in response to the local climate and resources to create an equilibrium of cycles and alliances that sustains life in a careful balance. With globalisation, humankind has created a carbon-hungry and open-ended ecosystem that overrides natural boundaries of climate and topography. Reliant on the import and export of goods globally to sustain life (to vastly different degrees of quality across the globe), this system's energy requirements and waste streams are unsustainable.

We now need to consider the wider value of landscape and open space to ensure it serves more purpose than just amenity.

## Design for resilience rather than equilibrium

Fundamental to designing for climate change is acknowledging how design parameters are changing. What was done in the past will not necessarily work in the future. No longer can dynamic systems be treated as if they are at equilibrium; rather, landscapes are continually evolving in response to changing environmental conditions. Design processes that do not recognise the need for ongoing adaptation, flexibility, and resilience will ultimately fail.

Resilience is the ability of an ecosystem to withstand or recover from disturbance or stress (Walker et al. 2004). Disturbances such as drought, heat, cold, flood, and disease and changes in species all influence or impair an ecosystem's capacity to perform specific functions and provide ecosystem services. The concept of resilience has its origins in the ecology of natural systems (as espoused by Odum in the 1960s), whereby ecological systems attain stability from their biomass, stratification, and complexity of function. Complex ecological systems consequently possess many protective mechanisms which help buffer disturbances and they are better able to recover from stress and more easily return to a stable, post-disturbance state. Accordingly, resilience is critical to any form of sustainable development in the era of rapid climate change.

Designing for resilience contradicts the 'designing for maximum yield' philosophy (Clark 1973). Agricultural, engineering, and economic models of many production systems are based on the premise of achieving a maximum sustainable yield from a given set of resources. Such production systems assume equilibrium conditions and do not allow for inbuilt redundancy, as resources are used for maximum efficiency.

Based on this understanding of natural systems, a resilient design solution would be one that features adaptive management frameworks that can respond to the changing needs of the environment and the people it supports. To illustrate this, we can explore the design of the proposed new township of Googong in Australia, where water movement and vegetation are planned to mimic the site's true natural templates.

Montgomery Creek is the main water course running through the 800-hectare Googong site. Over the past 100 years, it has been severely degraded through grazing and other destructive activities associated with agricultural land uses. A detailed site analysis unveiled the likely pre-development fluvial geomorphology and vegetation communities of this particular area, which can be referred to as the site's natural templates. These templates have guided the selection of future vegetation communities, habitat types, and fluvial morphology most likely to not only be resilient to prevailing site conditions, but also likely to have enough resilience to adapt to changing conditions as we move into the era of rapid climate change.

Water resources have been paramount in defining how the open spaces of the Montgomery Creek drainage corridor can be established and managed in perpetuity. A range of hydrological models have been established to understand water availability in likely future scenarios as the catchment is urbanised and also as weather patterns change. In contrast to a nostalgic landscape of predominantly mown green lawn and well-irrigated parklands, the design response balances this treatment with large areas of endemic Temperate Grassland communities which form the dominant landscape typology for Googong.

Understanding the site's existing and likely future hydrology has also brought confidence in the resilience of these new communities. The structural function of Montgomery Creek's 'chain of ponds' system and the stormwater runoff it experiences will provide a variety of wetting and drying regimes, which will encourage greater diversity of vegetation, integrate ecological productivity, and build natural resilience.

Biomimicry has informed the restoration approach for Montgomery Creek. Understanding the site's fluvial geomorphology has reduced the need for energy-intensive construction materials and methods in the restoration of the drainage corridor. The waterway channel will not be anchored to a defined course using boulders and concrete; rather it will be allowed to meander through the open space network as nature intended. Likewise with vegetation within the corridor, some species will become redundant after initial establishment and others will prosper. As with the anticipated movement of the creek's alignment, species migration is accepted and will be monitored as part of the adaptive management approach to the site.

In the context of natural systems, a designer's response to climate change is not necessarily through new technology: suitable design solutions and technologies already exist in nature. We have no other option but to provide less energy-intensive design solutions which provide a net benefit to the biosphere. The concept of applying biomimicry and learning from a site's natural templates is one response; however this must be coupled with a management approach which tolerates the change that comes with this. Some landscapes will fail and others will thrive, however if there is a sufficient diversity, these landscapes will be resilient and will have the capacity to respond to these changes with limited energy inputs.

As part of this new paradigm, designers, planners, engineers, and other professionals will be charged with educating clients and communities and gaining their acceptance. The era of urbanised areas being dominated by energy-intensive open space is behind us. We must look forward to a new paradigm—the era of the ecological landscape.

In the context of natural systems, a designer's response to climate change is not necessarily through new technology: suitable design solutions and technologies already exist in nature.

# Design and urban systems: the low-carbon commune

Christopher Choa

A few years ago, a young married couple went about choosing the right place to live. They were deeply concerned about environmental issues, committed to finding ways to minimise their environmental footprint, and vigilant about living among others who shared their values. And after looking around a bit, they found an extraordinary community that matched their aspirations.

Because of its compact organisation and shared resources, they rarely needed more than 20 amps of power during the course of the day. Because they walked everywhere, they didn't own a car. They didn't need one; they could walk to just about everything they needed—food, quiet open spaces, and places to socialise with their friends.

With this kind of frugal energy consumption, they had one of the lowest carbon footprints in the developed world. But their lifestyle choice wasn't just related to the environment; it was about social and economic choices too. They had both grown up in small towns, but in this new home they had a wider circle of acquaintances and more opportunities for rewarding work than they had ever known. Their children went to the local cooperative school, also an easy walk from where they lived.

Who were these people? And where was this place? Was it a commune high in the rocky mountains of Colorado? A rugged, low-energy settlement in Snowdonia, North Wales? The couple were good friends of mine, and they lived next door in a mid-town apartment building in Manhattan, the densest city in the United States and one of the denser places on the planet.

None of this should come as a surprise. Great cities are environmental machines because their density, mixed-uses, and transit options allow people to live in very close and productive proximity to work, amenities, and cultural assets. Manhattan has, by far, the lowest rate of private car ownership in the United States, simply because urbanity allows a very large number of people to get virtually everything they need within a five-minute walk or a fifteen-minute ride (New York City Department of City Planning 2006, p.4). When every person in the United States consumes an average of around eight tonnes of oil-equivalent per year for all of their daily and long-term needs (World Resources Institute 2008), Manhattan residents consume less than half of that (Tokyo Metropolitan Government 2006).

Great cities are environmental machines because their density, mixed-uses, and transit options allow people to live in very close and productive proximity to work, amenities, and cultural assets.

When you measure total energy (not just the need for residential and commercial power, but also transport, infrastructure, and the embodied energy of related goods and services), residents of great cities waste far less energy and open space resources on a per-capita basis than their rural and suburban counterparts living in single-family houses, given comparable income and lifestyle patterns. City residents share walls, floors, and ceilings with their neighbours, not only cutting back on energy losses but also reducing the amount of material required to build in the first place (Brown, Southworth and Sarzynski 2008).

For example, 40,000 residents in a suburban location with 18 residents per hectare require 2,222 hectares of land. Compare this to dense urban environments with 140 residents per hectare (about the density of the historic core of Venice), which need only 285 hectares for the same population. Those 40,000 suburban residents will typically and collectively travel two million kilometres a day, compared with their urban counterparts who will travel 700 kilometres a day, about 60 per cent less. The suburban location will produce 180,000 tonnes of carbon dioxide per year, compared to the urban environment's 65,500 tonnes per year (Brown, Southworth and Sarzynski 2008 and Vaughan 2009). And since carbon dioxide production is directly related to fossil fuel consumption, the comparable energy advantage of dense settlements over the less dense is clear.

Each resident of the largest 100 metropolitan areas in the United States is responsible on average for 2.24 tonnes of carbon dioxide in energy consumption each year, which is 14 per cent below the country's average of 2.6 tonnes per person (Brown, Southworth and Sarzynski 2008). And residents of Tokyo and some European cities produce much less than that. By their very nature, cities are centralised, making the transhipment of goods and services more efficient, reducing the fuel required by vehicles, and diminishing the number of roads required to serve a given population. Energy losses due to extended power transmission lines are reduced. Opportunities for advanced measures like district cooling plants are greatly increased.

I am concerned about adapting to climate change and how it might even be possible to mitigate climate change through strategic, high-performance planning and design. We are intensely focused on green technology, counting the minutes until we achieve grid parity, considering when geothermal wells and reverse heat pumps are most cost effective, and marvelling at the potential of new molten salt solar thermal systems. Renewable energy sources promise great benefits for large numbers of people. And once we have all this new technology, we won't need fossil fuels like we used to. That may be true. But the greatest, cheapest, most readily accessible source of renewable energy, by far, is the well-planned city.

Like you, I spend a lot of time imagining what the high-tech green cities of the future will look like—when we no longer need to depend so heavily on fossil fuels, or when we can no longer afford to. But I also know that if we're lucky, we can end up producing new cities that work remarkably like Manhattan, or like Rome, Paris, Istanbul, or St Petersburg: compact settlements that developed and thrived before cheap fossil fuels created less sustainable urban patterns. And we might be surprised to find that in a generation or two, after retrofitting with well-integrated mass transport, the urban cores of delirious new cities from Dubai to Shanghai perform at least as well, energy-wise, as London.

In parallel to the consideration of new green technologies, we should consider the elegant but powerful benefits of infrastructure. Massive wind turbine farms and expansive solar fields are great, but until we create smart grids that can absorb the spikes of the renewable energy inputs, we don't really have a useful system. By creating zoning and tax incentives that encourage the development of urban density over suburban sprawl, we also create the economic rationale for investment in mass transit, which in turn creates and magnifies environmental and energy benefits. By creating smaller block sizes in new cities we decrease the distances between intersections, reducing induced traffic on the streets and allowing the streets themselves to remain narrower, which in turn encourages easier pedestrian movement, minimising overall travel times and decreasing the need for cars in the first place.

Simple urban design initiatives can have extraordinarily powerful and positive consequences. Very recently, we passed a historic milestone: for the first time in history, the majority of our planet's population lives in cities. And the rate of urbanisation will continue to increase. In China alone, close to 400 million people will move from countryside to cities over the coming 15 years—the equivalent of a new city of a million people coming on line every two weeks (Jun 2007). This shouldn't be alarming; this is counter-intuitive good news for anyone concerned with future energy and natural resources.

As we contemplate ways to mitigate climate change and zero in on the sources and benefits of future energy, we should remember the obvious—the dense, well-planned city is itself a green machine and the most powerful integrator of economic, social, and environmental capital. And it's right at hand.

Simple urban design initiatives can have extraordinarily powerful and positive consequences.

# Land: climate change and terrestrial environments

## Isaac Brown

Changes in water and temperature regimes on land are the two fundamental drivers of climate change design. While future precipitation and temperature changes are reasonably understood, the great challenge lies in understanding the diverse ripple effect of ecosystem change that will follow. Ecosystem services such as agricultural productivity, flood protection, urban heat island control, energy and water supplies, and biodiversity are all threatened by climate-driven ecosystem change. The most apparent of these changes will be those that occur in our backyards, in the terrestrial landscapes where we live, work, and recreate.

Most existing land use has been constructed assuming a stable climate, not the substantial and rapid climate change we now face. Accommodating climate change will require new development designed for change, transforming inappropriate existing land uses and reducing current stressors on ecosystems (Joyce et al. 2008). The end game is to design climate change-adaptive land use that sustains the ecosystem services upon which we rely and accommodates biodiversity. The result will be new ecologically-appropriate land use forms and bold transformations of the terrestrial landscape.

## Natural lands and climate change

Changing regional climates are already beginning to transform ecosystem processes and patterns of species. Rapid temperature change combined with fragmented and degraded landscapes and insufficient conservation infrastructure will drive species to new ranges and many into decline and extinction (Ecological Society of America 2008 and Hannah, Midgely and Millar 2002). Preserving biodiversity requires a radically expanded habitat conservation infrastructure. The common perception of biodiversity protection must also evolve in the context of climate change: biota plays an integral role in nearly all ecosystem services from flood protection to regulating the global carbon balance (Millennium Ecosystem Assessment 2005). The following discussion explores some of the technical and cultural aspects of this emerging conservation design paradigm.

### Threats to biodiversity

Changes in ecosystems are expected to be so complex, interrelated, and difficult to model that a recent report by the United States Climate Change Science Program states the 'primary premise for [climate change] adaptive approaches is that uncertainty, change, novelty, and uniqueness of individual situations are expected to define the planning backdrop of the future' (Joyce et al. 2008, p. 3:62). The old environmental planning paradigm, which assumes that biodiversity and ecosystems can be managed based on relatively static climatic conditions, must be retooled to account for substantial and complex ecosystem change (Millar and Woolfenden 1999).

To protect biodiversity, a high performance conservation network must become ubiquitous in the landscape. This network must allow plant and animal species to migrate to new ranges and preserve enough existing ranges for species to adapt in place. Perhaps most importantly, this network must protect the natural patterns and processes that facilitate species movement and formation of new ecological associations (Joyce et al. 2008).

Natural processes such as flooding, windstorms, fire, seed dispersal, and species migration are major forces of ecosystem change that must be strategically integrated into conservation networks (Julius et al. 2008). Still, many plants and other less mobile species will not be able to move fast enough for the rapid changes predicted: some scientists are considering aggressive schemes to assist the movement of these species to new ranges (Hoegh-Guldberg et al. 2008).

The impact of climate change on species ranges will vary widely across different regions. In Mediterranean climates like that of California, for example, species have evolved historically over very small ranges, even through a long history of climate transition events (Grivet et al. 2007). In contrast, across eastern North America, species have evolved through continental-scale glaciations, driving the relocation of entire forest regions from Louisiana to Ontario in just the last 10,000 years (Braun 1950). Now, design and planning strategies must consider conservation infrastructure to help species relocate to new areas, based on global temperatures that are already higher than any in the last 5,000 years and are certain to continue to rise (Crowley 1996 and Hansen et al. 2006).

*Cities and biodiversity*

City footprints may also pose a significant hurdle to biodiversity adaptation and species migration. As they expand, cities increasingly impact regional biodiversity patterns and processes. For example, as coastal cities sprawl inland they often bisect narrow coastal eco-regions, creating major disconnections in the super-regional ecological fabric. This may have global-scale impacts on climate-induced species movement within these narrow coastal eco-regions.

This raises the question of whether habitat corridors should be reinserted through cities as a part of holistic urban sustainability planning. As the vast areas of low-performance industrial and suburban land in American cities become retooled for sustainability, there is ample opportunity to reinsert urban habitat corridors and other climate change adaptation infrastructure into cities at a metropolitan scale. The fact that outdated, energy inefficient industrial land use frequently lays linearly though cities along rivers lends itself well to creating such corridors.

*Climate design and conservation planning*

This new design and planning paradigm will alter land use patterns and the land development process and will fundamentally change conservation policy. It will require restoration of degraded ecosystems and likely the reclamation of some human land uses back to primarily ecological function. Species-by-species conservation approaches must be expanded to consider complex and unclear threats faced by broad segments of regional biodiversity. While complex modelling and planning processes are a long-term solution, simpler and more immediate strategies could be implemented, such as applying basic landscape ecology and biogeography principles when designing areas of urban expansion or land use conversion.

For example, leaving expanded corridors along stream courses that are set back from high flood lines to preserve adjacent upland corridors would allow more natural flooding processes and facilitate biodiversity adaptation across watershed scales. Catastrophic disturbance events such as 500-year floods are important forces of species distribution over long distances and time scales (Joyce et al. 2008).

Preserving a conservation network of corridors and core areas within and between major landforms, habitat types, or landscape ecosystems could preserve the fundamental pattern of biodiversity and ecosystem processes across eco-regions. Coordinating such strategies across multiple eco-regions or macro-watersheds could preserve natural patterns and processes across great distances. Such generous and precautionary conservation strategies may seem like a huge leap, but once more thorough understanding of climate change impact is reached, over-conserved areas could eventually be in-filled with additional development.

Although such a 'pull back' to protect natural infrastructure may be a significant social hurdle, it is an integral part of a whole systems approach to regional sustainability planning for climate change. It could also help encourage greater performance in other sustainability technologies. Dedicating more land to conservation could justify higher densities, improve community identity and aesthetics, and facilitate mass transit, more efficient agricultural practices, enhanced recreation opportunities, and increased conservation behaviour among communities.

## Built lands and climate change

Ensuring effective adaptation strategies for built communities must also include processes to evaluate impacts and risks and to establish appropriate infrastructure and integrated planning. Additionally, actively facilitating shifts in cultural perception may be increasingly necessary to achieve the rapid evolution of the built landscape. The following discussion focuses on the ecological and cultural challenges of adapting built landscapes and cities to climate change.

The United Kingdom is likely the leader in climate change adaptation planning through the activities of the UK Climate Impacts Programme. Their three-year project, Adaptation Strategies for Climate Change in the Urban Environment (or ASCCUE), applies adaptation assessment methodology to two contrasting cities: Manchester, a large and diverse northern city with a full array of urban characteristics; and Lewes, a low-lying southern coastal town in Sussex. Their approach evaluates the risks and impacts across each city based on a framework of neighbourhood-scale 'urban morphology units'. It also makes assessments across three 'exposure units': human comfort, urban greenspace, and the built environment. Their work aims to understand the risks and impacts and to establish risk screening methodologies. Since ASCCUE's completion, the Programme continues to develop many additional resources and outreach.

*Changing water regimes*

An important driver of land use adaptation will be new water regimes resulting from changes in weather, temperature, and ecosystems. Size and timing of storm events, soil moisture retention, groundwater levels, and altered snowfall and snowmelt regimes will affect water supply and hydrology management infrastructure. Hydrologic change will not be as simple as looking at only precipitation change; rather, it must be considered from an ecosystem perspective. For example, in areas where rainfall may remain constant but temperatures rise, vegetation patterns, wildfire frequency, and soil moisture levels may change, bringing watershed-scale variances that may increase flood events and landslides or alter groundwater supplies. Such complex relationships illustrate the need to thoroughly consider the ecosystem relationships of air, earth, water, biota, time, landscape pattern, and process in designing for adaptation.

In many locations, changes in annual flood heights, undersized or oversized stormwater infrastructure, reduced evaporative cooling, stress on urban vegetation, and countless other impacts are expected. Following historical hydrologic patterns is no longer an appropriate basis for stormwater design. Often, regional climate models have a hard time predicting the effects of climate change on precipitation patterns (Julius et al. 2008). Again, the best approach to designing long-lived hydrologic infrastructure might be a precautionary one: giving more generous setbacks to watercourses and minimising water use as a general rule regardless of supply are simple steps. If more generous setbacks from urban watercourses are coupled with wildlife corridors, seasonal land uses, parks, urban agriculture, or renewable energy generation, multiple adaptation benefits may be achieved while maintaining the land's economic value.

*Land and carbon sequestration*

Sequestering carbon from the atmosphere in biomass and soil is emerging as a major component of climate change reduction strategies. Planting trees, restoring grasslands, forests, wetlands (particularly peat-forming wetlands), and no-till agricultural practices are some of the less expensive and more beneficial carbon offset technologies. If combined with ecosystem restoration, carbon sequestration could assist both climate change reduction and adaptation of built and natural systems. Biomimicry design of high sequestering wetlands could lead to a new role for urban water features. Even the simple decision to increase tree planting and tree size in small-scale landscape installations is becoming a frequent consideration as climate change mitigation becomes more widespread.

*Urban heat island*

Another benefit of tree planting is urban heat island mitigation. Climate change will exacerbate this effect, which today can lead to more than a six-degree Celsius increase in urban air temperatures compared to the surrounding natural landscape (United States Environmental Protection Agency 2008). Vegetated and highly reflective surfaces reduce this effect, while trees provide the added benefit of shade at the ground level and on buildings, reducing energy use.

Another mitigation measure involves aligning land use with local climatic patterns to leverage the benefits of atmospheric cooling. This may include orienting urban centres with valleys to allow evening valley cooling to penetrate the urban core, placing water features upwind of urban centres in hot-dry climates, maximising urban soil moisture retention in hot-dry climates, and placing tall buildings at the upwind edge of cities to facilitate atmospheric mixing.

**ABOVE**
Alternative work-in-progress scenarios for subregional
urban growth in Arizona. The business-as-usual scenario
(left) depicts a traditional open space framework limited to
narrow, channelled watercourses. A present-day best practice
scenario (centre) includes expanded watercourses and large
but fragmented conservation areas limited to hilly areas. The
eco-cities development scenario (right) maximises ecosystem
services and climate change adaptation potential through a
reduced development footprint and an ecologically-diverse and
well-connected open space network.

*Mobile architecture*
Even the revived mobile architecture movement
may have increasing value as the climate warms
and populations grow. Since many of the ecological
problems of climate change are temporal in nature,
mobile architecture has the benefit of allowing
people to move out of the way of predictable
events. Designating mobile architecture zones
in areas predicted for sea level rise, flooding
during rainy seasons, increased fire in dry
seasons, or where seasonal species migration
must be balanced with growing populations could
satisfy the need for more land for people and for
accommodating natural processes.

*People connection*
Designing land use to improve cultural connections
with nature may also be beneficial to adaptation.
As the global population becomes more urban,
the cultural disconnection with nature and
ecosystem services widens. Many studies have
shown that contact with nature is correlated
with conservation behaviour and human health
(Kaplan 1995 and Kellert 2005). Most cities are
designed with nature at the fringe and natural
resource-based activities in surrounding rural
lands. Cities of the future could reduce the nature
contact deficit in high density areas by increasing
urban natural areas and natural resource-based
activities, such as urban farming. This closeness
to nature also means more direct contact
between people and climate change impacts
on ecosystems, potentially fostering greater
awareness and action.

For example, as an urban farm feels the direct effects of climate change, the close proximity of consumers to the farm brings broader understanding of the impacts. In the case of biodiversity, if urban natural areas contain iconic native species that are dying out because of climate change, residents would witness the impacts first hand and may be more concerned and aware of conservation. Leaving a wide floodplain rather than channelled watercourses through cites would allow people to better observe changing water regimes. Schools located near a natural area, an urban farm, or watercourse, could use these as learning tools in their curriculum. Instilling deeper knowledge of ecology among citizens is an important step in addressing the complexity of climate change. Keeping its impacts front and centre through integrated urban design will raise the awareness necessary to achieve climate change adaptive communities.

## Conclusion

Terrestrial ecosystems are dynamic and changing. They provide us with diverse services, such as flood and tidal protection, erosion control, urban heat island reduction, pest control, improved air quality and pollination. Climate change will drive dramatic ecosystem change and, with it, the services they provide. Our infrastructure and land use must now be retooled to accommodate these changes. No region is adequately planned for climate change impacts. Mitigation strategies must begin with evaluating existing regional land use performance, potential ecosystem changes, and climate change vulnerabilities. In many cases these strategies will involve developing new infrastructure to protect human populations from destructive changes and to protect biodiversity as habitats rearrange with changing regional climates. Planning approaches must promote regenerative strategies that rapidly transform land uses to support regional adaptation of both human and natural communities.

Fostering land use transformation will depend on achieving broad awareness of the ecological implications of climate change. Land use approaches in which urban areas and ecosystem services are designed as integrated systems could encourage greater awareness and local accountability when future impacts occur. Such approaches are now being adopted within the sustainable development movement, with mega-scale centralised infrastructure being exchanged for finer grain solutions, such as distributed energy generation, urban agriculture, multi-modal transit, and dispersed stormwater management. Additionally, integrating habitat and biodiversity equitably into cities could make climate change impacts on species more visible to more of the population.

We are at a critical point where the impacts of climate change are just beginning to be felt in our terrestrial landscapes. Many of our landscapes still feature ancient biotic communities and unaffected ecosystem services. We must act boldly to mitigate the destructive forces of climate change on ill-prepared land uses and conservation strategies.

LEFT
Reinserting natural areas and ecosystem services into urban areas can facilitate community engagement with nature. It can also offset high densities, promote understanding and admiration of natural systems, and increase conservation behaviour.

While adapting to climate change in existing cities will be complex, long term, and costly, we can look to areas of urban expansion for early implementation of climate-sensitive design approaches. The following case studies explore how this emerging design paradigm is being applied at the urban fringe. The first is the ecologically-designed Hunter Economic Zone, which showcases leading edge climate-adaptive design technologies. The second, Eagle Mountain, is an award-winning conceptual design study which explores climate-adaptive subregional growth.

# Case study: industry within the bush

The design of a new 1,000-hectare industrial estate offers a rare opportunity to create a visually-compelling, consistent and high-quality bushland landscape environment that conserves and supplements local fauna habitats and endangered vegetation communities.

The landscape response for the Hunter Economic Zone in Australia's Hunter Valley envisions industry within the bush, rather than an industrial estate with bush landscaping. To realise this vision, the design accommodates industry in a way that ensures the essence and substance of the bush as context remains strong and defined. The area's five signature vegetation communities present a diverse palette of colour, form, texture, and scale, while the landscape response appreciates the site's *genus loci* and works cooperatively with its existing environmental processes.

*Integrating water sensitive urban design*
A strategy of stormwater harvesting on individual lots and at the cluster scale will maintain runoff volumes at close to pre-development levels, conserving the existing ephemeral hydrologic regime and site ecology, including the habitat of the endangered Green-thighed Frog.

During times of heavy rain, swales and detention storages will buffer and slow stormwater runoff to protect local creeks from erosive flows. Where the underlying soils are conducive to infiltration, French drains and infiltration areas will encourage groundwater recharge. On-site detention basins on each lot attenuate flood flows and prevent the development from flooding downstream areas. No net increase in the 100-year discharge will result from the site's development.

A broad riparian conservation corridor runs through the industrial estate.

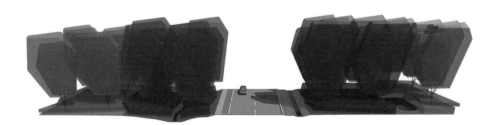

30-metre wide bushland corridors along roadsides conserve and supplement local fauna habitats and endangered vegetation communities.

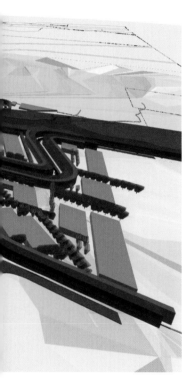

*Provenance plant material*
Using only plant material of local provenance mitigates dilution of the local bushland gene pool. A site-specific handbook identifies locally indigenous species that are aesthetically appealing, reliable to cultivate and cost little to grow, maintain, and replace. A plant procurement database compiles all information required to collect, propagate, and plant vegetation to inform future work by developers and landscape architects alike.

*Regeneration through soil strategy*
Specialist soil stripping and reinstatement processes will help regenerate bushland across the development, exploiting the viability of the burgeoning native soil seed bank sourced from local lands. Direct seeding of local provenance native grasses supplements these processes. Studies on site show a high success rate for bushland regeneration from relocated topsoil. This offers a relatively inexpensive and effective landscape restoration solution to deal with road verges, embankments, and other areas of development within the Hunter Economic Zone.

*Sharing the knowledge*
This landscape restoration approach requires a coordinated and informed civil contracting team to maximise conservation outcomes and to apply the methodology of topsoil stripping and reinstatement without compromising the fragility of the site topsoil. Plant operators and supervisors learn soil types, soil horizon depth and stockpiling techniques during on-site training sessions.

*Making connections*
Road networks not only connect with nearby townships. They form an environmentally and economically efficient network to service the most lots with the least roads and creek crossings. Road networks follow existing watercourses, where possible, forming bushfire protection zones, bushland management boundaries, and stormwater management corridors before discharging into conserved natural watercourses.

Studies on site show a high success rate for bushland regeneration from relocated topsoil.

# Case study: ecologically-sensitive development at Eagle Mountain

How can a new community in a pristine location facing extensive development foster ecologically-sensitive, socially-vibrant, and economically-successful subregional growth? A study of ideas explores the answers for California's Eagle Mountain.

Located at the meeting point of Interstate 10, an approaching urban fringe, and the last great wilderness of Southern California, Eagle Mountain may soon face a flood of urban sprawl. A new community development, no matter how internally green, will trigger an increase in the velocity and volume of this urban flood.

Given this context and risk, the conceptual response explores multi-scale planning infrastructure to safely accommodate an initial community of around 600 permanent residences, along with up to 300 additional environmentally-dependant mobile dwellings. It focuses on three core concepts: understanding spatial and temporal scales; applying principles of ecological design, adaptive reuse, and eco-permeability; and fostering vibrant and sustainable modes of living and working.

### *Context in scales*

Ecology and human impacts cross all boundaries and often have far reaching and complex consequences, so the concept maximises its benefit to ecosystems and urban systems at all scales. From its global, regional, vicinity, and community implications, through to its site and microsite effects, the design response reduces the on- and off-site ecological footprint and promotes a flourishing and equitable society.

### *Ecological design, adaptive reuse, and eco-permeability*

The design maximises indigenous biodiversity and landscape character. It explores the concept of eco-permeability, which strives to create permanent and mobile built forms and landscapes that respond to the indigenous spatial-temporal flux of natural patterns and processes and biotic movement. The design form aligns with the valley's natural alluvial and biotic processes accordingly.

### *Vibrant and sustainable modes of living and working*

The design envisions a comprehensively planned and truly sustainable community, with an economy initially based on the rehabilitation of unsustainable landscape features. Economic activity on site and in the valley is contained through strict controls on unsustainable environmental activities. These controls, coupled with regional population growth and mounting sustainability consciousness, gradually fosters an economy and development pattern founded on environmental sensitivity and impact mitigation. A culture of ecological living, social equity, and artistic inspiration emerges.

*No-pollution zone and eco-urban fabric*
The concept shapes the future of the region and represents a new era of infrastructure development. The vision combines the opportunity of expansive public lands, the last great open space between Los Angeles and Phoenix, little existing economic activity, and high vulnerability to urban sprawl to create a regional zone designated and elevated to the highest levels of sustainable use. It establishes a no-pollution zone called *NO-POL* in the region to promote a carbon-negative and ecologically-regenerative eco-urban fabric. This zone will reduce Southern California's impacts on global and local climate, biota, and natural systems, while fostering vibrant, healthy, and creative local communities.

*Ecological infrastructure*
The concept envisions a valley where a no-pollution transit system and electric vehicles replace most combustion engine vehicles. Centres called *greenstops* along Interstate 10 become districts of green technology and sustainability services, with local organic food, alternative fuels, and carbon sequestration facilities for the Los Angeles to Phoenix corridor.

Ecologically-unviable infrastructure and land use is decommissioned as new infrastructure is developed to create a valley-wide land use system framed by robust areas for natural patterns and processes creating an eco-permeable eco-grid.

Specifically, roads, aqueducts, utilities, and railways that bisect and channel alluvial fans are realigned and rebuilt to restore natural alluvial patterns and processes. Built form aligns with alluvial processes to preserve natural biotic patterns and improve biotic resilience to climate change by creating a continuous eco-grid fabric accommodating of species migration, succession, and adaptation. Historic rectangular agricultural fields are replaced with amygdaloidal forms that mimic natural alluvial patterns and processes.

Eagle Mountain's old township and disused mine site straddle an ecotone: a transition zone between the ecosystems of the mountains and the plains. The bisected area is returned to nature, to restore continuity of native biotic species adapted to the ecotone and to free species migration between and along the two adjacent ecosystems.

*Unique emerging activities*
Communities in the NO-POL zone feature development that is healthy, inspiring, and close to nature. Streets are quieter and narrower, catering not for cars but for smaller neighbourhood electric vehicles, transit systems, bicycles, pedestrians, and even horses. An industry develops initially around recycling and restoring the disused mine site and township, later shifting to tourism, the arts, education, and the greenstops.

The unique setting combined with its equidistant proximity to Los Angeles, Phoenix, and Las Vegas makes this an ideal location for an annual arts festival, potentially featuring monumental installations oriented to the landscape. Reuse of many mine roads for mountain biking, horse riding, and hiking in the neighbouring Joshua Tree National Park provides world-class recreation opportunities.

Wind farming and clean solar technology ultimately stimulates economic activity founded on renewable energy for the community and the region. Wind and solar farms are configured to mimic natural amygdaloidal alluvial fans. The existing town site is reduced, with development pushed down slope to restore and buffer the converging mountains and plains ecotone. Natural alluvial fans are re-established around towns and along the regional ecotone corridor, positioning towns within a healing natural landscape.

Existing town

Climate-adaptive town
footprint concept

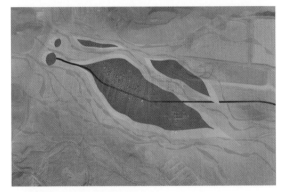

Existing subregion

Climate-adaptive
development concept

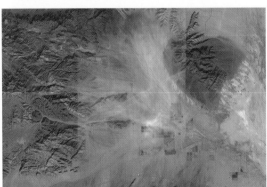

*Adaptable communities closer to nature*
Within the new community, dense living and
working areas are designed to encourage civic
vitality. Urban eco-permeability is achieved
through a system of greenways and habitat
nodes, encouraging wildlife and bringing
residents and visitors closer to nature.
Mobile architecture zones are designated along
old rail lines and in alluvial zones during the dry
season to allow people to live close to nature, but
in a way that is responsive to seasonal flooding
and biotic processes. During the wet season
mobile dwellings are brought into the community
and their impacts are restored through natural
alluvial processes. Some mobile dwellings
relocate via rail to fire-adapted oak woodlands in
the adjacent eco-region during the fire-free
wet season.

An outpost centre for restoration and recreation
activities is located on an abandoned prison site
within the ecotone corridor, just west of the new
community. Its green roof merges with the ground
to maximise eco-permeability through the corridor.

# Changing climates and the world's rivers and wetlands

Karen Appell, Christopher Benosky, Dr David Gallacher

Rivers and wetlands play a critical role in moderating global climate by capturing and storing atmospheric carbon, protecting biodiversity resources, mitigating flood impacts, and reducing urban heat island effects. However, global climate change is threatening these environments: environments already under pressure from human activities that drain natural water bodies, clear land for development, and introduce pollutants to wetland ecosystems.

## Definitions of rivers and wetlands

Wetlands occur where the ground is saturated long enough during the growing season to develop anaerobic conditions, creating hydric soils that in turn support wetland vegetation. These habitats can be found from the Arctic tundra to the tropics, and on every continent except Antarctica. Wetland typology varies widely because of regional and local differences in soil composition, topography, climate, hydrology, water chemistry, vegetation, and other factors. Because of this diversity, any definition of wetlands and rivers is necessarily quite broad. Currently, a commonly adopted definition is that given in Article 1.1 of the *Convention on Wetlands of International Importance* signed at Ramsar, Iran in 1971, also known as the Ramsar Convention.

> Wetlands are areas of marsh, fen, peatland or water, whether natural or artificial, permanent or temporary, with water that is static or flowing, fresh, brackish or salt, including areas of marine water the depth of which at low tide does not exceed six metres. (Ramsar 2007)

## Importance of rivers and wetlands

Rivers, once used as sewage disposal conduits, and wetlands, once regarded as unproductive wastelands, are now viewed as highly valuable ecosystems. In the United States in the 1970s, an awareness of human-induced impacts to rivers and wetlands and the associated environmental consequences prompted the enactment of various federal, state, and local legislation and executive declarations. More recently, as developmental pressures continue to increase and as we better understand the impacts of global climate change, other values of wetlands have come to be recognised, including carbon sequestration and storage, urban heat reduction, and economic, cultural, and social aspects, such as ecotourism and public education.

### *Wildlife habitat and biodiversity*

Rivers and wetlands inherently provide diverse wildlife habitat due to their natural variety of vegetation, water levels, and topographic features. In addition, wetlands and rivers are often closely linked to other ecosystems, with lakes and oceans on the lower end of the elevation gradient and upland forests and meadows flanking higher areas, further increasing the potential for biodiversity.

Wetlands and rivers provide a vital ecological resource for wildlife habitat, supporting high concentrations of birds (especially waterfowl), mammals, reptiles, amphibians, fish, and invertebrate species. In the United States, for example, wetlands cover only 3.5 per cent of the total land area, but support over a third of all nationally endangered species (Mitsch and Gosselink 2000, p. 920). Of the 20,000 species of fish in the world, more than 40 per cent (some 8,500 species) live in freshwater wetlands (Ramsar Convention Bureau 1996).

The heterogeneity of wetlands and rivers also accommodates endemic organisms that dwell only in narrow, specific habitat types. The Amazon River alone has 1,800 endemic species of fish (Ramsar 2000). Many endangered species are entirely dependent on single aquatic ecosystems, such as the as the Chinese sturgeon (*Acipenser sinensis*), which is solely dependent on the Changjiang River and its estuary.

*Flood storage and storm protection*
Floods occur throughout the world, causing loss of life and damage to property and agricultural resources. In 2004, the flooding of China's eastern provinces resulted in 1,280 deaths and damaged 7.7 million hectares of agricultural land, with direct economic losses estimated at RMB71.3 billion (Ministry of Water Resources 2006).

A river's natural flood storage occurs within its floodplain. Allowing waters to overflow into the floodplain provides additional flow capacity and flood storage, in turn reducing downstream flooding impacts. Wetlands also reduce flooding brought about by heavy rainfall by intercepting and storing stormwater, then slowly releasing it to stream channels via surface or groundwater flow. In this way, wetlands allow downstream areas to benefit from reduced peak floodwater levels during prolonged flood periods. A one-acre wetland can typically store about three-acre feet of water, equal to one million gallons (United States Environmental Protection Agency 2006).

*Water supply and water quality improvement*
Clean freshwater provided by rivers and wetlands
is the most important environmental service
for human populations. It is estimated humans
withdraw about 4,000 cubic kilometres of water a
year from freshwater systems—about 20 per cent
of the world's rivers base flow—for agricultural,
industrial, and domestic use. The total amount
of water withdrawn or extracted from freshwater
systems has risen 35-fold in the past 300 years
(Revenga et al. 1998).

Complex physical, chemical, and biological
processes in wetlands combine to create
a powerful environment for the recycling,
transformation, and immobilisation of pollutants.
In natural wetlands, water quality is improved
by effectively filtering and absorbing suspended
solids, heavy metals, and other contaminants.
This capacity drives the design for most
constructed wetlands to treat water pollution
in its variety of forms (Scholz 2006, p. 360).
Constructed wetlands can remove from 48 to
80 per cent of Biological Oxygen Demand,
suspended solids, nitrogen, and phosphorous from
water (Kadlec and Knight 1996, p. 893).

*Carbon sequestration and storage*
Natural ecosystems have the ability to capture
and store atmospheric carbon dioxide. As plants
grow, they absorb $CO_2$ from the atmosphere and
convert it to biomass. Carbon is contained in living
vegetation and also in litter, peat, and organic
soils and sediments that have accumulated, in
some instances, over thousands of years (Kusler
1999). In fact, wetlands are more productive
in terms of biomass production than any other
ecosystem, except tropical rainforests (Campbell
and Ogden 1999).

ABOVE
California's Upper Truckee River and Wetland Restoration project will restore natural river and
wetland processes; preserve and enhance habitat for wildlife and sensitive plant species; improve
water quality; and provide public access, recreation, and environmental education opportunities
consistent with natural resources sensitivities.

Wetlands can also provide longer-term carbon storage than other ecosystems because decomposition processes are inhibited by saturated wetland soils, high acidity (in bogs), and low temperatures (in tundra). For example, it is not uncommon to find 10 or more metres of unconsolidated organic matter in peatlands, and forested tropical peatlands in South East Asia are estimated to store at least 42,000 megatonnes of soil carbon (Hooijer et al. 2008). Furthermore, as sea levels rise, tidal marshes accrete to match the rise in water level (Trulio, Callaway and Crooks 2007), continually pulling $CO_2$ as sediments accumulate.

*Cultural, social, and economic benefits*

Aside from the environmental benefits, rivers and wetlands also provide important cultural, social, and economic benefits. The Ramsar website (2000) identifies many of these, including:

- Fisheries – two-thirds of marine fish, including many commercially important species, rely on coastal wetlands at some stage in their life cycle;

- Wetland products – products from mangroves include thatch for roofing, fibres for textile and paper-making, timber, fuelwood, medicines, dyes, and tannins;

- Tourism and recreation – recreational fishing involves 45 million people in the United States, spending US$24 billion annually; and

- Cultural and spiritual – approximately 30 per cent of internationally important wetlands have some archaeological, historical, religious, or cultural significance at local or national levels.

Together with environmental benefits, such as flood prevention and water quality improvement, the total value of wetlands globally has been estimated at US$14.9 trillion (Constanza et al. 1997).

## Climate change threats to wetlands and rivers

Climate change threatens rivers and wetlands. Impacts can be direct, such as changes to ecosystems resulting from rising temperatures; others are indirect, such as hydrological changes resulting from altered precipitation patterns. Furthermore, the effects of climate change on rivers and wetlands are likely to be exacerbated by other human activities including development and over-extraction. It is the cumulative effect of these stresses that ultimately jeopardise the functionality and survival of fragile wetland ecosystems. Bergkamp and Orlando (1999) provide a concise summary of the various climate change-induced impacts, which are described and expanded below.

*Hydrologic effects*

The Intergovernmental Panel on Climate Change (IPCC) (2001) noted various aspects of wetland hydrology likely to be influenced by climate change, including precipitation, evaporation, transpiration, runoff, and groundwater recharge and flow. Additionally, increased global temperatures are likely to exert an overall drying effect on wetland habitats. Hydrological change is likely to be the most significant climate change-related impact to wetland ecosystems, as hydrology is the single most important factor that determines wetland location and ecological structure and function. As a consequence of declining precipitation and increased evaporation, larger permanent wetlands may decrease in size or shift from wetland to upland habitat. Small ephemeral wetland systems, such as seasonal streams and vernal pools, may disappear completely. These transformations are of particular concern for wetlands in arid and semi-arid areas.

*Impacts of sea level rise*

Increasing global temperatures are predicted to cause a rise in sea levels, resulting from melting of the polar ice caps and thermal expansion of ocean water. The Fourth IPCC Assessment Report estimates sea-level rises up to 59 centimetres by the next century (IPCC 2007). Recent research suggests that this figure may in fact be an underestimate, with sea levels potentially rising by 0.8 to two metres by 2100 (Pfeffer et al. 2008).

Rising sea levels will affect the tidal regimes that control the hydrology of many coastal wetlands. These habitats are highly reliant upon the accumulation of organic matter to maintain their surface elevation with respect to sea level. As sea level rise accelerates, some wetlands may be unable to keep pace and consequently will be inundated or eroded to the point of converting to open water. As these ecosystems disappear, the rate at which sediment from the wetlands is removed and transported to adjacent water bodies such as rivers, bays, and oceans will increase (World Wildlife Federation 2008).

Related to rising sea levels is the expected increase in the frequency and severity of tropical storms. Storm surges associated with tropical storms can directly affect both tidal and freshwater wetlands through increased coastal flooding, habitat loss, increased salinity of estuaries and freshwater aquifers, modified tidal ranges in rivers and bays, atypical transport of sediments and nutrients, and patterns of contamination in coastal areas (Bergkamp and Orlando 1999). For example, in 2005, Hurricanes Katrina and Rita converted 562 square kilometres of wetlands and other coastal land to open water in the Mississippi Deltaic Plain (Farris et al. 2007).

*Changing temperatures*

Rising temperatures will likely result in direct increases in the water temperatures in lakes and rivers (Bergkamp and Orlando 1999). The strongest effect would be at high latitudes and in low-latitude boundaries of cold-water and cool-water species ranges and where extinction would be greatest (Watson, Zinyowera and Moss 1996). Small changes can have disastrous affects on rare and endangered plant and animal species as their temperature-sensitive nature leaves them with no alternative habitat, especially in isolated areas like montane and alpine wetlands.

## Consequences of impacts to wetlands and rivers

The consequences of climate change will affect the capacity of wetland and river ecosystems to provide their most important ecological functions. As the benefits that establish wetlands and rivers as such valuable resources are lost, their ability to mitigate climate change impacts slowly decreases, creating a cycle of further degradation.

*Global carbon cycle*

Destruction of tidal wetlands can greatly impact carbon sequestration and storage. Marsh vegetation does not contribute to continual carbon storage as it does not build up woody material from year to year, as trees do (Trulio, Callaway and Crooks 2007). However, large amounts of carbon can be released when vegetation is eradicated or burned to clear these areas for development. Furthermore, when tidal wetlands are excavated or otherwise disturbed, stored carbon is released into the atmosphere as carbon dioxide due to increased rates of oxidation of soils, leading to aerobic decomposition.

The global carbon cycle could also be adversely impacted by rising wetland and river temperatures. In particular, the warming of subarctic and boreal wetlands could lead to the melting of large areas of permafrost, increasing the rate of soil decomposition and releasing carbon dioxide (and another greenhouse gases, such as methane) into the atmosphere. Tranvik et al. (2002) list recent estimates of the total quantity of peat carbon stores that could be released as a consequence of global warming, with figures varying from between some 200 to 1,500 gigatonnes. To put these values into context, the IPCC (1990, p. 365) notes that our entire atmosphere contains just 750 gigatonnes of carbon, although this value is currently increasing at three gigatonne per year.

*Water supply issues*

Water supply is already a significant issue in many parts of the world, with recent studies estimating one billion people do not have access to safe and affordable drinking water, and 2.4 billion people live in conditions lacking adequate sanitation (Parliamentary Office of Science and Technology 2002). Water demand is likely to increase in the future in response to rising temperatures, increasing populations, and expanding agricultural and industrial activity. In arid and semi-arid areas, populations are largely reliant on aquifers for water supply. The recharge of aquifers through seasonal inundations of floodplain wetland areas represents an important process for the maintenance of these water resources (IPCC 2001), and the loss of these wetlands will have serious implications for maintaining water supplies in the future.

In snow-dominated regions, the majority of flow in rivers and streams is supplied by snow melt water. As global temperatures increase, this melt water will occur earlier in the year, shifting peak river flow periods from summer and autumn (when water demand is highest) to late winter and spring. Where storage capacities are insufficient, much of the winter runoff will be lost to the oceans. Given that more than one-sixth of the Earth's population relies on glacier and seasonal snow melt for water supply (Barnett, Adam and Lettenmaier 2005) this situation could have serious implications.

Measures to address these issues, such as dam construction to collect and store river water and for hydropower, will further impact wetland habitats. Dam construction increases habitat fragmentation, inhibiting the movement of plants and animals to other locations over time in response to changing temperature or water levels.

*Habitat loss*

Habitat loss due to climate change essentially concerns changes in wetland habitat types and can be caused by many different stressors, such as temperatures changes, altered hydrology, or impaired water quality. Development can be cited for the direct loss of natural habitat, but climate change impacts actually transform specific habitats so that the plants, soil conditions, and wildlife associated with that habitat are no longer present.

## Planning and design innovations

To combat climate change, it is imperative that
we adopt design and planning strategies to
protect and restore existing wetlands and rivers.
However, there is also great potential to contribute
further to mitigating climate change by creating
new self-sustaining wetland ecosystems that
can be integrated within our natural and built
environments. Regarding the protection and
restoration of existing wetlands and rivers, Kusler
(1999) proposes a number of strategies, including:

- Protecting natural wetlands systems;

- Conducting regional inventories management
  planning for wetlands of greatest importance
  as carbon reserves and for carbon
  sequestering;

- Controlling fires;

- Protecting low flows and residual water;

- Installing water control structures;

- Planting trees and other vegetation; and

- Restoring, enhancing, and creating wetlands to
  provide for additional carbon sinks.

These strategies provide a solid foundation
for integrating responses to climate change in
planning and design efforts, being straightforward
and simple to apply. However, more complex
trends and philosophies are emerging that address
fundamental issues of climate change, wetlands,
planning, and design.

*Trends in sustainable planning and design*

Planning efforts to mitigate climate change and
also to protect and preserve our existing wetlands
and rivers must not only be based on government
jurisdictions, but also in the context of the
broader ecological landscape, whether based
on watersheds, eco-regions, or other important
landscape units. Land management strategies
and public policies also increase the viability
and sustainability of water resources, further
mitigating the effects of climate change.

*Land management*

The ability of biological communities to respond
to changing conditions is largely moderated by the
spatial configuration of habitats within the larger
landscape, and by the scale at which individual
organisms perceive the landscape (Kiviat and
MacDonald 2004). Land management planning
usually considers the importance of contiguous
natural areas for functional habitat and to allow
for successful wildlife migration, but future
planning also needs to factor the importance of
connectivity to keep hydrologic patterns intact.

Without proper planning, groundwater flows can
be interrupted by below ground structures, natural
stream processes can be impaired by culverts
and hard structure banks, and wetlands can be
fragmented due to development pressures. By
maintaining natural processes, the snowball effect
of degradation that can be intensified by climate
change impacts can be avoided.

Preservation and planning for large contiguous
areas allows for better adaptation to climate
change, based on the simple fact that the
impact to a larger area is less noticeable that
the same impact to a smaller area. However,
smaller, fragmented areas should also be viewed
as potentially important habitat both for rare
and common species, and also as an important
amenity for humans (Kiviat & MacDonald, 2004),
especially in urban areas.

**ABOVE**
The South Bay Salt Pond Restoration is the largest tidal wetland restoration project on the West Coast of the United States. When complete, the restoration will convert thousands of former commercial salt ponds to a mix of tidal marsh, mudflat, managed pond, and other wetland habitats. The project will also provide flood management and opportunities for wildlife-oriented public access and recreation.

*Watershed planning*

Watershed planning is a large-scale planning methodology that ensures receiving wetlands and rivers are protected from the impacts of urban stormwater runoff including pollutants, excess sediment, and flood flows. As part of this process, development in each watershed is carefully planned, incorporating Low Impact Development (LID) technologies and total water cycle management.

LID practices promote the concept of planning and designing sustainable sites in concert with the natural surrounding ecosystems; in essence, LID treats rainwater as a resource to be preserved and protected by:

- Minimising site disturbance;
- Preserving important on-site ecological features;
- Reducing or disconnecting impervious cover;
- Flattening steep slopes;
- Utilising native vegetation in landscaping;
- Minimising turf grass lawns; and
- Maintaining natural drainage patterns, features, and characteristics.

Total water cycle management planning recognises the finite limits to a region's water resources and assumes greater importance as the level of demand approaches those limits. It is a holistic approach to balancing the competing demands placed on water resources. Key principles include recognising all potential sources of water, including wastewater and stormwater; using all water sources sustainably; allocating and using water equitably; and integrating water use and natural water processes, including maintaining environmental flows and water quality.

*Water sensitive urban design*

Water plays an important role in most design projects; as an aesthetic landscape feature, a drinking water supply, a wastewater stream, or as stormwater runoff. Therefore, to protect water resources, designs must focus on the sustainability of natural and urban water cycles. Planning and design that embraces this approach is known as water sensitive urban design (WSUD).

The WSUD approach to designing urban environments fully appreciates the issues of water sustainability and environmental protection. It reflects synergies within the urban built form (including urban landscapes) and the urban water cycle (as defined by the conventional urban water streams of potable water, wastewater, and stormwater). The foundation of WSUD lies in LID techniques and the idea of treating stormwater as a resource to be used and managed, creating and incorporating human-made ecosystems, such as rain gardens, biofiltration and retention systems, constructed stormwater wetlands, vegetated swales, and green roofs. Combining these WSUD ideas with LID techniques provides a hydrological design framework to detain, treat, and in some cases, reuse stormwater runoff before it enters the natural receiving water bodies.

The WSUD approach provides holistic sustainable management of the natural and urban water cycle, while integrating it with the design of the built form. The design transition from standard engineering practices to more sustainable approaches promotes the protection, preservation, restoration, enhancement, and creation of wetlands and rivers. WSUD helps define ways these features can be integrated into our built environments. This is explored in greater detail by Professor Tony Wong in his discussion on water sensitive cities.

*Public policy*

At all levels of government, an important part of the planning process involves the implementation of sound policies that promote holistic watershed management. To reduce the impacts on our wetlands and rivers and to help mitigate global climate change, policies and regulations must provide incentives for sustainable design approaches. Examples include adequate buffer and setback requirements; proper landscaping materials and landscape design; LEED elements and green building requirements; density increases or transfers; roadway and parking standards to reduce impervious surfaces; open space preservation; tree canopy goals; and changes to the development review processes and submittal requirements. Structuring policy and regulations to promote these practices will encourage the development community to protect and preserve our water resources.

To be successful, the planning process must also include public outreach, education, and involvement. Meaningful community participation is central to the success of any future planning efforts that focus on climate change. To ensure a plan can be implemented by local municipalities, as well as being accepted by environmental groups, neighbourhood organisations, developers, and concerned citizens, it must encourage integration of public opinion and create consensus. Establishing environmental stakeholder committees with local and regional representation to guide the planning process, performing stakeholder interviews, and organising public events to educate, share information, and solicit input for plan goals and opportunities are all essential tools.

## Looking to the future

Future design strategies must incorporate sustainable water management techniques and focus on natural resources. Research shows that restoring tidal wetlands or salt marshes is one of the most effective measures for sequestering carbon. While planting trees is often looked to as a way to take carbon from the atmosphere, marsh restoration may be even more efficient per unit area at removing carbon (Trulio, Callaway and Crooks 2007). In their review of North American wetlands, Brigham et al. (2006) state that 'estuarine wetlands sequester carbon at a rate about 10-fold higher on an area basis than any other wetland ecosystem due to high sedimentation rates, high soil carbon content, and constant burial due to sea level rise'.

Design in the face of climate change requires us to analyse and evaluate a complex set of variables, including:

- Sea level rise;
- Changing trends in precipitation patterns, storm frequencies, and storm intensities;
- Temperature variability and future trends;
- Water supply (from snow stores, glaciers, and groundwater, for example) now and in the future; and
- Increasing pollutant levels and concentrations of contamination.

The interconnected nature of these variables requires an integrated design approach with meaningful collaboration among many disciplines, bringing together planners, architects, engineers, and scientists versed in the context of design, as well as language of climate change. Only by merging these various practices and utilising the sustainable design tools available to us can adaptation and mitigation for global climate change be integrated in our future designs. These approaches will protect, enhance, restore, and create self-sustaining wetlands and rivers that interact and flow seamlessly between our natural and built environments.

The implementation of watershed planning, land management, and public policy will provide a framework to incorporate sound design principles into our future development projects. Fragile ecosystems will be protected and, in turn, can remain as resources that will help minimise the impact of global climate change.

# Coastal design and planning: areas of transition

## Vivian Lee

Coastal areas have typically been defined as the transition areas between land and sea (Food and Agriculture Organisation of the United Nations (FAO) 1998). However, the term *transition area* should not be misconstrued as insignificant areas to be passed over in favour of land or sea. Rather, coastal areas serve as the nexus of human interactions with each other and with nature, support vital economic and subsistence activities, and provide critical terrestrial and aquatic habitats that support rich biological diversity.

### Coastal functions

Coastal areas serve many functions, including carbon sequestration, economic, cultural and social benefits, and ecosystem services.

### *Carbon storage*

While freshwater wetlands play a role as carbon sinks, salt marshes and mangroves found on marine coastlines store more carbon per unit area, while also releasing negligible amounts of methane (Chmura et al. 2003). Carbon is contained in the standing crops of trees and other vegetation and in litter, peats, organic soils, and sediments, and it has been estimated that wetlands hold 35 per cent of the total terrestrial carbon (Kusler 1999). Tidal salt marshes can accumulate soil in tandem with sea level rise, increasing their adaptability to climate change impacts. Choi and Wang (2004) note that coastal wetlands could be more valuable carbon sinks per unit area than any other ecosystem in a warmer world due to their sequestration capabilities and lower methane emissions. These studies underscore the vital and complex role that coastal wetlands play in the global carbon cycle and, by extension, climate change.

Tidal salt marshes can accumulate
soil in tandem with sea level rise,
increasing their adaptability to
climate change impacts.

*Economic, social, and cultural centres*
Humans have long been attracted to coastal areas
as a source of food, water, natural resources,
and employment. In 2000, 10 per cent of the
world's total population—634 million people—
lived in low elevation coastal zones (McGranahan,
Balk and Anderson 2007). Approximately
65 per cent of cities with more than five million
inhabitants are at least partially in the low
elevation coastal zone (zero to 10 metres), and
in Asia, three quarters of the population lives
in these areas (United Nations Population Fund
2007). In the United States, around half the
population lives in coastal areas, at densities
five times greater than those of non-coastal
counties, and coastal counties are growing three
times faster than those elsewhere (United States
Environmental Protection Agency 2008).
People are drawn to the water for economic,
cultural, and social reasons and coastal
urbanisation is expected to continue.

LEFT
Coastal areas serve as the nexus of human interactions
with each other and with nature, support vital economic and
subsistence activities, and provide critical terrestrial and
aquatic habitats that support rich biological diversity.

Cities have traditionally been established along trading routes, which have historically been in coastal areas. Many of the world's major cities, as well as economic, cultural, and social activities are located in these areas (FAO 1998). Resource-based activities (such as coastal fisheries, aquaculture, forestry, and agriculture) and industrial activities (such as shipping and manufacturing) are frequently dependant on coastal resources. The success of local and national economies is closely associated with their proximity to coastal resources, whether from tourism or industrial activity.

Cultural resources are intimately tied with coastal areas; historic settlements, archaeological artefacts, and traditional foods and practices are found in these areas worldwide. Coastal areas draw people together for recreation and tourism, provide a sense of place, and are often a source of local and national pride as well as a way of life.

### Biodiversity and ecosystem services

Coastal areas are dynamic environments that lie at the intersection of land and sea systems. Unique coastal ecosystems such as marine, estuary, and coastal wetlands have very high biological productivity; approximately 90 per cent of the world's fish production depends on coastal areas during their life cycle (FAO 1998). Biological diversity is also associated with coasts, with many coastlines supporting migratory and non-migratory waterfowl and endangered reptiles.

In addition to biodiversity, coastal ecosystems such as mangroves and reefs help alleviate the impacts of natural disasters by mitigating storm tide surges and floods, controlling coastal erosion, and delaying shoreline retreat. For example, mangroves can withstand changes in water salinity, prolonged submersion, and inhospitable soil, moderating monsoonal tidal floods and protecting coasts through sediment accretion and land stabilisation (Harakunararak and Aksornkoae 2005).

### Threats to coastal areas

Every year, natural hazards cause tens of thousands of deaths, hundreds of thousands of injuries, and billions of dollars in economic losses around the world (Dilley et al. 2005). Natural hazards facing coasts include hurricanes, earthquakes, floods, landslides, tsunamis, shoreline erosion, land subsidence, and algal blooms. While these hazards occur regardless of human influence, development in coastal zones exponentially increases risks to human life and economic losses.

Every year, natural hazards cause tens of thousands of deaths, hundreds of thousands of injuries, and billions of dollars in economic losses around the world.

### Anthropogenic forces

In some cases, the very resources that have attracted people to coasts now threaten their functions: development pressures, deforestation, water extraction, dams, reclamation, and deviation of rivers have all taken their toll.

Urban development in coastal areas diminishes the area of fertile land and releases untreated sewage and other pollutants into the water, threatening coastal ecosystems. An index of potential threats posed by development to coastal ecosystems has been developed, based on five global indicators: population density, cities, major ports, road networks, and pipelines (Burkett et al. 1998).

According to this research, roughly half the world's coasts are facing moderate or high threats from development. These threats include point and non-point pollution, direct and indirect destruction of coastal ecosystems, changes in freshwater flows from dams, aquaculture, tree harvesting, overfishing, and introduction of species from ballast water. Economic infrastructure activities such as reclaiming land, building ports, roadways, energy facilities, shoreline stabilisation, and agricultural operations all pose cumulative threats to coastal resources (National Oceanic and Atmospheric Administration (NOAA) 2007).

Development can have unintended destructive impacts. Deforestation, for example, may result in diminished biodiversity. Less immediately evident, deforestation also reduces the land's ability to stabilise soil, resulting in erosion and siltation at other locations. Siltation of rivers increases flooding hazards as it reduces rivers' ability to hold water. Destruction of mudflats also increases flooding risks as they normally dissipate wave energy and protect salt marshes and coastal defences, in addition to providing valuable habitat for migratory birds (UK Biodiversity Group 1999)

Urban development in coastal zones exposes humans to storms, floods, and cyclones. In turn, development can damage the natural defences of coastlines, such as mangrove forests. Urbanisation along coastlines is happening especially quickly in China and other parts of the world such as Bangladesh, where more than 40 per cent of the land area is within 10 metres above sea level (McGranahan, Balk and Anderson 2007).

*Impacts of climate change on coasts*
Coastal areas that are already threatened by human activity and natural hazards are under greater pressure from the impacts of global warming. Research conducted by Nicholls et al (2007, p. 4) indicates that urbanisation, coupled with a mean sea level rise of half a metre, could more than triple the number of people exposed to coastal flooding by 2070.

The distribution of expected climate change impacts will vary as different regions will face varying levels of risk. For example, coastal regions that have major lagoon systems may be impacted by saltwater intrusion and changes in freshwater flows, which may impact species that are the basis for aquaculture. South, east, and south-east Asian coastal cities are expected to be at greatest risk of river and coastal flooding (IPCC 2008, p. 83). Other impacted areas are the southern Mediterranean, Africa, the Caribbean, Indian Ocean islands, and the Pacific Ocean small islands. Impoverished and marginalised communities in poor countries are expected to face the greatest risks of climate change impacts.

Economic infrastructure activities such as reclaiming land, building ports, roadways, energy facilities, shoreline stabilisation, and agricultural operations all pose cumulative threats to coastal resources.

Aside from impacts to human life and property, sea level rise could cause the loss of important ecological systems. By 2080, sea level rise could potentially contribute to the loss of up to 22 per cent of the world's coastal wetlands, and losses of up to 70 per cent could be expected when sea level rise is considered in tandem with destruction associated with human activity (Nicholls, Hoozemans and Marchand 1999). Saltwater intrusion associated with sea level rise will alter the composition of delicate ecosystems and potentially contract freshwater habitats in other areas (Burkett et al. 2008), in addition to threatening the amount of freshwater supply.

Rising sea surface temperatures and changes in ocean current circulation, freshwater flows, and the frequency, locations, and duration of extreme climate events are other impacts associated with climate change (Kay and Alder 2005, p. 50). The cumulative impacts of these changes may have far-reaching biophysical and socioeconomic impacts.

## Adaptive design

The significant risks posed by climate change to coastal regions demands an integrated response. It is clear that the current trend of coastal development is not sustainable and that it places strain on already stressed coastal ecosystems and resources. Decisions about land use planning and priorities must favour intelligent coastal development that manages and minimises the impacts of development.

Cohesive urban design can help inform smart decisions about land use and coastal planning. While changes to the shoreline have been introduced by coastal developments all over the world in the past decades (a trend that will inevitably continue), proper planning of coastal ecosystems, hydrodynamics, and sediment dynamics will exert a positive impact on the moulding of new coastal form. Advanced computer modelling tools can aid the configuration of land forms, diagnosing the flow fields in the nearshore region and predicting the littoral sediment transport, thereby enabling the design of robust land form to minimise impedance to water circulation and disruption to sediment balance.

Other best practices such as increasing pervious areas and mimicking pre-development hydrologic processes have become an integral part of urban design works to alleviate the pressure exerted to the stressed environment and concomitantly improve the vulnerability of coastal developments towards natural hazards. Research confirms that the water quality and overall health of water bodies within a watershed declines significantly as impervious surfaces cover more than 10 to 30 per cent of a watershed (NOAA 2007).

RIGHT
Design in coastal regions should take place within the larger context of integrated coastal zone management. This does not necessarily mean a complete ban on use of the coastal area; rather, it can encourage the framing of open space armature along the waterfront, as exemplified by Southport Broadwater Parklands on Australia's Gold Coast.

Design in coastal regions requires the incorporation of climate change mitigation and adaption measures and should take place within the larger context of integrated coastal zone management. Non-structural measures include adaptation through managed retreat, such as coastal setbacks, density restrictions, phased out development, and rolling easements (IPCC Working Group II 2001). Setbacks involve limiting development at a minimum distance from the shoreline, and density restrictions and phased out development help limit urbanisation. This does not necessarily mean a complete ban on use of the coastal area; rather, it can encourage the framing of open space armature along the waterfront, as exemplified by the Southport Broadwater Parklands on Australia's Gold Coast.

Design in coastal regions requires the incorporation of climate change mitigation and adaption measures and should take place within the larger context of integrated coastal zone management.

The stronger adaptability of open space realm towards evolving coastal environment caused by climate change offers an opportunity for planners and designers to shape a more interactive coastal region between humankind and nature and to create more diverse habitats and recreational programs to celebrate coastal resources. Rolling easements are a responsive measure to allow land development, provided that it does not hold back the sea. This easement 'rolls' landward as rising sea levels encroach on land, thus limiting development pressures and ensuring public access to coastal areas.

In response to the growing pressures facing coastal regions, informed designers advocate coastal design that promotes the rehabilitation or restoration of degraded coastal wetlands or the creation of new wetlands. In eastern coastal Shenzhen, China, a coastal resource analysis and evaluation contributed to an overall masterplan for the area, which includes an extensive system of protected areas, country parks, preserved historical sites, and restored wetland habitats. 'Coastal squeeze' is reduced by incorporating natural setbacks and restoring wetlands to provide natural buffers against the future impacts of climate change.

Dune management is another critical activity related to climate change mitigation. Sandy beaches and their associated dunal systems are under increasing pressure as the world's coastal population continues to grow. Dunes serve as buffers between the ocean and inland areas and provide valuable habitat as well as public beach amenities. Vegetative cover on foredunes prevents wind erosion and sand from blowing inland. The demand for public facilities and recreational space in dunal areas must be balanced against the need to provide adequate buffer zones to accommodate erosion and to protect sensitive dune vegetation communities. At the Southport Broadwater Parklands, the dunal quality of the site's shoreline is maintained and native grasses and groundcovers are used throughout the site.

Increasing the height of coastal infrastructure such as bridges or seawalls is a proactive structural measure and an important consideration in offsetting sea level rise (IPCC Working Group II 2001). In England, the Blackpool Promenade seafront was designed to be responsive to changes in sea level, as well as the associated increased risks of storm surges and wave activities. Coastal defences at the site mimic natural barriers, creating a multipurpose public realm that functions both as seating space and as sea defence.

## The coast ahead

Coastal design must adapt to natural and anthropogenic forces as sea levels continue to rise and as people continue to be drawn to coasts. The combined impacts of climate change and urbanisation on coastal areas are projected to be serious and broad ranging. These potential environmental, social, and economic impacts demand a coordinated and comprehensive response. Forward looking planning and design can avoid 'locking in' poor coastal defences and help preserve natural coastal barriers, improving the resilience and flexibility of coastal areas to respond to increased risks in a changing world.

**LEFT**
In England, the Blackpool Promenade seafront was designed to be responsive to changes in sea level, as well as the associated increased risks of storm surges and wave activities. Coastal defences at the site mimic natural barriers, creating a multipurpose public realm that functions both as seating space and as sea defence.

## Case study: balancing environmental and social sustainability with economic progress in coastal Shenzhen

In response to Shenzhen's breakneck urban growth and expansion, the Shenzhen Planning Bureau commissioned a study to evaluate the ecological, recreational, cultural, and historical resources within some 300 square kilometres of its vulnerable eastern coastal area. A masterplan was then developed to balance environmental and social sustainability with economic progress in the study area, which encompasses over 140 kilometres of coastline, containing 23 natural sand beaches, the Qiniang, Maluan, Paiya, and Wutong Mountains, and several old villages and historical sites.

A multidisciplinary team of ecological and environmental planners, plant specialists, hydrologists, wetland specialists, GIS specialists, economists, and urban planners worked together to survey ecological, environmental, historical, cultural, and recreational resources, representing and classifying each using GIS and scientific categorisation.

Natural defences along the coastline are kept where possible and a system of parks provides ecological and recreational amenities. The most environmentally sensitive regions of the study area are designated as *country parks*, which cover areas supporting extensive patches of ecologically-valuable forest habitats and reservoir water catchments. *Coastal parks* are designated as places where visitors can enjoy the natural environment and cultural heritage and provide landscape and ecological linkages between country parks. Finally, *wetland parks* are designated for restoring valuable wetlands to more natural habitats for nature conservation, recreation, and education.

Natural conservation and coastal protection through these parks forms the backbone of the resulting masterplan. Existing mangroves are protected by maintaining the tidal link between the sea and mangrove habitats and redirecting reclamation activities to other areas of the bay. The park planning system and restoration strategies strengthen Shenzhen's internal resilience to the future impacts of climate change and sea level rise, offering a balanced approach to natural and human resources on a regional scale and reconnecting the city with the coast.

LEFT
In eastern coastal Shenzhen, China, a coastal resource analysis and evaluation contributed to an overall masterplan for the area, which includes an extensive system of protected areas, country parks, preserved historical sites, and restored wetland habitats. 'Coastal squeeze' is reduced by incorporating natural setbacks and restoring wetlands to provide natural buffers against the future impacts of climate change.

# Urban regeneration and climate change

## Heather Cheesbrough

Tackling climate change has been made a key priority of the English planning system (Department for Communities and Local Government (DCLG) 2007). This government action has helped bring about a greater appreciation and understanding from practitioners, regulatory bodies, and local government of the critical role planning and development has in reducing and mitigating the potentially catastrophic impacts arising from major planetary upheaval. The strong policy lead aims to reduce emissions, stabilise climate change, and take account of unavoidable consequences. While it has led to a more united focus in plan making and scheme delivery, this has inevitably caused delays for development as significant amounts of supporting work and studies to examine the many potential facets and outcomes of climate change are now required under the English evidence- and justification-based planning system.

Further national policy guidance that articulates this message and sets the framework for more detailed local area-based plans encompasses *Planning Policy Statement 1: Delivering Sustainable Development* (DCLG 2005), *Planning Policy Statement 22: Renewable Energy* (DCLG 2004), and *Planning Policy Statement 25: Development and Flood Risk* (DCLG 2006). In addition to these specific topic-based policy documents though is the entire thrust of the planning system, which in 2004 was transformed from one based on land use to one of multi-layers, complexity, and integration. Called spatial planning, this revised approach to town planning brings with it the fundamental requirement to consider the implications of development on the nature, character, and role of place:

Spatial planning goes beyond traditional land-use planning to bring together and integrate policies for the development and use of land with other policies and programmes which influence the nature of places and how they can function. (DCLG 2008)

This requires planners and designers to have an in-depth understanding of a place and of how development and human actions over time will have an impact on it and the wider environmental context. This brings with it new responsibilities, processes, and working methods. Fundamental to these is the requirement to consult early in the plan-making process and actively engage with a much greater range of stakeholders as well as the public. Such stakeholders include statutory bodies such as the Environment Agency, with a key role in flood management, and English Nature, responsible for the conservation and enhancement of the natural environment and promotion of biodiversity. Other critical stakeholders are the water, power, and telecommunications utility companies for infrastructure planning and delivery, transport bodies, and local strategic partnerships. This last group consists of a broad range of public, private community, and voluntary bodies, including health, police and crime, and education.

Addressing the effects of climate change and seeking how to minimise them is now a central tenet in the preparation of development plans. The work requires a multi-agency approach and an integrated and imaginative response to a place's inherent strengths and opportunities. This has seen the development of a range of thoughtful and complex projects rooted in the content of a place; responding to strengths, weaknesses, threats, and opportunities, which allows the evolution of a plan unique to its context and character.

One such project is the Stratford and Lower Lea Valley (LLV) Area Action Plan. Commissioned by the London Borough of Newham in partnership with the Development Agency, this plan seeks to provide a regeneration strategy for an area of severe multiple deprivation, which is currently experiencing massive change and evolution through the construction of the London 2012 Olympic Park.

The LLV is an area of east London with huge opportunities and complex problems rooted in the history of industry, environmental degradation, population change, and migration. The de-industrialisation of the 1980s onwards has created large tracts of derelict land with negligible inward investment. Major infrastructure of rail and road creates barriers to movement at the local level and this is exacerbated by a network of waterways flowing north-south, which, although attractive and in places ecologically interesting, constrain movement and access.

The three town centres underperform and present a limited offer of shopping and services and a poor-quality environment dominated by road and vehicle movement. Open space is highly deficient and there is a lack of housing choice with an extremely high proportion of social housing and very little aspirational executive-style homes to appeal to and attract the professional sectors. This is reflected within the local population's low skills base and poor education and qualification attainment.

In bringing forward regeneration in the LLV, up to 50,000 new homes are proposed with corresponding community facilities and services. Two of the three town centres are subject to major regeneration proposals and massive public transport investment is taking place with the new Stratford International railway station, Docklands Light Rail improvements, and the recent approval of Crossrail, which will connect east and west London with a high-speed link. Central to these regeneration plans is the reuse of large tracts of inefficiently used land, bisected by waterways and isolated by infrastructure barriers.

This requires planners and designers to have an in-depth understanding of a place and of how development and human actions over time will have an impact on it and the wider environmental context.

In developing the structuring principles for the LLV Area Action Plan, increasing accessibility to the waterways and the retention of a significant proportion of the adjacent derelict land as new public open space were identified as key drivers. Historically, the many tributaries of the River Thames have been culverted and hidden away, becoming highly polluted and unattractive. Now their potential is being recognised as bringing value through their unique character and as an important leisure, recreational, and wildlife resource.

The plan proposes that the hard edges of the River Lea be minimised by reinstating natural green edges to attract wildlife and encourage biodiversity. This will help address climate change in several ways; by helping to mitigate the impact climate change will have on habitats (through destruction and changes in species distribution), and by creating new and more numerous places for wildlife. The soft edges will also act as a method of flood-risk management, a particularly critical issue as much of this area is identified as an area of high flood risk.

**LEFT**
The Stratford and Lower Lea Valley Area Action Plan seeks to establish a regeneration strategy for an area of severe multiple deprivation, which is currently experiencing massive change and evolution through the construction of the London 2012 Olympic Park.

The whole issue of flood-risk management is a familiar and complex issue for many of the United Kingdom's towns and cities, with many brownfield sites identified for regeneration located in zones of high flood risk. Government guidance strongly directs development away from these areas, with rigorous sequential testing required before development, particularly residential, can be permitted. In the LLV where the pressure to develop and regenerate is intense, coupled with a very ambitious housing target, the solution will involve careful consideration of all the elements that facilitate sustainable development.

The priority will be for development that minimises vulnerability to climate change and provides resilience, while providing social cohesion and inclusion. Waterways and open space will play a critical role, managing flood risk by their incorporation into sustainable drainage systems. The soft river edges will also provide greater permeability to slow water runoff and help reduce flash flooding, while the surrounding open space, generous waterside banks, and gently sloping sides increase overall river capacity to absorb rises in sea levels.

**LEFT**
Historically, the many tributaries of the River Thames have been culverted and hidden away, becoming highly polluted and unattractive. Now their potential is being recognised as bringing value through their unique character and as an important leisure, recreational, and wildlife resource.

Green open spaces and landscaping will also help with urban cooling to combat the urban heat island effect brought about by the projected temperatures increases. However, underlying this approach is the careful balance that needs to be struck between these more land-extensive uses and the need to develop land intensively to accommodate the ambitious housing numbers, with their associated community facilities and employment space.

Green open spaces and landscaping will also help with urban cooling to combat the urban heat island effect brought about by the projected temperatures increases.

While patterns of urban development are central to this equation of regeneration, climate change, and sustainable communities, architectural solutions will also have a key role to play in delivering mixed-use typologies which successfully integrate family housing at first floor or higher levels with less vulnerable uses, such as commercial accommodated on the ground floor. The widespread use of green roofs and walls is also being encouraged for buildings to reduce flash flooding by slowing down water drainage and providing water storage.

Patterns of urban development also have a critical role to play in the reduction of carbon emissions through minimising the need to travel, promoting sustainable forms of transport, and encouraging walking and cycling. The LLV suffers from poor local connectivity and this must be remedied if people are to access the services they need to begin to address the causes of severe multiple deprivation. Therefore, promotion of sustainable patterns of urban development also greatly informed the structuring principles of the area action plan, with higher intensities of development focussed around the existing town centres to optimise good accessibility to public transport, shops, facilities, and services.

New walking and cycling routes to connect previously inaccessible areas with key activity nodes such as Underground stations and town centres are also proposed. Within this new network, the plan proposes to incorporate and upgrade the important primary route of the Greenway; an elevated walkway and cycle path built on top of the embankment of the Northern Outfall Sewer. This route, although renovated in the 1990s, suffers from poor natural surveillance, with very restricted access for the mobility impaired or those with small children; however, its major potential as an east-west connector, giving access to the Olympic Park and beyond, is now properly recognised and promoted.

The LLV Area Action Plan also proposes parking restrictions and car-free development to reduce carbon emissions in areas of high public transport accessibility, with the aspiration that this will assist in maintaining the existing low car ownership levels as a more affluent population moves in.

A reduction in carbon emissions is also being pursued through the promotion of zero-carbon development, with a proposal for a Carbon Challenge site at West Ham. By 2016 all new housing in the United Kingdom will need to be zero-carbon rated, however at this time the ability for volume house builders to meet this standard is yet unproven. Carbon Challenge is the government's response to this by working in partnership with landowners, planning authorities, and developers to identify and develop appropriate sites for zero-carbon housing. Within the LLV this development would also help provide a new type of housing designed and built to attract professional and higher income residents, which would assist in the broad policy aim of creating mixed and balanced communities.

In conclusion, urban design and regeneration have a central role in reducing and mitigating climate change and this need not be incompatible with urban regeneration. Undertaken with commitment, they can actually provide the stimulus for innovation, the attainment of higher environmental standards, and a focussed approach to delivering sustainable development. As a consequence, development has higher costs from emerging green technologies, as green roofs, energy generation, and water management solutions are particularly expensive. The latter two initiatives are often only viable at larger sites and this will require new heights of partnership working between developers, so far not experienced.

The issue of additional development costs also needs to be fully appreciated by planning authorities who often have unrealistic expectations of what a developer can contribute in terms of community planning gain, such as the provision of affordable (social) housing and community and strategic infrastructure. This is particularly pertinent in times of economic downturn and requires some tough prioritising and decision making. However, necessity is the mother of invention and we must continue to develop creative solutions and challenge attitudes and behaviour in both the planning and development industry and the wider population, not only to maintain momentum, but also to accelerate the significant progress made to date if we are to have any chance of a healthy long-term future for the planet.

# Creating environments that engage

## Cathryn Chatburn

### Reflecting on the past

In the late nineteenth century and early twentieth century, attitudes to architectural design and urban planning changed significantly in response to technological innovations, the needs of an expanding, increasingly mobile and urbanised population, as well as the desire to create new and better homes for all.

New concepts of urban living were developed without knowledge or concern for the finite nature of our natural resources. Industrialisation created urban environments built on the mass extraction of resources from nature. Traditional building techniques and crafts were rejected in favour of new technologies and more cost-effective manufactured materials capable of mass production and fast-paced delivery.

Reference to historic urban forms and vernacular architectural solutions—often a response to local climate and distinct environmental and social conditions—were not a significant concern. Neither was the long-term impact of more extensive urbanisation in the quest to deliver more socially-conscious, healthier, and attractive places for people to live and work.

At the turn of this new century, these same aspirations remain—to provide an improved quality of life for all. But concern about the impact of continued rates of urbanisation upon the health of the planet and its inhabitants is refocusing attitudes towards the way we build. The United Nations Earth Summit of 1992 alerted world governments to the environmental and ecological problems associated with continued urban growth and focused international, national, and local concern on how we live and grow as a global community.

The complex and interconnected nature of the environments we occupy is now universally recognised, as are our local and international spheres of influence and contribution to climate change. In the same way that modernism foresaw a brave new world in which mechanisation and industrialisation provided the key to the future and in which planners, architects, and theorists imagined new urban frameworks through which communities would live out more fulfilled lives, today's designers are reimagining the future to reduce the environmental footprint of our activities to deliver more sustainable development.

**RIGHT**
In terms of offering platforms for sustainable living, multi-unit dwelling models as they are currently delivered present few opportunities for occupiers to creatively engage with their environments.

## Sustainability: the design agenda of the twenty-first century

The Brundtland Commission's 1987 report provides the basic definition of sustainable development. This has been the premise for emerging policy and behavioural attitudes globally since its release. Importantly, it highlights the significance of intergenerational equity, advocating an approach to development that requires solutions to be considered in the context of their immediate and future impacts and fostering environments that encourage long-term social responsibility. Achieving this goal requires development models capable of physically delivering environments to support and foster community engagement and the adoption of more sustainable patterns of living over time.

Across Europe, the legacy of well-intentioned, large-scale, post-war urban development provides stark examples of the complexities of social and urban planning. Many of the buildings, estates, and new towns of this period have been in a state of decline or dereliction and are themselves the focus of studies and new masterplanning initiatives to regenerate and recreate them as more attractive and vibrant places to live.

In the most extreme cases, wholesale demolition has been required. This is a disappointingly unsustainable fate for such relatively young environments, generating significant volumes of material waste and damaging the social structures of communities only just regaining their identity and cohesion as working systems of social interaction. The British Government's study, *Towards an Urban Renaissance*, highlights how the lack of robust social frameworks to support and nurture communities is a major flaw of these past efforts.

ABOVE
The legacy of well-intentioned, large-scale, post-war urban development in Edinburgh's Craigmillar district.

People make cities but cities make citizens. The city, the town and the urban neighbourhood provide the framework for weaving together shelter, education, health, work and leisure, within the context of a strong participatory democracy. If this urban framework is neglected, people and communities struggle and investment is wasted.
(The Urban Task Force 1999)

Combining the lessons learnt from these most recent experiments in urban planning with the emerging environmental agenda (more specifically the energy and resource efficiency requirements to arrest climate change) is critical to create environments that will ultimately provide the platforms for the required behavioural change.

Physical issues of size, mix, layout and density, building forms, movement patterns, materials, and resource efficiency are all being considered in the quest to define new models to guide the development of more sustainable urban settlements. The outcomes to date strongly advocate the compact city model: a high-density, mixed-use urban form proposed with integrated public transport, high-quality public spaces, and energy-efficient buildings.

Significant progress has been made in understanding this typology and how it might work; in particular, how renewable energies might be adopted and how materials, water, and waste efficiencies might be managed and integrated into built forms. As these changes have been understood, they have been translated into an increasingly prolific catalogue of government policies, objectives, and targets used to inform and drive professional practice and change the nature of built forms and patterns of urbanisation globally.

However, policies are emerging at varying rates and the development industry and its customers tend to respond to change only when 'encouraged' by mandatory requirements or fiscal incentives. A stronger approach is needed to govern the way development moves forward; one informed by community and 'consumer' engagement.

In countries with historically high single-family home ownership and where land is not scarce, the compact city model requires communities to embrace not only changes in the physical nature of their environments but also changes to well-established patterns of living. We now need to explore more rigorously the creation of homes that collectively support the compact city model, meet the aspirations of diverse and changing population needs, and allow for greater levels of sustainable living.

*Creating flexible frameworks for sustainable living*

The city is not static; it is a dynamic system in which the key to its long-term health and success, or its intelligence, will be its capacity to adapt to change. Like an ecological system, the key to this capacity is diversity. (Briggs 2005)

In terms of offering platforms for sustainable living, multi-unit dwelling models as they are currently delivered present few opportunities for occupiers to creatively engage with their environments. While they improve land efficiencies, deliver a critical mass of population to support infrastructure, and offer efficiencies of scale to support the adoption of decentralised and greener energy options, they do not provide occupiers with long-term solutions that respond to the changing dynamics of their lives and that of the city.

Today's multi-unit dwelling models are characteristically rigid, being a collection of distinctly defined and prescribed spaces, with limited diversity and fixed walls. As neighbourhoods, they lack certainty and flexibility in terms of accommodating the essential elements of social infrastructure and meaningful recreational space—the building blocks of a community.

Many high- and medium-density developments offer residents inadequate private access to external space from individual dwellings, little opportunity for urban agriculture or workable private or shared gardens, and few options for childrens' play. They often present poorly to the adjacent public realm and are inflexible in their design, delivering individual units with fixed parameters within which the occupier is restrained, with little opportunity to adapt the built form over time as lifestyle requirements and land use opportunities change. They provide few facilities to comfortably accommodate alternative modes of transport, such as bicycles. And their homogeneity and bulk dulls their distinctiveness and identity, limiting their contribution to the creation of attractive cityscapes at a human scale.

Creating sustainable cities requires a rethinking of built form as an 'architecture of engagement'. This reimagining sees developments as a 'living lattice' of growing and evolving neighbourhoods, with built form frameworks that respond to residents' needs as their lifestyles and circumstances change. The delivery of a constructed shell is the start: its form will evolve as residents and businesses move in and change over time.

Buildings are thought of in terms of their layers and as a collection of expandable and flexible spaces. Fixed frames form their skeleton. Within this new built form, internal and external apartment walls can be moved. External edges are structurally designed to accommodate garden beds where small vegetable patches can be cultivated. Residents can create meaningful private outdoor space as an extension of their indoor living areas, catering for childrens' play needs as they grow.

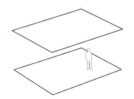 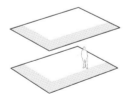   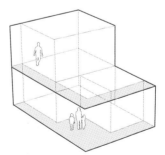

Platforms for life: Building occupants choose the extent of space they require.

Cultivated edges: External edges are designed to accommodate additional weight to support more substantial planting opportunities.

Flexible space: Internal walls are designed for ease of realignment to enable occupants to redefine their interior and exterior space.

ABOVE
Flexible frameworks for sustainable living and how they might come together to build a dynamic neighbourhood structure.

Blank external elevations can be furnished with a revolving ladder of tiered planting beds, like hanging gardens. Further garden space can be established on roofs and transformed for weekly markets where residents can trade home-grown produce and other goods.

In the ground layer, a diverse range of communal amenities can be provided, such as car sharing stations and well-furnished bicycle parking and storage facilities. Real time public transport schedules can be made available, as well as live feed information on the building's energy, water, and waste performance.

This new type of built form will bring greater levels of 'urban stewardship' as long-term relationships between the city and council bodies, developers, landlords and residents evolve. Accordingly, social responsibility and environmental management systems would be established as part of body corporate agreements.

Many exciting opportunities exist to reconsider models for more compact living. Encouraging more sustainable lifestyles requires more than delivering high-density development figures and land efficiencies. Good urban design is after all the process of shaping physical settings for life. Effective sustainable urban design has the capacity, when considered comprehensively, to deliver the frameworks within which lives can begin to be lived more sustainably.

Observers widely recognise an essential ingredient of behavioural change is the notion of long-term social responsibility and individual ownership of the premise of living sustainably as a community (Brundtland Commission 1987). If the environments on offer to people do not engage and incorporate opportunities to encourage the required behavioural change, sustainable urban solutions will continue to fall short. Urban dwellers of the future should not simply be submissive recipients of fixed ideas of urban planning; rather, they should be offered environments that facilitate their role as agents of change.

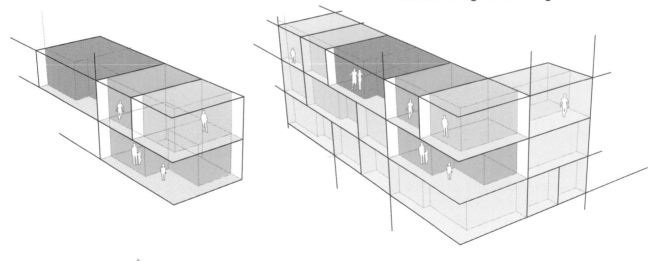

Diverse composition: Units are able to extend vertically and horizontally within the built form framework.

# Urban form and low-carbon buildings

## Lester Partridge and Jason Veale

A responsibility rests on all designers to develop buildings and urban precincts which mitigate the human causes of climate change. While parts of the building industry have enthusiastically embraced green rating tools, emissions from the building sector represent a high proportion of global emissions: 48 per cent (Architecture 2030 2009) in the United States and 23 per cent in Australia (Centre for International Economics 2007). In Australia, commercial building emissions are rising faster than those from transport, agriculture, manufacturing, non-energy-related mining, and residential buildings (Department of Climate Change 2009). With estimates that over 50 per cent of the population will be living in urban areas by 2010, it is essential that urban design helps, rather than hinders, buildings to reduce their emissions in the coming decades.

The impact of buildings on the environment has led to the introduction of sustainability rating tools such as LEED in the United States, BREEAM in the United Kingdom, Green Star in Australia, and HK BEAM in Hong Kong. These parametric tools assess buildings against a range of sustainability criterion including management, indoor environmental quality, energy, water emissions, transport, and materials. Buildings awarded a star rating under these schemes often achieve 30 to 40 per cent energy or greenhouse emissions savings compared to a business as usual benchmark set by the tool. These benchmarks are often based on larger, fully-air conditioned buildings rather than the whole sector. Gathering data on larger buildings is easier as their owners are often more conscious of their market perception and aware of the cost savings and therefore more willing to participate in energy reduction schemes. Ironically, the analysis in this chapter suggests that in temperate climates it may be the smaller, simpler buildings that tend to use less energy per square metre.

Governments around the world are targeting long-term emissions reductions of 50 to 80 per cent compared to 1990 or current levels (the benchmarks and targets vary). There are no specific global targets for the building sector, however given the contribution to global warming and studies that identify the building sector as having the most cost-effective energy savings opportunities (McKinsey & Company 2008), a long-term reduction of at least 80 per cent is realistic and carbon neutrality is feasible with the use of renewable energy.

The steady rise in commercial building emissions in cities during the twentieth century was primarily due to the discarding of passive design considerations in the pursuit of low-cost construction techniques and maximising return on investment. Energy was cheap and paid for by a future, unknown building owner and tenant so energy efficiency was not considered.

While a return to a strict indigenous vernacular is not feasible due to labour costs, architectural considerations, the need for low maintenance, and the expectations of occupants, there are lessons to be learnt for designers of modern buildings in higher-density areas. The use of materials and form to insulate and provide thermal storage; the design of layouts and facades to promote breezes; and the greater use of shading and orientation to reduce heat gains are strategies largely forgotten by designers of high-rise buildings—until the advent of the green building rating.

The challenge now for urban designers is to develop an evaluation framework and climate-responsive masterplans for the urban form that allow buildings to approach carbon neutrality using these passive techniques reinterpreted for twenty-first century living and working.

Developing a strategy to achieve a low-carbon urban form requires addressing all aspects of carbon emissions in the urban environment. This includes not only building energy consumption, but also transport, waste generation, recycling, and material use. In the case of high-density versus low-density developments, these can have opposing influences. For example, low-density developments may allow greater solar access and cross ventilation, yet increase energy, transport, and materials use. These competing issues of operational energy emissions and transport emissions suggest an optimum point exists for each climatic zone. An analysis of the competing pressures and strategies to lower the total emissions is best explored for a particular climate.

The steady rise in commercial building emissions in cities during the twentieth century was primarily due to the discarding of passive design considerations in the pursuit of low-cost construction techniques and maximising return on investment.

## Optimising emissions in a temperate climate

Sydney has a temperate climate with an average daytime summer maximum temperature of 28 degrees Celsius and a winter average minimum of 8 degrees Celsius. It has a large high-rise central business district (CBD) surrounded by medium-density residential and old industrial areas, which are gradually being converted to residential and commercial developments for smaller companies and a mix of other uses. Beyond the CBD are residential suburbs with a density among the lowest of western cities and six smaller satellite CBDs. Waterfront areas adjacent to the CBD and old industrial areas south of the city are undergoing rejuvenation, with building heights up to six storeys, generous green space, lower noise levels, and increased use of natural ventilation for office buildings.

The Australia-wide breakdown of emissions from commercial buildings in Figure 01 is representative of Sydney's CBD buildings (Australian Greenhouse Office 1999). Figures show a high proportion of emissions for cooling, mechanical ventilation, and lighting. Combining these with heating, improved passive design of Sydney buildings could make significant savings on up to 84 per cent of their energy use.

However, Sydney's high-rise CBD, with its noise, air pollution (albeit moderate by international standards), poor solar access, wind tunnelling in certain areas, and small proportion of green space makes it difficult to rework building design with passive design techniques to reduce energy use.

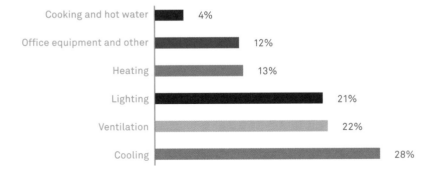

| | |
|---|---|
| Cooking and hot water | 4% |
| Office equipment and other | 12% |
| Heating | 13% |
| Lighting | 21% |
| Ventilation | 22% |
| Cooling | 28% |

FIGURE 01
Commercial building greenhouse emissions share by end use 1990.

Turning to residential dwellings, Figure 02 shows that perhaps contrary to the general belief, high-rise apartments in the state of New South Wales actually emit more greenhouse gas per person than low-rise apartments and even detached houses. The relatively high proportion of mechanical ventilation, cooling, and artificial lighting used in high-rise office and apartment buildings is strongly influenced by the urban density where these buildings tend to be located.

Conventional CBD office buildings can significantly reduce their energy use with improved glazing, external shading, highly-efficient mechanical systems and lighting, and cogeneration systems to produce low-carbon power. Figure 03 is based on modelling carbon reduction strategies for office buildings (operational energy only, not energy embodied in construction materials, waste, and the like) and illustrates the scale of emissions achievable with each strategy.

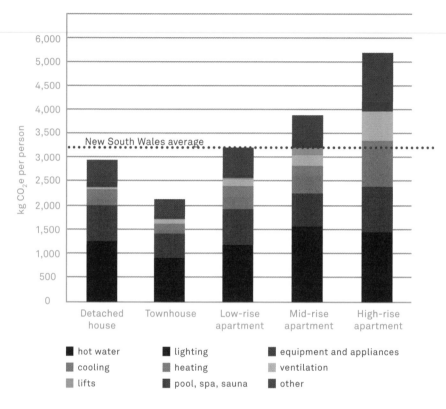

**FIGURE 02**
Greenhouse emissions per person for various residential types. The values are derived from typical residential developments assessed using the Building Sustainability Index and data published by Myors, O'Leary, and Helstroom (2005).

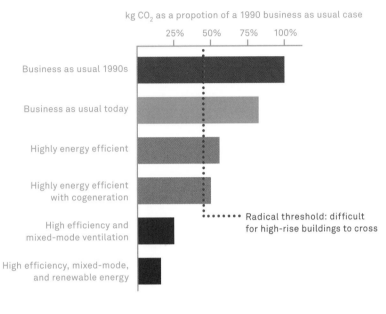

kg CO$_2$ as a propotion of a 1990 business as usual case

Business as usual 1990s

Business as usual today

Highly energy efficient

Highly energy efficient
with cogeneration

High efficiency and
mixed-mode ventilation

High efficiency, mixed-mode,
and renewable energy

Radical threshold: difficult
for high-rise buildings to cross

**FIGURE 03**
Greenhouse reduction achievable for office buildings
using various strategies

The radical threshold nominated in Figure 03 indicates the point at which the cost of reduction becomes excessive with primarily technological solutions. This point marks only a 50 per cent reduction; carbon neutrality would require expensive renewable energy such as photovoltaic cells on-site or off-site wind power. Reductions below this point can only be attained with radical design changes, which can only be achieved with an urban form different to the CBD of western cities, where office and apartment buildings are generally located.

Naturally ventilated or mixed-mode buildings are suited to CBD fringe and suburban environments, where the reduced density of the built form provides opportunities to maximise natural ventilation and daylight penetration. In temperate climates, these types of buildings have the potential to consume the least energy and correspondingly emit the least carbon per person or per square metre.

**Characteristics of conventional high-rise office and apartment buildings**
- Land costs are high so the building form maximises floor area and reduces surface area.
  Bathrooms and utility areas cannot be naturally ventilated.
- External shading is difficult as buildings are built to the boundary and shading devices many storeys in the air must be very strong due to high winds and are expensive to maintain.
- Offices have few open windows due to noise and air pollution. Offices are open plan which means organising staff to operate windows is difficult.
- Car parking is underground to save space and bathrooms and equipment rooms are deep within the building to maximise the perimeter for valuable office space, living rooms, and bedrooms.
- Glass areas are increased to maximise views and allow light into deep floor plates, increasing the solar gain and heat load on air conditioning systems.
- A large proportion of the floor plates of office buildings and all bathrooms and utility spaces, must be artificially lit during the day as there is inadequate penetration of natural light.
- Occupants have come to expect very tight control on the indoor humidity and temperature which drives up energy use and requires very complex mechanical systems.

Figure 04 illustrates the huge savings in the largest energy user (cooling systems) in a low-rise office building that is naturally ventilated with air conditioning only used in hot periods (mixed mode) compared to a mid-rise, fully-air conditioned office. The mixed-mode building is able to open windows and have moderate external shading, as the lower building height means the shading has less structural requirements to withstand wind pressure and it is easier to maintain than taller buildings. With ventilation and shading, it is able to achieve far lower annual cooling energy use with lower performance glazing, which is a cost saving over the taller building.

Some non-residential buildings have begun to reverse the twentieth century trend of extensive air conditioning by slowly removing areas where highly-controlled comfort is not necessary. In Sydney's northern beaches, the headquarters of health product manufacturer Blackmores has passive design features that reduce the need for air conditioning, maximise natural ventilation of all spaces, and turn off artificial lighting when there is sufficient daylight outside.

In north-west Sydney, the new Rouse Hill Town Centre is a shopping centre, entertainment quarter, and mid-rise residential development with a public transport hub. Despite western Sydney's warm-hot summers and cool winters, the centre has reversed the air conditioned mall concept and provides comfortable conditions with open streets, covered open air walkways between shops, and extensive use of natural light. Only individual shops use air conditioning when needed. In Melbourne's Docklands, the National Australia Bank headquarters uses a thermal chimney to naturally ventilate breakout spaces, which allows for a wider floor plate than a building with cross-flow ventilation.

These examples share a common design strategy—they have moved beyond conventional systems tweaked to be more energy efficient and they avoid using energy by significantly reducing the area subject to mechanical ventilation, cooling, heating, and lighting. They are also located in areas outside the CBD and away from high levels of noise and air pollution.

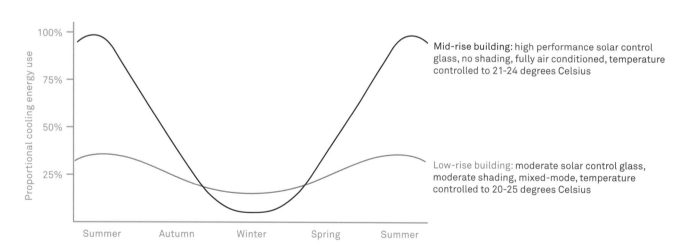

**FIGURE 04**
Typical annual proportioned cooling energy use for a mid-rise and a low-rise office building

At Blackmores headquarters, passive design features reduce the need for air conditioning, maximise natural ventilation of all spaces, and turn off artificial lighting when there is sufficient daylight outside.

Despite western Sydney's warm-hot summers and cool winters, the Rouse Hill Town Centre has reversed the air conditioned mall concept and provides comfortable conditions with open streets, covered open air walkways between shops, and extensive use of natural light. Only individual shops use air conditioning when needed.

The National Australia Bank headquarters uses a thermal chimney to naturally ventilate breakout spaces, which allows for a wider floor plate than a building with cross-flow ventilation.

## An urban form for low-carbon buildings

An urban form that provides opportunities for low-carbon buildings can take cues from some recent urban in-fill in Sydney and other cities around the work. The city fringe has areas where demand is strong for office space and higher-density residential living, with access to public transport links into the CBD and sufficient land away from busy main roads. Urban designers may consider the following to allow buildings maximum opportunity for low emissions:

- Ensuring new development controls density, traffic, and use to provide lower noise and air pollution;

- Where changes to streets are possible, aligning streets to allow for favourable building orientation;

- Maintaining distances between buildings and controlling building heights and form to improve solar access and allow gentle breezes to flow into buildings rather than being channelled through wind tunnels; and

- Increasing green space to improve air quality.

The City of Sydney's *Sustainable Sydney 2030* plan hints at this type of urban form and aims to develop a series of green village hubs adjacent to the CBD and has a city-wide greenhouse reduction target of 70 per cent below 2006 levels by 2030 (City of Sydney 2008). The plan will lift densities above their current low levels in some areas and provide a mix of land use and activities.

## A balancing act

Reducing density to lower building operational emissions may compromise the patronage of mass transit systems and the viability of increasingly popular distributed energy (such as cogeneration and trigeneration), which rely on density to minimise energy used to pump heated and cooled water to buildings. Figure 05 shows the relationship of transport energy to density or activity density for various suburbs of Sydney: proximity to the CBD increases as activity intensity increases (Newman 2006). This is supported on other data of major world cities, which shows an increase in fuel use as average density decreases. The volume of building materials may also increase with the increased surface area of buildings.

Higher-density urban environments lend themselves to district energy production where transmission losses are minimised. However, their efficiency is enhanced in extreme climates where continuous operation of cooling or heating is required year round.

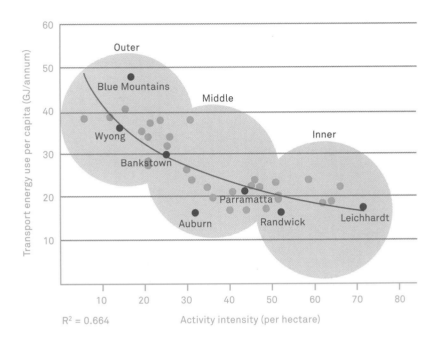

R² = 0.664

**FIGURE 05**
Activity density and transport energy in Sydney suburban areas

An increase in surface area and potentially greater use of heavyweight materials for thermal mass may also increase the emissions embodied in building materials. Given calculating embodied emissions is far more complex than operational emission, the literature has not settled on rules of thumb to determine when an increase in embodied emissions outweigh operational savings. The general view is that a moderate increase in embodied energy from the use of materials designed to reduce operational emissions will still provide an overall emissions reduction. A fair comparison would also need to consider the emissions from additional concrete volumes required for the structural systems of high-rise buildings. A major downside of this theory is that emissions must be reduced now to alleviate the impact on global warming; waiting more than twenty years for additional materials to have a net benefit may be too late.

These competing issues of operational energy emissions and transport emissions suggest an optimum point exists for each climatic zone. Balancing the variables requires consolidated modelling of a single variable. Total carbon modelling is a useful tool to compare different urban design options and bring in other factors such as biodiversity, social cohesiveness, water use, and resource depletion, to name a few. This is explored in greater detail by Steve Kellenberg and Honey Walters in their discussion on measuring carbon performance and climate stable practice.

## Other climates

The extreme cold climates of places such as Toronto dictate that buildings need to minimise heat loss and maximise solar gain for the majority of the year. Minimising the facade-to-volume ratio suggests high-density urban form with greater provision for solar access.

Similarly, constant hot and humid climates such as Singapore dictate that buildings need to minimise heat gain and solar gain all year round. Natural ventilation is feasible for residential buildings, however the high humidity is a barrier to using natural ventilation to provide comfort in office buildings. Therefore for office buildings, minimising the facade-to-volume ratio and enhancing protection from low-angle sun with shading and overshadowing again directs the urban designer to high-density urban form. District trigeneration cooling systems can be used to lower the building's carbon emissions.

For external spaces, in the same way that houses in tropical climates have extensive shading and try to create space between the dwellings to allow breezes to pass between, urban form in the tropics should consider maximising the flow of breezes between buildings and providing good external shading. Overshadowing of open spaces provides respite from the sun, however heavy overshadowing may reduce amenity for public spaces depending on the cultural context and urban design.

In Hong Kong, all major new developments must have their air ventilation assessed to determine their effect on vital summer breezes passing through narrow laneways. This requirement has arisen in response to the impact of urban development on microclimatic conditions within narrow laneways. The design of Hong Kong's urban fabric now promotes breezes and wind tunnel effects during summer by capturing breezes and deflecting them into smaller laneways.

An urban form for the tropics may consider a combination of compact, high-density buildings that provide some overshadowing arranged in such a way to allow air to pass through the city as a whole for pedestrian comfort.

Despite efforts in recent years to improve the energy efficiency of the built environment, emissions from the building sector are increasing in cities across the world: at best, they are plateauing in Europe (Levine et al. 2007). There is certainly a case to be made for not over emphasising the true scale of the problem or indicating that the solutions are out of reach. However, in the building sector, there is no escaping the last 60 years of increasing use of energy-intensive systems and how this has been encouraged by the urban form of our cities.

The switch back to very low-carbon buildings may well require a change to the way our cities are arranged. A new urban form in temperate climates that supports green buildings can be seen in much the same way as an individual building—letting the light in and the air through, facing the winter sun, reducing exposure to the summer sun, and most of all, keeping it simple. Fortunately, there are signs in urban renewal areas that this is happening and these principles are consistent with public transport planning, liveability, air quality, and diversity of land use.

### Fundamentals of reworking building design

- Small floor plates, high ceilings, close access to facade openings.
- Greater surface area to allow utility areas on the perimeter for natural ventilation and allow cross ventilation of occupied spaces.
- Heating energy may rise with increased surface area unless insulation and glazing performance is improved. A careful balance of heating, cooling, and ventilation energy use would be required.
- More external shading to reduce heat gains. Office buildings use cooling in Sydney even in winter due to internal heat loads and a lack of external shading.
- Greater consideration of orientation in office buildings, particularly the location of core and utility areas.
- Potential move away from the current trend of very open plan offices to smaller areas, where a smaller group of office workers can collectively manage opening control and maintain minimum fresh air levels.
- Change to an adaptive thermal comfort model for workers.
- Thermal comfort experts are exploring the possibilities of an adaptive comfort approach for offices, which allows the internal temperature to rise and fall with the seasons rather than holding it at a constant range (usually 21 to 24 degrees Celsius) throughout the year (Nicol and Pagliano 2007). The conventional practice of using a constant temperature range not only increases energy use; conventional air conditioning systems that deliver cooled air throughout a building have difficulty providing satisfactory internal conditions for office workers with different comfort expectations. In other words, the current energy-intensive and expensive approach is not significantly better at delivering comfort than the more radical approach of allowing the internal temperature to rise and fall with the seasons (for example, between 20 to 25 degrees Celsius), using a combination of natural ventilation and air conditioning when the temperature falls outside this range.

# Measuring carbon performance and climate stable practice

## Steve Kellenberg and Honey Walters

Mitigating the harmful effects of climate change requires the stabilisation of greenhouse gas (GHG) concentrations in the atmosphere at a level that prevents anthropogenic interference with the climate system: a minimum of two degrees Celsius above pre-industrial levels, according to the United Nations Framework Convention on Climate Change and the Intergovernmental Panel on Climate Change (2007). This value corresponds to atmospheric $CO_2$ concentrations of 350 to 400 parts per million (ppm). In 1990, global $CO_2$ concentrations were approximately 353 ppm, the value of goals set in legislation such as the California Global Warming Solution Act of 2006 and the Kyoto Protocol.

One of the most important steps in mitigating the effects of climate change is quantification. The exercise of performing a GHG emissions inventory does not necessarily need to involve counting every pound of $CO_2$ equivalent emissions, but it should be conducted at a level robust enough to identify the source types peculiar to the project or area in question and capture their relative contribution. This data can serve as the basis for evaluation systems that analyse mitigation strategies to determine the areas with the greatest potential for emissions reduction. Overall, a clear understanding of the total magnitude of emissions and composition, coupled with an evaluation system, are essential to developing reduction goals, identifying effective mitigation strategies (and potential reductions and costs), and monitoring implementation (successes and failures).

The emergence of regulations mandating reductions in GHG emissions, along with the growing concern and awareness of climate change and sustainability, have increased pressure to plan and design new communities (and retrofit existing ones) that reduce carbon footprints and achieve identified goals. Consequently, fundamental strategies for urban form, transportation, energy, and policy development are being reconsidered and redefined across the globe.

Primary land development components that effect GHG emissions levels are project location (specifically in relation to primary job and service centres), urban form (the degree of a project's organisation around job and service centres and higher-density land uses), transportation (external linkages and connectivity within the project and multi-modal choice), and building energy (increased energy efficiency within the building stock and the addition of renewable energy on the building and freestanding within or close to the community). A secondary tier of emissions are attributable to public realm energy requirements, water treatment and conveyance of domestic and wastewater, and construction processes.

The key to gauging performance in terms of climate stabilisation, lowering $CO_2$ and other GHG concentrations in the atmosphere, and achieving sustainability objectives is the utilisation of measurement tools and associated policy development. However, up until recently, no specific tools have existed for agencies, government entities, and developers to identify and evaluate the myriad reduction choices and quantify valid costs and benefits. For this reason, models, policies, and GHG analytical methodologies and mitigation strategies have been developed over the last few years to assist in the overall goal of climate stabilisation.

## Sustainable Systems Integrated Model

The Sustainable Systems Integrated Model (SSIM) is organised around the core themes of mobility, energy, water, building technology, socio-cultural assets, ecology, and carbon footprint and the project design features of each. The model roles up into a community-wide set of indicators, including total energy use, water demand, vehicle miles travelled, and the resulting total GHG emissions. Various strategies and measures may quickly be recombined and modelled with immediate outputs for carbon and water footprint, as well as related initial and ongoing cost impacts to both the master developer and constituent builders.

The methodology provides a multi-step process utilising the latest modelling and cost-benefit analysis techniques to construct a sound, defendable, and affordable whole systems sustainability and carbon reduction strategy. Through this process, a new community developer is able to:

- Develop a quantified, defensible basis for carbon, water, and other sustainability representations;

- Optimise the environmental value of the sustainability program;

- Minimise cost relative to the benefits achieved;

- Develop a low-carbon development strategy; and

- Achieve exemplary status as a sustainable new community.

## Stage one: masterplan optimisation

SSIM starts by using a GIS-based modelling tool to compare the sustainability merits of alternative urban form solutions. Using a customised palette of land use types, street types, pathways and bikeways, community facilities, and amenities, a conceptual sketch is drawn for each scheme. Each palette item is a prototype with relevant assumptions such as density, building types and mix, and spatial dimensions built in to its definition. A spatial analysis model is used to measure aspects of urban form such as built form density, land use mix, walkability and proximity to transit and amenities, and number of dwelling units and each scheme is evaluated to ascertain which has the lowest inherent carbon footprint per worker or resident, highest level of local trip capture, land use balance, and the like. This is done using a business as usual scheme and then recalibrating the model with alternative plans until ultimately a preferred plan evolves. Based on the outputs, various modifications and improvements to both the masterplan framework and land use program can be analysed.

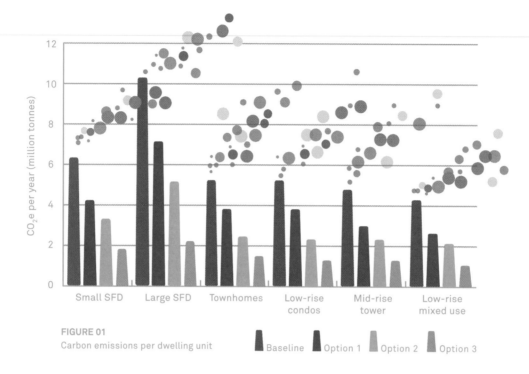

**FIGURE 01**
Carbon emissions per dwelling unit

Baseline   Option 1   Option 2   Option 3

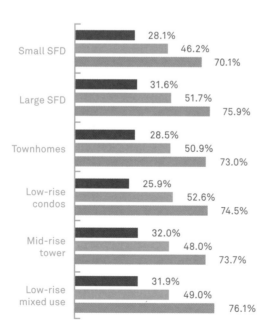

**FIGURE 02**
Percentage carbon reductions relative to baseline

Carbon footprint per capita is utilised, as well as total emissions, since several urban form-related mitigation strategies require higher densities, which may result in higher total emission quantities, but lower emissions per capita or dwelling unit. A primary tool in this step is the 7Ds local trip capture calculator developed by California-based transportation planners Fehr & Peers, which takes into account density, diversity, design, destination accessibility, distance to transit, demographics, and development scale. Methods employing the first four of these variables have been in relatively general use over the past several years and are based on gross Institute of Transportation Engineers' vehicle trip generation rates, followed by reductions in vehicle miles travelled (VMT) based on characteristics of land use, density, connectivity, and the like. The full method assesses all seven characteristics and directly estimates trips by vehicle, transit, pedestrian, and bicycle modes. The goal of this step is to find the urban form and land use density mix that achieves the highest possible local trip capture (30 to 70 per cent) and related reductions in VMT and mobile emissions.

## Stage two: primary systems modelling

After a preferred masterplan framework is selected a more intensive evaluation of sustainability practices and measures can occur. This step answers three questions: for each core theme, what energy reduction targets should be evaluated; which combination of project design features are required to achieve each target; and which combination of project design features allows us to achieve reduction targets in the most cost-effective manner. The sub-models developed for each core theme push for increasingly higher levels of resource efficiency, while tracking the conceptual cost and environmental benefit of each solution set. The core themes currently modelled include:

- Residential building energy;
- Retail building energy;
- Office building energy;
- Industrial building energy;
- Water – domestic, storm, waste, recycled, and grey;
- Transportation;
- Green building; and
- Public realm energy.

Other core themes being developed for SSIM include:

- Ecological systems and open space programming;
- Socio-cultural infrastructure; and
- Urban heat islands.

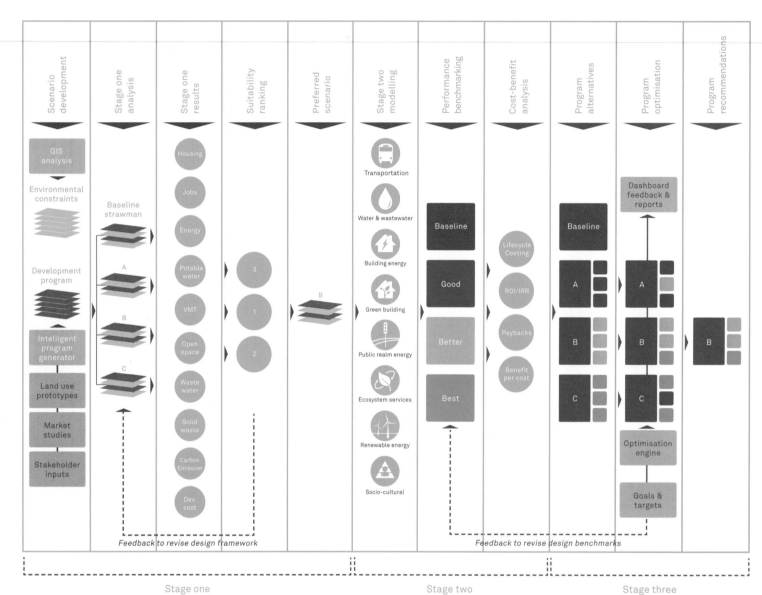

FIGURE 03
The stages of SSIM

Firstly, a base case of conventional development and building practices is defined, such as energy consumption per year, acre feet of water per year, and metric tonnes of $CO_2$ equivalent per year. Then good, better, and best levels of increasing sustainability efficiency are defined for each core theme. Models for each core theme are run to define which combination of strategies, measures, and technologies are required to achieve each target.

For building energy, the good scenario typically avoids photovoltaic or other renewable energy technologies and relies mostly on passive design, building shell enhancements, and more efficient heating, ventilating, air conditioning, and water heating systems. The better scenario adds photovoltaic energy to the degree that for residential developments, the size of the system provides a first-day positive cash flow. For the best scenario, photovoltaics and solar hot water are added to the degree that a net-zero electrical home is achieved. Targets and design features vary by project and client goals, but building energy reductions can range from 25 to 80 per cent.

For transportation, three families of project design features are typically created—internal multi-modal measures, external multi-modal measures, and employer-to-housing linkage measures. These design features range from neighbourhood electric vehicle programs, to off- and on-site shuttle systems and transportation management programs, which can further reduce VMT levels by another 5 to 25 per cent from those achieved in step one.

For each project the sub-models are recalibrated for local conditions, including climate, backbone electricity sources and rates, common regional practices, and transportation fleet characteristics. Each package of design measures is then measured on both a first-cost and life-cycle cost basis. These costs are compared to the percentage improvement achieved by each package and a cost-benefit ratio is ascertained, which determines what combination of design measures realise the highest reduction in resource use or carbon footprint at the lowest incremental cost. Decisions can then be made on what packages to include in a candidate Master Sustainability Program.

**Stage three: master program synthesis**
In the previous task, the team defines and models good, better, and best packages of design measures for each core theme and provides outputs related to environmental benefit, first-costs, life-cycle costs, monetised cost-benefit, and benefit per US$1,000 invested for each package. SSIM can then be used to combine individual core theme options into a set of comprehensive, all-systems Master Carbon Reduction Program (MCRP) alternatives. At least three MCRPs are constructed with the following outputs provided for each:

- Total building energy savings;

- Total public realm energy savings;

- Total reduction in VMT;

- Total water savings;

- Total reduction in GHG emissions;

- Total initial costs; and

- Total ongoing monthly costs.

As a part of the evaluation of master program alternatives, various cost allocation scenarios are developed and reviewed with the team and client. The following cost allocation categories are typically defined and populated:

- Increased costs or savings to residential building construction (in cost per square foot and percentage over base costs);

- Increased costs or savings to non-residential buildings (in cost per square foot and percentage over base costs);

- Increased costs or savings to the master developer;

- Increased costs or savings to third party energy or infrastructure entities; and

- Increased costs or savings to the Master Homeowners Association.

On the basis of this information, analysis of core theme packages continues until a MCRP is defined that is consistent with the goals, business plan, and financial model of the developer.

Each MCRP is also evaluated against any project-wide carbon reduction targets that have been set. Often a MCRP achieves a total carbon reduction goal of 15 to 25 per cent (including mobile emissions) on the basis of core theme packages alone. If a higher carbon reduction goal is targeted then a freestanding renewable energy or carbon sequestration offset can be explored. SSIM offers calculators for wind turbine farms, photovoltaic plants, carbon sequestration farms, and district cogeneration and trigeneration systems that can ascertain the size, cost, and area requirement for each or a combination there of. These renewable energy alternatives are independent of building systems and typically are freestanding facilities requiring separate financial analysis. The SSIM model is an excellent platform for evaluating alternative scenarios to achieve carbon footprint targets while identifying related costs and acreage.

Figure 04 summarises a MCRP for a 6,000-dwelling new community in Northern California. It indicates that a 56 per cent reduction in residential building energy was achieved as well as a 66 per cent reduction in domestic water import. Vehicle miles travelled were reduced by 13 per cent, with a total carbon footprint reduction of 26 per cent including mobile emissions and 55 per cent not including mobile emissions. Cost impacts on the building stock were significant but scaled to be close to cash flow positive for residential and amortised within 10 years for commercial. The net cost to the master developer was a savings of US$13 million dollars due to the reduction in infrastructure cost (primarily in water treatment) that could offset all other developer costs incurred for the program.

## In summary

The SSIM model provides a unique architecture for evaluating large-scale, complex projects. The process is somewhat labour intensive, requiring careful calibration for each region and multiple competency experts (for each core theme), team meetings, and workshops. But once calibrated with sub-model inputs, the integrated final stage allows for effortless recombination of measures and targets with immediate cost-benefit outputs. Thus, a development team can analyse and select the best conceptual MCRP for their project (consistent with regulatory program requirements) and update the selected program over time to address changes in public policies and priorities and advances in technology.

| | Baseline plan | Adjusted plan | Improvement |
|---|---|---|---|
| Residential building energy | 38,000 kilowatts/hour | 17,000 kilowatts/hour | 56% |
| Commercial building energy | 590,000 kilowatts/hour | 300,000 kilowatts/hour | 49% |
| Domestic water | 2,900 acre feet/year | 980 acre feet/year | 66% |
| Transport VMT | 710,000 VMT/year | 618,000 VMT/year | 13% |
| Carbon footprint (excl. transport) | 40,300 metric tonnes $CO_2e$ | 18,000 metric tonnes $CO_2e$ | 55% |
| Carbon footprint (incl. transport) | 303,700 metric tonnes $CO_2e$ | 226,100 metric tonnes $CO_2e$ | 26% |

Residential cost = 12% increase in construction $/square foot with net positive cash flow
Commercial cost = 6.5% increase in construction $/square foot with 10-year amortisation
Developer cost = -US$13 million (net savings)

FIGURE 04
Carbon reduction achievement and targets for a 6,000-dwelling new community in Northern California. When a carbon reduction program does not achieve targets due to cost issues, offsets such as carbon sequestration and freestanding wind and solar renewable power can also be evaluated.

# Case study: how SSIM measures the sustainable design of a new town in China

## Steve Kellenberg and Honey Walters

The sustainable development movement has caught on in China, where the planning of eco-towns has recently become a popular trend among local governments and developers. Owing largely to new national regulations requiring eco-town planning, often times planned eco-towns are missing the 'eco' completely. How do we know if a so-called 'eco-town' is actually in line with the principles of sustainability?

SSIM is being applied to verify the sustainable design of a new town in Tianjin in China's Tanggu District. Located within Tianjin's Binhai New Area, the Tanggu District has been identified by the Chinese Government as 'the next growth engine of China', following on from Suzhou in the 1990s.

Beitang New Town is situated on around 10 square kilometres, with existing conditions consisting of residential development, limited commercial development, and significant portions of environmentally degraded, undeveloped land. The Tanggu District's history of industrial development has seriously affected the environmental condition of the area, which was once home to healthy wetlands. In light of this situation and inspired by the popularity of 'sustainable planning', local authorities have committed to achieving greener development as they aim to become the new commercial centre of northern China.

Several alternative master plan options for Beitang New Town have been developed, creating different variations of district centres, land use combinations, transport routes, ecological conservation areas, and green belts. Sustainability goals and targets have also been set for residential and non-residential building energy, transport and mobility, and whole systems water planning.

A series of 'sustainability indicators' were chosen during alternative development to provide a comparison through which a preferred masterplan alternative could be chosen. Indicators included the number of residents, population density, open space connectivity, overall open space percentage, walkability to job centres from public transport, and water consumption. Once the best performing and thus preferred alternative was chosen, the next step was to determine how to improve the base plan—and to determine how much it would cost.

The next step involved identifying tiered intensity measures for water use, building energy, alternative energy, public realm energy, ecology, and transportation, which were categorised as good, better, and best and subsequently investigated and tested within SSIM. The project's energy modelling team provided various levels of application for green building measures; the water team modelled different methods of water reuse and water savings; and the transportation team investigated options for alternative transportation and road networks. The cost and benefit of all of these measures were tested within SSIM.

The last step of the SSIM process was demonstrated by selecting several combinations of good, better, and best measures for each sustainability system, leading to a total project calculation of energy, water, vehicle kilometres travelled, and total greenhouse gas emissions generated. This last stage involves analysing the various measures to determine the greatest benefit for the initial and long-term investment. In most cases, implementing the most intense measures for each system results in a cost-prohibitive program. SSIM determines how much is possible within a reasonable cost range.

Result so far show that over 50 per cent energy savings are possible depending on the cost impact found acceptable, and that water use could be reduced by 40 per cent with a cost savings of RMB16 million (approximately US$2.35 million). The most intense program also shows a 50 per cent reduction in private car use and a 36 per cent reduction in greenhouse gas emissions.

Though SSIM has been used for several projects in the United States, its application to a project in China is truly groundbreaking. As a work in progress, SSIM is currently being updated and refined for Beitang New Town as the masterplan develops. While quantifying sustainability and measuring the effectiveness of a sustainable master plan or 'eco-town' remains a difficult task, SSIM presents itself as a comprehensive planning tool that provides a compelling way to answer the question—what makes a development sustainable?

## Case study: how methodologies to quantify project-generated GHG emissions influence land use development in California

New standards have been set for analytical methods and mitigation strategies to reduce GHG emissions through work with the California Air Pollution Control Officers Association (CAPCOA), which represents all air quality districts in California. Federal Courts have ruled that GHGs must be analysed and the California Environmental Quality Act (CEQA) was amended to mandate the analysis of GHG impacts and the implementation of reduction strategies. A project's cumulative GHG contribution is unlike any other issue addressed under CEQA in light of the impact's global nature. No guidance was available to define adequate analysis or mitigation until CAPCOA's highly anticipated CEQA & Climate Change resource guide, released in January 2008 and underpinned by a report on Greenhouse Gas Analytical Methodologies and Mitigation Strategies.

The methodologies are used to evaluate a project's contribution to global climate change for the purposes of environmental impact assessment. Methods were developed and tools were identified to quantify emissions generated by construction activities: vehicle trips associated with proposed land use development, area-source emissions associated with on-site space heating, water heating, and landscape maintenance, and indirect emissions associated with energy consumption. Applicability of the newly-developed analytical methods to different project types was evaluated and example calculations were provided. In turn, a quantitative threshold framework was established to determine whether proposed land use developments would be consistent with California's GHG reduction goals, while accommodating projected economic and population growth. These methodologies and metrics help local governments evaluate the potential of proposed development projects to contribute to global climate change, while fulfilling the purposes of CEQA.

**LEFT**
A quantitative threshold framework was established to determine whether proposed land use developments would be consistent with California's GHG reduction goals, while accommodating projected economic and population growth.

Also provided was a comprehensive list of mitigation measures currently in practice and under study which reduce GHG emissions associated with land use development and planning and infrastructure projects. A full description of each measure is featured and applicable project types and emission sources are identified. The feasibility of each measure was assessed for their reduction effectiveness, technological and logistical availability, and economic cost. In addition, the potential of any measures to cause secondary adverse or beneficial impacts to air quality was evaluated, such as increased ozone precursor emissions from using alternative fuels in construction equipment, reduced ozone precursor emissions through minimising vehicle miles travelled, and increased off-site energy consumption and associated indirect air pollutant emissions.

This demonstrates how implementing measures into project design and land use planning can bring quantifiable reductions in GHG emissions. Measures identified mitigate emissions on and off site from mobile, area, and stationary sources and address regional- and local-scale projects. Categories of measures include transportation and circulation, parking, commercial and residential building design, neighbourhood layout and density, land use planning, mixed-use development, energy efficient building components, construction practices, social awareness measures, and planning policy. Many of these measures are consistent with the concepts of new urbanism and neo-traditional development.

**ABOVE**
Our knowledge of the traditional values of open spaces and landscape needs to be bolstered with an understanding of the ecological functioning of urban landscapes and their role in sustainable water management, microclimatology, food production, and the facilitation of carbon sinks.

# Water sensitive cities: a roadmap for cities' adaptation to climate and population pressures on urban water

## Professor Tony Wong

Urban communities face future uncertainties in water supplies caused by a combination of climate variability, population growth, and climate change. Protecting the water environment and managing its resources sustainably will help make our cities more resilient to climate change, while accommodating higher population densities.

Best-practice urban water management is complex and requires planning to protect, maintain, and enhance the multiple and interdependent benefits and services offered by the total urban water cycle:

- Supply security;
- Public health protection;
- Flood protection;
- Waterway health protection;
- Amenity and recreation;
- Greenhouse neutrality;
- Economic vitality;
- Intra- and inter-generational equity; and
- Demonstrable long-term environmental sustainability.

From an integrated urban water cycle planning and management perspective, the framework for water conservation and protection of aquatic environments is shaped by the following broad principles:

- Minimising the import of potable water;
- Minimising the export of wastewater;
- Optimising the use of stormwater; and
- Finding the appropriate scale to best achieve these three principles.

Cities have access to a range of water sources, in addition to the established convention of capturing rainfall runoff from rural and forested catchments. These alternative water sources for cities include groundwater, urban stormwater (from catchment runoff), rainwater (from roof runoff), recycled wastewater, and desalinated water. Many of these sources are within city boundaries and ready access to this diversity of water sources in water sensitive cities may be framed under the general theme of cities as water supply catchments.

The integration of urban landscape design with sustainable urban water management, through the practice of water sensitive urban design (WSUD), presents opportunities to build ecological landscapes to buffer the impact of climate change and increasing densities on natural aquatic environments and to preserve and re-establish ecosystem services. WSUD brings sensitivity to water into urban design, ensuring its due prominence and integrating the disciplines of engineering and environmental sciences associated with water services and the protection of urban-based aquatic environments. Water sensitive cities provide ecosystem services for urban and surrounding natural environments.

Community values and the aspirations of urban places govern urban design decisions and therefore urban water management practices. Fundamental to a water sensitive city is its social and institutional capital, which is reflected in its community living an ecologically-sustainable lifestyle cognisant of the ongoing balance and tension between consumption and conservation; in its industrial and professional capacity to innovate and adapt as reflective practitioners in city building; and in its government policies, which facilitate its ongoing adaptive evolution as a water sensitive city.

Therefore, a water sensitive city may be characterised by three key attributes:
1. Access to a diversity of water sources, underpinned by centralised and decentralised infrastructure;
2. Provision of ecosystem services for the built and natural environment; and
3. Socio-political capital for sustainability.

In a water sensitive city, each of these attributes is wholly integrated into the urban environment through urban design and planning.

## Cities as water supply catchments

Many cities exclusively depend on water resources derived from the capture of rainfall runoff from largely rural or forested catchments. Communities are increasingly susceptible to increasing temperatures and too little moisture in the soil and to climate variability, drought, and climate change. Continuing the conventional approach, such as by building dams, is often not the most effective option. The dependency of cities on soil moisture in catchment areas for their water supply must be broken. Although in many regions the effect of climate change on rainfall is uncertain (and may not necessarily reduce rainfall), it is more likely that climate change will increase global temperatures and thus have a more certain effect on soil moisture in traditional water supply catchments, making them drier. This will reduce catchment runoff during storm events.

A strategy built around diverse water sources and a mixed water infrastructure will allow cities the flexibility to access a portfolio of sources at least cost, in terms of environmental impacts and other externalities. Each alternative water source will have its own reliability, environmental risk, and cost profile. In a future water sensitive city, each source can be optimised (even on a short-term basis) through infrastructures associated with water harvesting, treatment, storage, and delivery. This would include centralised and decentralised water supply schemes, from a simple rainwater tank for non-potable use to city-scale indirect potable reuse schemes and a pipeline grid linking regional reservoirs.

It takes time to build a diverse infrastructure throughout a built-up area—and this does not address the immediate short-term water crises facing many cities. Governments have tended to focus on large, centralised infrastructure, such as desalination plants and indirect potable substitution schemes which return treated recycled water to water supply storage areas. These are important elements of a diverse water portfolio but can often have higher operating costs than decentralised schemes.

An important component underpinning a diversity of infrastructure is the secondary supply pipeline for non-potable water (sometimes referred to as the third pipe system or dual supply). Water delivered via a secondary supply system helps to promote a fit-for-purpose approach to water use, with non-potable water from a variety of local sources, such as stormwater, groundwater, and recycled wastewater replacing potable water used in toilet flushing, laundry, garden watering, and open space irrigation.

**A strategy built around diverse water sources and a mixed water infrastructure will allow cities the flexibility to access a portfolio of sources at least cost, in terms of environmental impacts and other externalities.**

It costs less to provide the secondary supply pipe in greenfield developments than it does to retrofit existing developments. At present, greenfield development opportunities are often not taken up for the lack of a suitably cheap alternative non-potable water source for non-potable demands. However, recycled wastewater is often the only source considered and financial assessment is based solely on the present cost of water recycling technology without recognising the significant reduction in the cost of water recycling technologies over the past five years—and this trend is likely to continue. Furthermore, assessments of the feasibility of current projects do not consider that the costs and reliability of alternative sources, such as stormwater, could be considered as a long-term component, where it may just be one of an interchangeable suite of alternative water sources of varying cost and reliability.

The provision of a second water supply pipeline for non-potable water is fundamental to accessing recycled water in the future. Its implementation would be made easier by policies requiring greenfield development and urban renewal redevelopment projects (including new buildings) to be fitted with a dual water supply network, even if sources of non-potable water may initially be stormwater or sewer mining rather than the ultimate aim of recycled wastewater.

## Cities providing ecosystem services

Landscapes are the product of varying natural and human-induced forces, interacting within regional and global ecosystems. Open spaces in the public domain are essential, however these urban landscapes must be functional beyond providing spatial amenities. Our knowledge of the traditional values of open spaces and landscape needs to be bolstered with an understanding of the ecological functioning of urban landscapes and their role in sustainable water management, microclimatology, food production, and the facilitation of carbon sinks.

The concept of the ecological landscape helps to define ecologically-functioning landscapes as a continuum framework that encompasses the perspectives of nature conservation through to the creation of urban ecologies. Three broad themes characterise the design objectives, distinguished by the degree of urban density and complexity:

- Nature conservation – to build and conserve biodiversity in flora and fauna in terrestrial and aquatic environments;

- Natural and urban interface – to manage the natural and urban environment interface, protecting high conservation areas and mitigating and rehabilitating the environmental impacts of urbanisation. Here the focus is on the transition of natural environments into a more complex and balanced landscape of natural and human-induced features that integrate physical, biological, and social considerations; and

- Urban ecology – to further urban design where the role of biomimicry in constructing green infrastructure influences the urban landscape and involves anthropogenic and natural features that provide for ecosystem services, art, and science.

Protecting environments from where water is diverted for urban consumption and to where treated wastewater and stormwater is discharged is an essential objective of sustainable water resource management. Managing the impacts of urban development on the water environment requires attention to the three streams of the urban water cycle: drinking water, wastewater, and stormwater. The growth of WSUD in stormwater management over the last 10 to 15 years has been remarkable. Within this relatively short timeframe, the philosophy, technology, and language of WSUD has evolved to industry standards and is referenced in policies across all levels of government in Australia and internationally.

Stormwater treatment technologies, such as constructed wetlands and bioretention systems (commonly referred to as rain gardens), are implemented at a range of spatial scales, from buildings and allotments to regional public open space and multiple use corridors. These elements are becoming mainstream features of stormwater quality management and through close collaboration with landscape architects and urban designers it has been possible to incorporate these technologies into the urban form.

The rehabilitation of degraded urban waterways is another important issue of WSUD and many factors influence their condition. Waterway health management typically consists of a mixture of catchment-wide initiatives (such as WSUD strategies) and on-site works (such as channel stabilisation and the creation of in-stream and riparian habitats). Catchment management initiatives underpin the protection and improvement of waterway health—and improving water quality underpins all waterway health initiatives.

## The social and institution capital of a water sensitive city

WSUD as a framework for sustainable urban water management is well-founded and ongoing research is expected to further WSUD technologies for improving stormwater quality. However—and this is essential—technology based on physical science research alone will not deliver the desired outcome. The capacity of institutions themselves to advance sustainable urban water management is only now being recognised as an important part of many technological solutions. Brown (2004) argues in her study of local institutional development and organisational change for advancing sustainable urban water that unless new technologies are embedded into the local institutional and social context, their development in isolation will not be enough to ensure their successful implementation in practice.

Institutional reform for integrated urban water cycle management remains elusive. Like most reform agendas, it requires the consideration of options that are not immediately clear, technically or otherwise. The socio-institutional dimension of WSUD, while instrumental in effective policy development and technology diffusion, is still a largely underdeveloped area of research. Brown and Clarke (2006) analysed the historical and socio-technical drivers of WSUD's development across Melbourne, Australia. Melbourne was selected as a case study because it is often informally identified as a leading city, nationally and internationally, in urban stormwater management and WSUD. Additionally, this work has drawn on contemporary social science thinking on the diffusion of technology in other fields.

This research revealed the growth of WSUD in Melbourne is the result of a complex and sophisticated interplay between key champions (or change agents) and important local variables. In particular, the champions represent a small and informally connected group of individuals from government, academia, and the development industry who have pursued change from a best practice management ideology consistently underpinned by local science and technology advancement.

However, the existence of champions alone is not enough to explain the development of WSUD. There are also a number of instrumental variables representing a mixture of historical accident and intended advocacy outcomes. Over the last 20 years these have included the rise of environmentalism, strategic external funding avenues, and the establishment of a number of industry-focused cooperative research centres to bring researchers and industry practitioners together. These associations and networks have helped to formalise the objectives of improving stormwater quality, increasing large developers' receptivity to WSUD in the marketplace, and developing strategic capacity building tools that include methods for envisioning future water management scenarios, water quality modelling software, and design charts and guidelines.

Community acceptance and broad political support for WSUD is fundamental if it is to be implemented faster and if industry's technical capacity and ingenuity in complex urban environments is to be improved. There has been a growing focus on the role of communities in refining WSUD's characteristics and developing its strategies. Public art highlights community relationships with water and the general intrinsic values of water and furthers community awareness and participation in decision-making on urban water management. Some projects have profiled community attitudes and openness to water reuse and pollution prevention to inform local WSUD policy development. Others have focused on implementing community participatory action models, including scenario workshops for envisioning sustainable water futures and different types of community-based forums designed to deliver jointly developed strategies and local WSUD plans.

The pursuit of sustainability through ecologically-sustainable development is aimed at initiatives to protect and conserve natural resources, to provide resilience to climate change, and to promote lifestyles and supporting infrastructure that endure indefinitely because they neither deplete resources nor degrade environmental quality. While such ambitions may seem unattainable, they set a challenge that leads to environmental, social, and economic benefits as we edge towards the ultimate goal of sustainability. They represent a paradigm shift in urban design. In relation to urban water management and climate change adaptations, the shift is towards integrated urban water cycle planning and management based on the principles of water sensitive urban design for sustainable urban water management and for building water sensitive cities.

# Case study: water sensitive urban design in Singapore

The Singapore Government has embarked on a project to convert Marina Bay, located within the heart of Singapore City, into a freshwater reservoir for harvesting stormwater from metropolitan areas. Undertaken by the Public Utilities Board of Singapore, this significant undertaking will transform the city of Singapore into a water supply catchment. In preparation for the closure of Marina Bay and its conversion into a freshwater reservoir, the Public Utilities Board has a mission to protect water quality in the Marina Reservoir.

Through its Active-Beautiful-Clean (ABC) Waters Programme, the waterway corridors of Singapore are being progressively retrofitted to become high quality, active landscapes for community recreation, education, and connection. These landscapes are also functional in their capacity to improve the quality of stormwater runoff and to deliver a clean water environment.

Delivering a clean and healthy water environment is a catchment-wide effort extending beyond the administrative jurisdiction of the Public Utilities Board. In May 2006, as part of the ABC Waters Programme, the board commenced its development of an implementation framework to institutionalise water sensitive urban design in Singapore.

The framework for stormwater management, referred to as the ABC Waters Design Guidelines in Singapore, draws on insights from social science on the theory of transition. In this case, the transition is towards advancing sustainable urban water management from traditional approaches (which are often based on a single management objective that considers stormwater as a source of potential hazard to public safety) to a multifaceted approach founded on the many socio-technical considerations that influence the sustainable management of urban stormwater at the city scale.

Singapore has already developed a diversity of water supply around its Four National Taps Strategy and an extensive water reclamation system. The ABC Waters Programme's holistic approach to sustainable stormwater management integrates urban planning with the protection, management, and conservation of the water cycle by implementing its own masterplan and set of design guidelines.

The documentation and analysis of the rapid transition of water sensitive urban design from concept to policy in Melbourne during the years from 1990 to 2006 provided a useful framework from which to develop the approach to this project. As noted by Brown and Clarke (2007), the insights gained from their study of Melbourne are of direct relevance to other cities, as the Melbourne scenario:

> ...also represents many of the significant pressures faced by modern cities today, including: rapid population growth; decreasing household occupancy ratios; ageing infrastructure; water supply stresses; degraded waterway health; complex and sometimes unclear administrative configurations and variable levels of commitment to environmental management across government agencies and departments.

In their study, Brown and Clarke identified eight interdependent enabling factors, all critical elements in facilitating the rapid uptake of water sensitive urban design in Melbourne:

1. Socio-political capital – aligned community, media, and political concern for improved waterway health, amenity, and recreation;
2. Bridging organisations – dedicated organising space that facilitates collaboration across science and policy, agencies and professions, and knowledge brokers and industry;
3. Trusted and reliable science – accessible scientific expertise, innovating reliable and effective solutions to local problems;
4. Binding targets – a measurable and effective target that binds the change activity of scientists, policy makers, and developers;
5. Accountability – a formal organisational responsibility to improve waterway health and a mandate to influence practices that lead to such an outcome;
6. Strategic funding points – additional resources dedicated to the change effort;
7. Demonstration projects and training – accessible and reliable demonstration of new thinking and technologies in practice, accompanied by knowledge diffusion initiatives; and
8. Market receptivity – a well articulated business case for the change activity.

These eight enabling factors provide a robust organising structure for considering the issues pertinent to water sensitive urban design and gaps that need addressing.

In formulating the framework to implement the ABC Waters Design Guidelines, the project team first set out to identify and assess local attributes and to establish the readiness of institutions in Singapore to support successful water sensitive urban design, benchmarked against the eight key enabling factors. The project team then formulated incentives and activities to address any inadequacies, including:

- Reviewing and developing catchment management objectives and incorporating these into the corporate objectives of government agencies whose functions impact on catchment management;
- Developing uniform standards and engineering procedures for designing water sensitive urban design measures (or ABC Waters design features in the Singapore context) for stormwater management;
- Establishing industry capacity building initiatives, such as training courses and construction of demonstration projects;
- Engaging government agencies as stakeholders in the planning, design, and construction of demonstration projects; and
- Strengthening local scientific research efforts.

# Transit-oriented development: land use and transportation planning in the context of climate change

**José G. Mantilla, with a case study by Damien Pericles and Ann-Marie Mulligan**

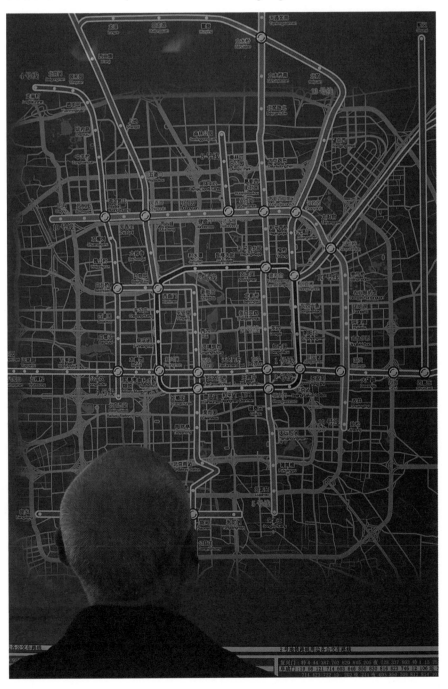

Transit-oriented development can play a crucial role in reducing greenhouse gas emissions by promoting urban growth in a way that reduces the need for travel and advances the use of energy- and emissions-efficient modes of transportation. Scientific evidence shows people in transit-oriented development drive 20 to 40 per cent less than those in traditional development. However, since single strategies tend to have a modest effect on reducing travel and greenhouse gas emissions, transit-oriented development will only yield considerable benefits as part of a comprehensive set of economic, regulatory, planning, technological, infrastructure, and behaviour-focused initiatives.

## Transportation and climate change

Mobility is an essential human need. The ability to move people and goods promotes human survival and social interaction and is almost universally acknowledged as one of the most important prerequisites to achieving improved standards of living (Greene and Schafer 2003, Intergovernmental Panel on Climate Change (IPCC) 2007, and World Business Council for Sustainable Development (WBCSD) 2004). Mobility systems are essential facilitators of economic development since they create opportunities that would otherwise be unavailable to producers and consumers. Transportation networks capable of providing efficient, economical, reliable, safe, and secure movement of people and goods make the very existence of cities and occurrence of global trade possible (WBCSD 2004). Enhanced personal mobility increases access to essential and non-essential goods and services, while enhanced goods mobility provides consumers with a widened range of products and services at more affordable prices.

Transportation activity has grown strongly over the past decades and it is projected to continue increasing. Transportation is associated with greenhouse gas emissions, air pollution, congestion, noise, community and equity effects, ecosystem impacts, and deaths, injuries, and physical damage (WBCSD 2004). Mobility has thus come at a price economically, environmentally, and socially. Accordingly, the transportation sector faces a challenging future, particularly given the projected growth in travel demand, its high dependence on oil, and its significant and growing contribution to world energy consumption and greenhouse gas emissions (IPCC 2007).

The transportation sector accounts for almost half of world oil consumption and is responsible for 13 per cent of total anthropogenic greenhouse gas emissions and 23 per cent of world energy-related emissions. More than three quarters of transportation emissions come from road vehicles; automobiles alone account for almost half the total for the transportation sector (IPCC 2007). Hence, individual travel choices and behaviour have a significant cumulative impact on the global climate.

Transportation emissions have increased at a faster rate than those for any other energy using sector during the past decade and are forecast to continue growing strongly. Also, around three quarters of the projected increase in world oil demand between 2005 and 2030 is expected to come from the transportation sector (Energy Information Administration (EIA) 2008 and International Energy Agency (IEA) 2008).

Estimates predict that in 2030, unless there is a major shift away from current patterns of travel and energy use, transportation emissions will be approximately 80 per cent higher than in 2002, with the highest rates of growth in the developing world (IEA 2008, IPCC 2007 and WBCSD 2004). Consequently, reducing transportation greenhouse gas emissions must be a primary objective for any comprehensive climate change mitigation strategy (Feigon et al. 2003 and Greene and Schafer 2003).

## Urbanisation and development trends

Urbanisation has been extremely rapid in the last decades, especially in the less developed regions of the world (United Nations (UN) 2008). A parallel trend to urbanisation has been the decentralisation of cities, which have spread out faster than they have grown in population as people search to maximise privacy and individual space (Feigon et al. 2003).

This dispersed development trend played a central role in developed countries such as the United States and Australia during the second half of the twentieth century, where it was the result of deliberate planning and became known as 'predict and provide'—predict travel demand and provide infrastructure, generally roads (Goodwin 1999 and Vigar 2002). Although less deliberate and organised, this pattern is becoming increasingly prevalent in developing countries. In China, cities are following the trends and patterns of the United States, the most automobile-dependent country in the world (Cervero and Day 2008).

Together, urbanisation and decentralisation have created cities planned and built on the assumption that people own automobiles and will use them for most of their travel needs (Ewing et al. 2008). These cities, characterised by a functional separation of land uses, do not support non-motorised transportation, such as walking and bicycling, and are not well served by public transit, making alternatives to the automobile inconvenient and often uneconomical (Feigon et al. 2003). Importantly, transportation costs for those living in decentralised areas are consistently higher than for those living in more compact development (Feigon et al. 2003).

As a larger share of the built environment follows this pattern, travel demand (expressed in number of trips and distances) has significantly increased, accompanied by rapid growth in automobile dependency and a concurrent decline of non-motorised and transit modes as a share of total urban travel (WBCSD 2004). Population growth has been responsible for only about one quarter of the increase in automobile travel over the last decades (Ewing et al. 2008). A larger share has resulted from higher numbers of people travelling exclusively by automobile to meet their travel needs and making longer and more frequent trips as homes are located farther from workplaces, schools, and other destinations, such as shopping and entertainment locations (Feigon et al. 2003, Ewing et al. 2008, and Turcotte 2008).

## Automobile dependency

Economic growth has also contributed to changing travel patterns; as incomes have risen, people have shifted from walking and bicycling to public transportation to motorised transportation, such as motorcycles and automobiles (Schafer 2000 and IPCC 2007). Automobile travel now accounts for 15 to 30 per cent of total trips in the developing world, but 50 per cent in Western Europe and 90 per cent in the United States (IPCC 2007). The world automobile fleet grew from about 50 million to 650 million between 1950 and 2005, five times faster than the growth in population, and is projected to grow to 1.4 billion and 2 billion automobiles by 2030 and 2050, respectively (IEA 2008 and IPCC 2007). Relative to the year 2000, the world automobile fleet is expected to double by 2030 and triple by 2050.

In the United States, automobile travel has grown three times faster than population since 1980 (United States Environmental Protection Agency 2006). In China, annual automobile sales have increased threefold from 2001 to 2006 and automobile travel has increased fivefold during the last two decades (Cervero and Day 2008 and WBCSD 2004). In 2006, China became the world's second-largest vehicle market after the United States (Energy Information Administration 2009). Crucially, there is significant scope for continued expansion of China's vehicle fleet, since there are only 30 automobiles per thousand people in China, compared to about 850 automobiles per thousand people in the United States and about 590 automobiles per thousand people in Western Europe (Davis et al. 2009).

Automobiles are significantly more energy and emissions intensive (on a per passenger-kilometre basis) than public transit; the difference is even greater relative to non-motorised transportation (Davis et al. 2008, Department for Environment, Food and Rural Affairs 2008, and IPCC 2007). Scientific evidence strongly suggests that technology alone will not allow the transportation sector to meet emission reduction targets because technological improvements in automobiles and fuels are likely to be at least partially offset by continued growth in automobile travel (Greene and Schafer 2003 and WBCSD 2004). Furthermore, even though every passenger-kilometre in public transit is equivalent to multiple passenger-kilometres in an automobile, automobiles are allocated a disproportionately high amount of space to move a disproportionately low number of people (Newman and Kenworthy 1999 and Holtzclaw 2000).

The combination of decentralised development and construction of road infrastructure has resulted in land being consumed at a rate almost three times faster than population growth. Therefore, the amount of land available for emissions sequestration has been reduced, while transportation emissions have increased by the promotion of an emissions-intensive mode (Ewing et al. 2008).

A recent study in Canada shows that travel accounts for 40 to 60 per cent of the life-cycle greenhouse gas emissions of urban developments (Norman et al. 2006). In urban areas, promoting a shift to more energy- and emissions-efficient modes can considerably reduce transportation greenhouse gas emissions and thus constitutes an essential component of a climate change mitigation strategy (IPCC 2007, Ewing et al. 2008, and Feigon et al. 2003).

It is important to highlight that a significant share of automobile trips cover relatively short distances (less than five kilometres) that could be easily accommodated by alternative modes. Since greenhouse gas emissions are directly proportional to the amount of fuel consumed, it is crucial to sharply reduce the growth in automobile travel across the world's urban areas. To achieve this, it will be necessary to reverse long-standing decentralised development patterns and redefine the transportation user hierarchy (that is, considering pedestrians first, then bicyclists, then public transit users and, lastly, automobile drivers) to encourage a reduction in travel and a shift in mode choice (Ewing et al. 2008 and Whitelegg, J. 2008, personal communication, 12 November).

## Transit-oriented solutions

Transit-oriented development is proposed as the catalyst for this shift in travel mode choice and as the foundation of an integrated transportation and urban growth management strategy. The concept of transit-oriented communities is hardly new and is evocative of the transit villages of the late nineteenth century (Costello et al. 2003 and Cervero et al. 2004). However, there is no universally accepted definition of transit-oriented development, mainly because the characteristics that define it are highly dependent on location-specific features (Cervero et al. 2004).

Transit-oriented development is broadly defined here as development that promotes urban sustainability through an environment that advances a reduction in the need for travel (trips and distances), enhances accessibility to goods and services, provides a variety of travel alternatives, and preserves or augments the market share of low-emitting modes of transportation. In this context, transit-oriented development is characterised by coordination of land use and transportation planning; higher average 'blended' densities; a mix of land uses; ready access to goods and services via a variety of travel modes; strong population and employment centres; interconnection of streets; and the design of structures and spaces at a human scale (Ewing et al. 2008, Cervero et al. 2004, and Arrington and Cervero 2008).

The scientific literature strongly suggests that single initiatives tend to have a modest effect on changing travel behaviour and reducing greenhouse gas emissions. The synergistic nature of many strategies means that the key to achieving sustainability goals is to cluster a suite of them as a package (IPCC 2007, Greene and Schafer 2003, and Ewing et al. 2008). Transit-oriented development will, therefore, be effective only when supported by a comprehensive set of policy, regulatory, planning, economic, technological, infrastructure, and behaviour-focused elements that make non-motorised transportation and public transit use a feasible and desirable mobility option for urban residents to access the services they need and want (Feigon et al. 2003). The set of initiatives to be implemented will vary across regions, depending on each location's demographic, geographic, climatic, economic, political, and cultural conditions.

A crucial strategy to promote transit-oriented development is to strengthen local institutions (Sperling and Salon 2002). Some cities like Stockholm, Portland, Hong Kong, Singapore, and Shanghai are pursuing sustainable mobility goals by coordinating land use and transportation planning and providing high-quality public transportation; a crucial and often overlooked factor to provide a viable alternative to the automobile (Abbott 2002, Cameron et al. 2004, Cullinane 2002, Lundqvist 2003, and Willoughby 2001). A key quality aspect of public transit is frequency of services, which may attract new passengers to public transportation just as new road infrastructure induces automobile travel (Akerman and Hojer 2006).

Cities in developing countries provide substantial and largely untapped opportunities for the creation of sustainable urban forms and the prevention of automobile dependence, given the current trend of urbanisation and decentralisation and the prevailing high-density, mixed land use and low automobile ownership and use levels (Cervero and Day 2008 and Gwilliam et al. 2004). Curitiba in Brazil and Bogotá in Colombia are prime examples of coordinated regional land use and transportation planning (Cervero 2005a, Cervero 1998, and Gilat and Sussman 2003). The accompanying case study discusses Bogotá's balanced approach to sustainable urban and transportation planning to enhance accessibility, affordability, and living conditions for low-income groups.

Urban development patterns were initially characterised in terms of their density, diversity, and design (Cervero and Kockelman 1997). More recently, destination accessibility, distance to transit, and parking supply and cost have been added as important considerations (Ewing et al. 2008). These variables have a significant impact on the travel of individuals and households, mostly through their effect on distances travelled and mode of choice (Ewing and Cervero 2001 and Ewing et al. 2008). In the United States, for example:

> ...trip frequencies appear to be primarily a function of socioeconomic and demographic characteristics, and secondarily a function of the built environment; trip lengths are primarily a function of the built environment and secondarily of socioeconomic and demographic characteristics; and mode choice depends on both. (Ewing and Cervero 2001 and Ewing et al. 2008)

Transit-oriented developments will only yield benefits if they are part of a regional system that locates a variety of land uses and destinations, such as housing, employment, educational institutions, shops, and entertainment around the transit network (Cervero 2007 and Feigon et al. 2003). This enhances access to goods and services and allows an even spread of trip origins and destinations, producing efficient bidirectional transit flows that avoid peak-period transit vehicles being full in one direction and nearly empty in the other, as is the case in many United States and Australian cities (Cervero 2005a).

## Transit-oriented development: key climate change mitigation strategy

Many rigorous empirical studies of the link between urban development and travel patterns show that, even after accounting for income and other socioeconomic and demographic differences, residents of transit-oriented communities drive significantly less and walk, bicycle, and ride public transit more than their counterparts in traditional communities (Arrington and Cervero 2008, Cervero et al. 2004, Ewing et al. 2008, and Feigon et al. 2003). Even though the level of travel reduction and shift to alternative modes is highly dependent on local and regional conditions, such as urban form and accessibility, most of the evidence shows that people in transit-oriented development drive 20 to 40 per cent less (Ewing et al. 2003, Feigon et al. 2003, Ewing et al. 2008, and Bartholomew 2007).

This is mostly attributed to shorter distances between destinations—allowing people to live within walking or bicycling distance of some of their destinations, such as work, school, shops, and parks—and easy access to transit to reach farther destinations. Hence, automobile ownership is lower, automobile trips are shorter and less frequent, and non-motorised and public transportation have a larger share of the overall travel demand (Arrington and Cervero 2008). Community-oriented travel within neighbourhoods is not dealt with in detail in most studies, and bicycling and walking are generally disregarded. As a result, Ewing et al. (2008) suggest that the potential reductions in automobile travel are probably underestimated.

---

### Initiatives to promote the success of transit-oriented communities

- Integrate land use and transportation planning at the local and regional level to promote access to goods and services.
- Enhance access to integrated goods and services (employment, school, health, recreation) within the development to maximise community-oriented travel.
- Manage travel demand, including soft measures to promote voluntary travel behaviour change, and hard measures to lock in the benefits.
- Implement pedestrian- and bicycle-friendly land use initiatives and facilities that support local, community-oriented travel, such as walkable and safe urban spaces and dedicated bicycle paths.
- Integrate non-motorised transportation and public transit to enhance their mutual effectiveness, such as by placing bicycle facilities at transit stations and bicycle racks on buses.
- Provide access to high-quality, frequent, and safe public transportation for longer-distance trips.
- Encourage mobility on demand initiatives, such as car and bicycle sharing programs.
- Develop innovative strategies for land acquisition and development.
- Introduce financial incentives and disincentives to give transit-oriented development a competitive edge in urban real estate markets by using instruments such as location-efficient mortgages and employee-preference housing.
- Establish market-responsive and flexible zoning for increased densities and mixed uses
- Implement flexible parking policies, such as parking limitations, pricing, adaptive reuse of parking lots, and unbundling of housing and parking costs.
- Provide transit incentives.
- Expand telecommunications services to facilitate reductions in work and shopping travel.
- Reallocate existing road space for walking, bicycling, and public transit facilities.
- Introduce disincentives to automobile use via traffic calming, road user charges, operating restrictions, automobile-free districting, and road design mechanisms.

The potential for transit-oriented development to reduce transportation greenhouse gas emissions will depend on the share of new development and redevelopment that takes place in the future and the degree to which density, diversity, design, destination accessibility, distance, parking strategies, and complementary policies and initiatives are adopted (Ewing et al. 2008). Population forecasts indicate that significant new development or redevelopment will take place in urban areas around the world (UN 2008). In the United States, it is estimated that more than half the development 'on the ground' in 2025 (and approximately two-thirds of that in 2050) is yet to be built (Nelson 2006). This places transit-oriented development in a unique position to provide a 'low-cost climate change mitigation strategy because it involves shifting (the nature of) investments that have to be made anyway' (Ewing et al. 2008).

Recent studies estimate that comprehensive transit-oriented policies could reduce transportation greenhouse gas emissions from current trends by seven to 10 per cent in 2050 (Ewing et al. 2008). Other studies provide even higher reduction estimates of five to 25 per cent by 2050 (Marshall 2008, Stone et al. 2007, and Dierkers 2005). These estimates do not include building-related energy and emissions savings or the greenhouse gas sequestration from forests preserved by compact (rather than decentralised) development.

**ABOVE**
Residents of transit-oriented communities drive significantly less and walk, bicycle, and ride public transit more than their counterparts in traditional communities.

This is significant since high-density urban development is less energy and greenhouse gas emissions intensive than low-density suburban development on a per capita and surface area basis (Norman et al. 2006 and EIA 2008). An important consideration is that the 'long-lived nature of buildings and infrastructure, which limits the short- and medium-term benefits of transit-oriented development, makes emissions benefits permanent and compoundable' (Ewing et al. 2008). Reducing transportation greenhouse gas emissions will require a combination of initiatives, from automobile and fuel technologies, to economic policies, to infrastructure investments, to behaviour changes, to land use and transportation planning integration. These and other measures provide significant opportunities for reducing greenhouse gas emissions but are not sufficient in isolation. Transit-oriented development can play a crucial role in reducing transportation emissions by promoting urban growth in a way that reduces the need for travel and advances the use of more energy- and emissions-efficient modes of transportation to meet people's travel needs.

Additional benefits of transit-oriented development include improved air quality, reduced congestion, preserved land and open space, protected water quantity and quality, improved health and physical activity, affordable housing and liveable communities, equitable accessibility and mobility, and reduced road and other infrastructure costs. Transit-oriented development can thus promote environmental, social, and economic sustainability objectives. It can also support the establishment of resilient communities, better prepared to withstand issues like peak oil production and potential increases in fuel prices. Importantly, the technology and knowhow for transit-oriented development exist today, as it is based on long-standing principles, and can thus be readily applied to reduce the impact of urban transportation on climate change.

# Case study: integration of affordable housing and transportation planning in Bogotá

Bogotá, the capital of Colombia, has gained worldwide recognition for implementing one of the most sustainable and innovative urban transportation programs in the world, featuring a high-speed and high-capacity bus rapid transit (BRT) system called TransMilenio. The city's land use and transportation programs were framed around planning for *people and places* instead of *movement*, adopting a balanced approach that stressed accessibility as well as mobility. The principles of transit-oriented development were embraced under the premise that accessibility (for all sectors of the population) and priority to people instead of automobiles were essential to building a functional, liveable, and sustainable city (Cervero 2005a).

Bogotá has a population of around seven million people occupying around 30,000 hectares. With a population density of around 13,500 people per square kilometre, it is the ninth densest city in the world (City Mayors 2009). Mixed land use patterns provide access to goods and services within relatively short distances. The city's high density and diversity, combined with a mild climate, make non-motorised and public transportation particularly attractive. In 1998, approximately 70 per cent of automobile trips were less than three kilometres and over three quarters of overall daily trips were less than 10 kilometres in length (IPCC 2007 and Cervero 2005a). Given the high levels of congestion in the city, non-motorised and public transportation can be faster than the automobile for a large proportion of trips.

The success in promoting sustainability goals in Bogotá is largely due to the strengthening of local institutions and the implementation of a variety of policy, planning, infrastructure, and economic elements. Bogotá has used a balanced approach that combines soft measures that encourage non-motorised and public transportation with hard measures that provide disincentives to automobile use, such as license plate restrictions, parking management, and automobile-free districting. As such, investment priorities have focused on pedestrians first, followed by bicyclists, then public transit riders, and lastly automobile users. The city actively promotes pedestrian and bicycle access by providing green connectors: grade-separated pedestrian and bicycle ways that connect residential and commercial areas to other areas and to public transit. During the first three years since bicycle ways were introduced in the late 1990s, the share of daily trips by bike grew from about half a per cent to about four per cent (Hook 2003). Today, Bogotá has the most extensive network of bicycle ways in Latin America (over 300 kilometres), the world's longest pedestrian corridor (17 kilometres), and the world's biggest car-free day.

Bogotá began operating TransMilenio in 2000, building upon Curitiba's success with dedicated busways. TransMilenio is the centrepiece of Bogotá's transportation system and is credited with 'transforming aesthetically displeasing busway corridors with severe pollution and safety problems into modern busways with significantly lower travel times, noise levels, accidents, and emissions of air pollutants and greenhouse gases', all achieved without operating subsidies (Estupiñán and Rodríguez 2008).

TransMilenio station location and access are key to the success of the system: many public squares, libraries, parks, and recreational facilities are located within a half kilometre of busway stops; parking is limited to the end stations of the busways; sidewalks and bicycle ways feed most stations; and around half the stations are served by pedestrian overpasses. As a result, 70 per cent of TransMilenio users reach stations by foot or bicycle (Cervero 2005b) and 10 to 20 per cent of TransMilenio riders are former automobile drivers (Cervero 2005a and Gilbert 2008).

TransMilenio is characterised by its low cost (relative to rail investments), high ridership, and accessibility benefits (Rodríguez and Targa 2004). As of 2008, TransMilenio comprised nine lines covering 84 kilometres with exclusive right-of-way, operated more than 1,000 articulated buses across 114 stations, and carried 1.4 million one-way trips per day at an average speed of 27 kilometres per hour (three times the average vehicle speeds during the peak commuting period in 1999) (Rodríguez and Mojica 2008). TransMilenio weekday ridership is almost two times that of the subway system in Washington, D.C., at a fraction of the construction and operating costs and with less than half of its distance of track (TransMilenio 2009 and Washington Metro 2009). The use of dual carriage ways (allowing buses to overtake each other), enclosed boarding stations with high-level platforms, and off-board fare collection systems allow TransMilenio to have a throughput of about 36,000 persons per direction per hour, a number that matches that of many high-quality metro rail systems (Cervero 2005a and Hook 2006).

A critical element of Bogotá's urban and transportation planning has been to site new housing settlements near peripheral TransMilenio stations and along regional bicycle networks, to provide accessibility and mobility to the vast population of low-income households who do not own automobiles. As in many Latin American cities, a significant portion of the population of Bogotá lives in informal settlements on hillsides with difficult access and few public services. Average daily commute times for residents of informal housing are between two and three hours, including sometimes strenuous walking due to the peripheral location and limited availability of public transportation. In addition, workers seeking jobs in more central locations pay multiple fares for informal paratransit connections to the city, consuming as much as 15 per cent of their income (Cervero 2005a). In 2000, the city government estimated a deficit of approximately 450,000 homes for low-income households.

In response to these problems, the government introduced Metrovivienda, an innovative land-banking and poverty-alleviation program (Cervero 2005a). As of 2008, three Metrovivienda projects have been built, providing housing for close to 12,000 families, and expansions to current and new projects are in different stages of planning and construction (Metrovivienda 2009). Under the program, the city acquires land in open areas well in advance of the arrival of TransMilenio to avoid the price inflation brought by access to public transit: recent studies show significant appreciation of property values with proximity to TransMilenio stations (Rodríguez and Targa 2004 and Rodríguez and Mojica 2008).

The city provides public services (water, sewage, gas, electricity, and roads) and open space and then sells the property to developers (at higher prices to recover infrastructure costs), with the condition that housing is provided at prices affordable to people within the two lowest income groups (Cervero 2005a and Metrovivienda 2009). The population is divided into six income groups, with groups one and two classified as poor under Colombian law. Metrovivienda housing for group one is priced up to 50 minimum wages (21,685,000 Colombian pesos or approximately US$10,770*) and for group two between 50 and 70 minimum wages (30,359,000 Colombian pesos or approximately US$15,079) (Metrovivienda 2009).

Metrovivienda provides two parallel benefits to residents by building communities near TransMilenio stations: legal and improved housing with amenities and community features, such as bicycle and pedestrian ways, parks, and libraries, which are generally available only to higher income groups; and high-quality public transit services that improve access to major economic, cultural, and recreational centres in the city. A recent study estimated that (for those moving from illegal housing to Metrovivienda) the number of jobs reachable within an hour's travel time increased threefold and commuting costs decreased by around 50 per cent (Cervero 2005a). Travel costs declined mainly because former residents of illegal housing have gone from paying multiple paratransit fares to paying only the TransMilenio fare (Gilbert 2008).

The TransMilenio and Metrovivienda programs highlight the broader social, economic, and environmental benefits of integrating affordable housing and transportation planning in developing countries, while focusing on people rather than automobiles. Low-income groups in Bogotá gained improved access to employment, education, shopping, and other services, while enjoying a reduction in the joint costs of housing and transportation (that can represent as much as two-thirds of their income) (Cervero 2005a). A critical environmental benefit is the reduction in vehicle travel and transportation emissions, thus improving local air quality and reducing the impact of transportation on climate change. Although Metrovivienda has only provided homes for a relatively small number of families to date, it is a positive step forward and showcases the sustainability benefits provided by the integration of land use and transportation planning.

* As of July 2009, US$1 = 2,013 Colombian pesos

# Case study: the No Excuse Zone and CycleCity Strategy

## Damien Pericles and Ann-Marie Mulligan

Using Sydney as a case study, the CycleCity Strategy provokes a paradigm shift in urban modal transport, founded on the benefits of cycling for the individual, the community, the economy, and the environment.

Transport currently accounts for 34 per cent of Australian household emissions (Australian Greenhouse Office 2003). And each year, air pollution from cars causes between 900 and 2,000 early deaths and between 900 and 4,500 cases of bronchitis, cardiovascular, and respiratory disease, costing between A$1.5 billion to 3.8 billion (Bureau of Transport and Regional Economics 2005). Bicycles, as a zero emission form of transport, offer the potential to significantly reduce Australia's transport emissions.

Traffic congestion currently costs A$9.4 billion and is projected to increase to A$20.4 billion by 2020 (Bureau of Transport and Regional Economics 2007). Much smaller in size than cars, bicycles are an effective decongestant to urban traffic problems.

In Australia, physical inactivity costs tax payers A$15 billion a year (NSW Premier's Council for Active Living 2007) and is the second most significant cause of ill health in Australia (Mathers, Vost and Stephenson 1999). Active modes of transport such as cycling and walking are effective ways of getting adequate physical exercise (Badland and Schofield 2005).

Based on a series of test rides, a zone around Sydney's Central Business District (CBD) has been mapped to measure the distance a healthy person can cycle within half an hour. Called the No Excuse Zone, it provocatively suggests if a person lives within this zone and works in the CBD, they should cycle to work at least a few days a week. Subsequently, the cities of Brisbane and Melbourne have also been mapped, with No Excuse Zones established for both urban centres.

CycleCity proposes a new level of infrastructure for cyclists that maximise the bicycle's effectiveness as a means of mass transit: a series of strategically-located, fully-separated bicycle paths that are safe, efficient, and direct. Like the No Excuse Zone mapping, they operate on a radial model centred on major employment centres. Informed by established commuter patterns, these paths weave through existing urban conditions, utilising existing disused infrastructure, open space, drainage corridors, and back streets. And they are informed by key destinations, such as employment centres, universities, hospitals, stations, schools, and the like.

CycleCity aims to positively change the impact and stranglehold motor vehicles have on Sydney. It envisions streets with a constant stream of movement, yet they are peaceful; streets that are safe for children and seniors to move along; and streets which re-engage community participation in open space. In this respect, CycleCity is proposed as an urban activator.

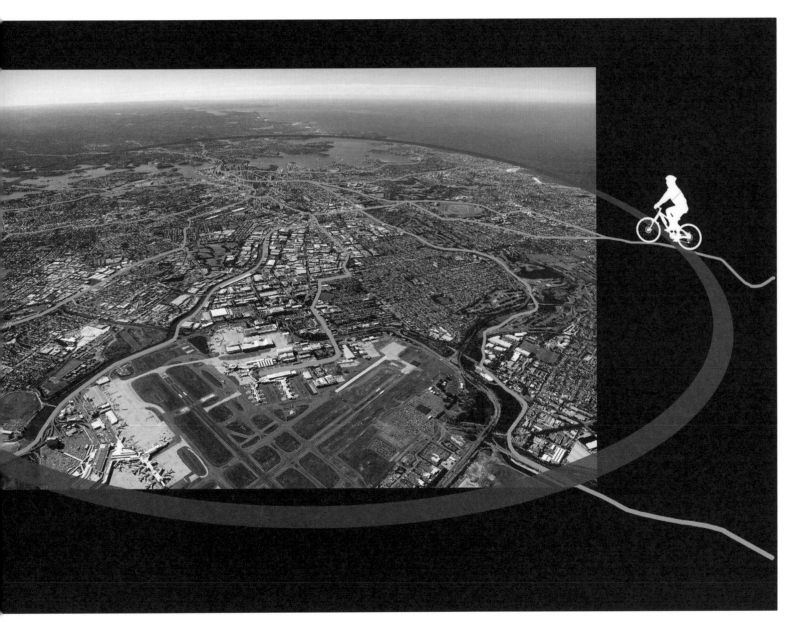

**ABOVE**

CycleCity proposes a new level of infrastructure for cyclists that maximise the bicycle's effectiveness as a means of mass transit: a series of strategically-located, fully-separated bicycle paths that are safe, efficient, and direct.

Preliminary economic analysis has quantified the significant benefits to be gained by increasing cycling and implementing the CycleCity concept:

- Increased physical activity levels and the associated increased health benefits; and
- Reduced cost of transport externalities, including air and noise pollution, road traffic injuries, congestion, and climate change mitigation.

Analysis focused on quantifying the benefits if more journeys to work were made by bicycle. An ambitious target was set: halving commuter car trips originating from within the No Excuse Zone and destined for the CBD by 2031.

Examination of journey to work data from the 2006 Census of Population and Housing reveals almost 32,000 commuter car trips are made between the No Excuse Zone and Sydney's CBD each weekday. If 50 per cent of these commuters shift from cars to bicycles by 2031, CycleCity could deliver economic benefits of more than A$257 million (net present value) for commuting trips to Sydney's city centre alone. Benefits include reduced vehicle operating costs, less congestion, externality benefits such as reduced air and noise pollution, and climate change mitigation.

These figures indicate up to A$250 million could be spent over 30 years to improve bicycle facilities in inner Sydney, with the benefits outweighing the costs. In addition, 160,000 tonnes of greenhouse gas emissions would be saved between 2010 and 2040.

Implementation of CycleCity could also bring considerable additional savings not quantified by this economic analysis, such as:

- Benefits for other types of transport trips, such as those for shopping and recreation, as around 66 per cent of personal transport is used for non-commuting purposes (Australian Greenhouse Office 2006);
- Benefits to the existing transport network, as public transport users switch to cycling creating additional capacity. This could delay the need for additional capacity to be built into the public transport system, known as deferred infrastructure savings; and
- Benefits to personal savings, brought, for example, by decreases in travelling time and transport expenditure, through reductions in the need for car ownership.

Sydney's CBD already has a lower proportion of trips made by car compared with regional cities in Australia. The implementation of CycleCity in these regional centres has the potential to bring greater benefits.

# Economic and planning responses to climate change

Jasmin Abad, Ellen Nunez, Eli N. Pincus, Vivien Wu, Yang Fan, Chris Yoshii, Jessie Zhang

The twenty-first century may be remembered as the period in history when humankind realised the value of its relationship to Earth and its climate. As a society, we are realising that the ever-accumulating mass and interconnectedness of economies in an era of globalisation demands recognition of the effects of climate change and necessitates intelligent design and planning.

This discussion explores several economic and planning responses to climate change: land use, building and energy use; carbon footprint reduction; and cost-benefit and life cycle analysis. It goes on to highlight some of the issues of resettlement planning for those displaced by the environmental effects of climate change.

## Land use, building use, energy use

Undeveloped green spaces and ecosystems contain enough vegetation to store carbon dioxide and purify water, using only solar and biological energy. Similarly, land left in its natural state requires little or no additional energy. But human activity—residential, commercial, and industrial land use—changes the natural state of land and increases energy consumption. Land use significantly contributes to, if not determines, the energy demand and subsequent carbon emissions and climate change impacts of a particular location.

Basic human activities, as presented in Figure 01, account for all deliverable energy around the world. US government energy statistics report that the residential, commercial, and transportation sectors account for 14 per cent, 8 per cent, and 27 per cent, respectively, of world energy consumption (Energy Information Administration 2008), with the industrial sector accounting for the largest share at 51 per cent.

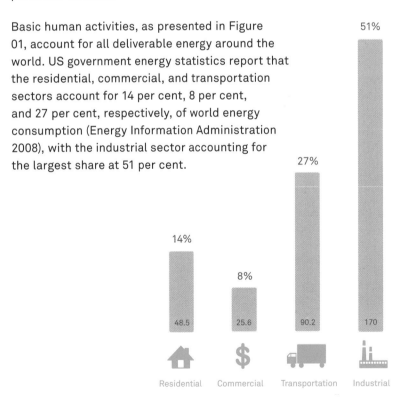

FIGURE 01
Total world delivered energy consumption by end-use sector, excluding energy used for electricity generation. Measured in quadrillion British Thermal Units. (Energy Information Administration 2005)

Table 01 demonstrates how different housing types utilise energy in the United States. Approximately 80 per cent of residential energy use is consumed in single-family homes, the highest compared to other housing types (Energy Information Administration 2004). This is because single-detached family structures require more energy per unit for cooling, lighting, and space and water heating. Dwellings with fewer occupants per unit also have a higher percentage of units heated with electricity, resulting in lesser efficiency on a delivered basis.

Multi-family units account for 38 per cent of all housing units, but consume only 15 per cent of the energy used in this sector. Mobile homes, which use liquefied petroleum gas, account for seven per cent of the housing stock, but comprise five per cent of all residential energy use (Cymbalsky 1998). On an energy use per household level, mobile homes are also less efficient than denser multi-family dwellings.

In terms of commercial use structures, 40 per cent of total building energy is consumed by retail, service, and office buildings. Civic facilities such as schools use 13 per cent, which is much more than hospitals and other medical buildings combined (Energy Information Administration 2003). The remaining categories or 'all other buildings' account for the other half of sector use.

As far as community scale developments are concerned, there is increasing evidence that higher-density, mixed-use compact developments are more accessible, encourage pedestrian activity, and are therefore more energy efficient (Tarnay and McMahon 2005). Table 02 illustrates the rationale for specific land use strategies as they are applied to such developments. Consequently, more developers are embracing the compact, mixed-use concept as a market selling point; not only in terms of higher returns but also for longer-term value appreciation.

In summary, land use planning takes into consideration principles that not only address specific efficiency and cost issues but climate change issues as well. As Table 02 clearly suggests, land use planning, climate change measures, and smart planning all relate to creating sustainable communities.

| Type of residential buildings | Number of households (million)[1] | Energy used (quadrillion BTU) | Energy used per household (million BTU) | Percent of total energy used[2] |
|---|---|---|---|---|
| Single family | 77.7 | 9.2 | 118.4 | 80% |
| Multi-family | 38.1 | 1.7 | 45.3 | 15% |
| Mobile homes | 8.6 | 0.6 | 66.9 | 5% |
| Total | 124.4 | 11.5 | N/A | 100% |

TABLE 01
Average energy consumption in the United States by housing type ([1]US Department of Housing and Urban Development & US Census Bureau 2006, [2]Energy Information Administration 2004)

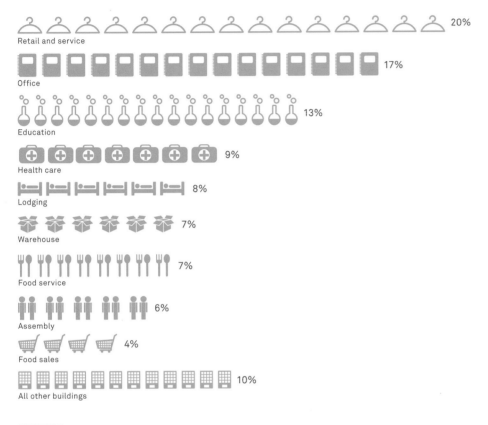

Retail and service     20%

Office     17%

Education     13%

Health care     9%

Lodging     8%

Warehouse     7%

Food service     7%

Assembly     6%

Food sales     4%

All other buildings     10%

FIGURE 02
Energy use in the United States by commercial building type (Energy Information Administration 2006)

| Land use strategy | Defining characteristics | Mitigating features |
| --- | --- | --- |
| Connectivity | Smooth grid-like pattern rather than road network that ends up with cul-de-sacs | Limits carbon emissions, traffic congestion and distance between homes |
| Walkability | Core destinations in close proximity and reduce additional need for infrastructure | Pedestrian-friendly places and neighbourhoods promote healthier lifestyle and builds community |
| Density | More buildings clustered together, with consideration on how buildings are clustered in a specific plot and area of development | Creates the drive for businesses to provide better goods and services, further creating smaller and unique shops that serve the community |
| Mixed uses | Visual spread throughout the community by combining retail, commercial and services with residential and offices in the same building or area | Generates a diversity of people; people of all ages, sizes, income, cultures and races, making developments unique and creating a sense of belongingness |
| Accessibility | Availability of different modes of transit, with train and light transit instead of highways and roads | Makes a community more financially viable, placing people in close vicinity to shops and businesses |

TABLE 02
Land use and efficiency features of high-density mixed developments

## Carbon footprinting our way to a better future

Carbon footprinting measures the impact human activities have on the environment and reveals the greenhouse gas generated daily by the burning of fossil fuels (Wiedmann and Minx 2007). As a key consumer of electricity and energy and contributor to carbon dioxide emissions, the built environment has profound impacts on climate change (US Green Building Council 2008). Reducing a building's carbon footprint can generate measurable environmental and economic benefits; it is an increasingly important concern of real estate investors and occupants. Strategies that target carbon footprint reduction are continuously being developed as more businesses and cities strive for carbon neutrality.

Greening building is widely regarded as a greenhouse gas mitigation measure with diverse energy efficiency techniques. Carbon footprint reduction has become integral to most green building certifications, such as Leadership in Energy and Environmental Design (LEED), the Building Research Establishment Environmental Assessment Method (BREEAM), and the Comprehensive Assessment System for Building Environmental Efficiency (CASBEE). Intentions are to include requirements for carbon footprinting to significantly reduce greenhouse gases beyond the baseline level in rating green buildings (Pyke 2008).

Carbon footprinting measures the impact human activities have on the environment and reveals the greenhouse gas generated daily by the burning of fossil fuels.

Increasing emphasis on green buildings has also placed more attention on the larger community; a single green building in isolation has marginal impacts on the community's costs of infrastructure and services. In many cases, an appropriate urban form is required that will enable buildings to achieve their green potential. The holistic approach has been reflected in LEED for Neighbourhood Development, a new LEED rating system that integrates the principles of smart growth, new urbanism, and green building into neighbourhood design (US Green Building Council 2008).

Planning measures that reduce carbon footprints include higher-density developments, transit orientation, mixed land uses, and walkability. Increased land use intensity and non-motorised transportation usage can significantly reduce regional greenhouse gas emission. Cities such as Portland, San Francisco, New York, and London are spearheading this field (The Climate Group 2008). Emerging Asian cities are also experimenting on similar ideas in their burgeoning new town developments. Abu Dhabi's MASDAR carbon-neutral city (Thomson Reuters 2008) and Shanghai's Dongtan Eco-city are among the leading pioneers of this program (The Observer 2006). While the practicalities of these developments remain yet to be discovered, their ambition and pioneering endeavour to combat climate change have gained global market recognition.

Overall, the focus on buildings and land uses is critical to achieving global carbon footprint reduction because they present immediate opportunities for action with long-term consequences. This discussion suggests that design and construction of the built environment are essential components of efforts to mitigate and adapt to climate change. It also exemplifies our ability to work with nature in addressing common concerns.

## Cost benefit and life cycle analysis of going green

Planning for a zero-emission world is not yet the industry norm; very few are convinced of the financial and market benefits of climate-sensitive design. The many variables that go into a property's financial cost and rate of return are already a mouthful and for developers integrating climate change costs, green features and alternative products give the impression of very high additional financial burden.

But a broad study by Davis Langdon and Seah International (Matthiessen 2006, cited in Broughton (ed. ULI) 2008) concludes that comparatively, average construction costs for green buildings versus non-green buildings are insignificant; design and construction costs do not have to increase in order to enjoy green benefits. To be sure, current design standards and techniques already satisfy about half of the minimum LEED requirements. A number of notable examples illustrate how the numbers work.

- Green buildings can have significant impacts on cost savings. Texas Instruments' Richardson Texas manufacturing facility cut construction costs by US$220 million and estimates annual operating savings of US$4 million by adapting green building design and construction processes.
- Green features can lead to savings on capital costs. Dell Children's Medical Centre in Austin Texas (part of the Seton Family of Hospitals chain) collaborated with Austin Energy to build a gas-fired turbine combined heat and power plant to deliver power, steam, hot water, and chilled water for hospital use. The plant is able to achieve 80 per cent energy conservation efficiency.

Presented below is a cost-benefit analysis framework of climate-conscious developments; considered a valuable tool, not only from an investment point of view, but also in terms of insurance and valuation purposes, public awareness, and other social goods. While cost-benefit analysis is arguably reductionist and has inherent simplifications and assumptions, it is a valuable and dialectical process that can be adapted to project-specific needs or extrapolated as a benchmark or reference point.

### Cost analysis

The direct contribution of buildings and developments to anthropogenic climate change is through carbon-intensive energy usage and demand. In the United States, buildings are responsible for 40 per cent of energy and raw material consumption and at least 30 per cent of greenhouse gas emissions (Royal Institute of Chartered Surveyors 2008). A building's largest single operating cost is usually energy, commanding approximately 30 per cent of the operational expenses (Eicholtz 2008). Therefore, investing in features up front which maximise energy efficiency and minimise fossil fuel dependency would cut electricity bills and alter the mix of energy sources such that it costs less and emits less.

Identifying and tabulating the initial building costs is known as first-costs analysis. This is usually a straightforward and intuitive process. One compares the greener or more environmentally-beneficial product with the industry standard counterpart product, and establishes the nominal cost difference. Once this is undertaken for all project factors in scope, the investor can then make a decision or use the information for other financial analysis. However, the disadvantage of the first-cost method is that it does not capture the potential benefits over time.

| Project | The Plaza at PPL Centre | The Dalles Middle School | The Seattle Justice Centre |
|---|---|---|---|
| Architect | Robert A. M. Stern | Heinz Rudolf | NBBJ |
| Client | PPL Corporation | The Dalles School District | City of Seattle |
| LEED consultant | Atelier Ten | Heery International | GC/CM |
| Completion | 2003 | 2002 | 2002 |
| Project area | 252,000 square feet | 96,000 square feet | 280,000 square feet |
| PSF | US$220 | US$104 | US$247 |
| Cost premium | 1.0% | 0.50% | 4.0% |

TABLE 03
Notable cases illustrating the cost benefits of going green

| Category | Average increase or decrease |
|---|---|
| Energy savings | 25% to 35% |
| Operating costs | -8% to -9% |
| Return on investment | +6.6% |
| Occupancy rates | +3.5% |
| Rent | +3% |

TABLE 04
Average benefits resulting from green
developments as opposed to conventional
developments (Drummer 2008)

| Category | Average cost increase |
|---|---|
| LEED consultant | US$25,000 |
| Design and certifications | (Up to 10%) |
| Building commissioning | Up to US$20,000 |

Table 05
Increased costs of obtaining LEED
Certification (Drummer 2008)

A more sophisticated and comprehensive framework is the life-cycle cost analysis. The long-term energy savings and other environmental benefits afforded by a green development can be recorded in the life-cycle cost analysis, by discounting costs to net present value and including projections for operations and maintenance. In one landmark study, it was shown that if up-front costs increased two per cent and the balance were invested in green capital, the life-cycle savings is equivalent to 20 per cent of total construction costs (Kats 2003). This means that the financial benefit of environmental design is 10 times the marginal financial cost of the investment.

*Benefits analysis*

These costs or investments in green design lead to economic benefits that can be examined in the following framework.

The construction process itself has the potential to yield economic benefits: investing in more environmentally rigorous construction saves energy and resources. A better plan or design decreases operating costs and increases savings. Furthermore, a better plan or design makes for a less wasteful, more energy-efficient layout and provides high-quality systems that insure against future energy cost increases (Eichholtz, Kok and Quigley 2008). Finally, the decreased energy usage or fossil fuel usage mitigates greenhouse gas emissions and contributes to low or near-zero carbon footprints.

Most of the economic and climate benefits of green development are manifested over time as the building operates (aside from benefits from a better construction process). For a more representative bird's eye view of a project and its cost-benefit ratio, the financial savings must also be discounted to net present values.

An investor in a real estate project is likely seeking to maximise benefits and minimise costs; however, the menu of available environmental features has many associated costs. The Urban Land Institute proposes a spectrum of 'shades of green' possibilities for the developer (Kellenberg and Schweitzer 2007). The sceptical end of the spectrum would be concerned, at the very least, with recovering the premium of the green features; at the other end, the most ecologically-conservative approach would be to build with the highest possible environmental standards.

*The green continuum*

Many possibilities and potentials for green continuum exist:

* Guaranteeing end user preference, fully recouping green premium;

* Choosing the plan with lowest first-cost;

* Choosing the plan with lowest life-cycle cost;

* Choosing the plan with the highest environmental benefit at lowest life-cycle cost; and

* Planning and building with highest possible environmental benefit.

## Illustrating costs, benefits, and value

The growing popularity of green and sustainable developments has led to a spate of information being published on the cost savings of building green. The savings realised due to green development accrue over time and therefore investment in a green project should be assessed considering the entire life of the project rather than only the initial outlay (Kats 2008).

A widely accepted conclusion is that green developments are only marginally more expensive than non-green developments and that the loss from the initial investment in a green development can be recouped over the long term. However, in order to keep costs low it is imperative that the building plans are originally designed with green building practices in mind.

Some of the major benefits provided by green developments include energy, water, and waste savings; increased occupant efficiency and health; decreased operational and maintenance costs; decreased detrimental effects on the environment (decreased carbon dioxide emissions); increased return on investment; and tax breaks.

The LEED rating system has been the most widely accepted green rating system for US developments. The Sustainable Building Task Force reports that overall cost premiums for a LEED certified building average just under two per cent (Kats 2008). One should note, however, that these costs are expected to be more than compensated for over time in the form of the savings from green developments discussed earlier.

An iconic example of a successful green development that temporarily increased costs, but ended up in huge monetary savings over time, is the Silicon Valley headquarters of Adobe Systems Inc, where green upgrades have brought the following benefits:

- Decreased energy use by 35 per cent;
- Decreased natural gas usage by 41 per cent;
- Decreased domestic water use by 22 per cent; and
- Decreased landscape irrigation by 76 per cent.

The total cost of upgrading Adobe's headquarters came to US$1.4 million. However, the company was granted rebates of US$389,000 and is saving around US$1.2 million per year. These figures yield a payback in less than 10 months and a Return on Investment of 121 per cent.

Table 06 displays a cost-benefit comparison for many facets of the improvements. Adobe's headquarters is a prime example of a company that has not only helped the world's environment, but also managed to profit from its increased environmental scrutiny.

As the benefits of developing green become increasingly well known and the fragility of the world's ecosystem more publicised, it can be expected that the trend in green building will continue to grow. Not only is developing green environmentally friendly; it is also economically beneficial when looked at over the entire lifetime of the project. The new trend is green and companies would be wise to jump on the bandwagon if they expect to remain competitive in the ultra-competitive landscape of today's business world.

| Upgrade | Cost (US$) | Annual saving (US$) |
|---|---|---|
| Modified tower cooling staging and sequencing | 575 | 12,272 (and a 50% decrease in energy consumption) |
| Installation of web-based, weather-station-automated irrigation controllers with a drip irrigation system | 3,610 | 9,001 |
| Installation of waterless urinals | 35,374 | 6,338 (5,396 rebate) |
| Garage lighting to fluorescent bulbs | 156,878 | 86,198 (40,558 rebate) |
| Rewired rooms and offices for lighting zone control and reprogrammed relay controls for demand-response programs | 83,000 | 28,000 (2,887 rebate) |

TABLE 06
Cost-benefit analysis of the green upgrade of Adobe's headquarters (Golan 2008)

# Case study: beyond economics – resettlement planning responses

Resettlement is often an unavoidable consequence of natural disasters—some caused by climate change—that leave, for example, many coastal and low-lying communities homeless, jobless, and outside developed social networks. Ferris (2007, pp. 4-5) explains that although the displacement of people is not directly caused by climate change, it produces environmental effects that make it difficult for people to survive where they are. This concept is further articulated by modelling the impact of climate change on the displacement of people.

1.  Increased severity and sudden onset of natural disasters displaces people.
2.  This causes explicit long-term effects over time, meaning people's livelihoods are no longer sustainable, forcing migration to other places.
3.  This leads to increased conflict over resources, in turn displacing people.
4.  This causes environmental effects to which the government responds inappropriately, thus forcing people to leave their communities.
5.  This causes negative long-term environmental effects, which the government and international community tries to alleviate through the construction of large-scale development projects, which displaces people.

Anke Strauss from the International Organisation for Migration reports that 50 million people will be displaced by 2010 as a result of natural disasters (Ferris 2007, p. 1). This represents an increasing trend and therefore, it is essential to come up with purposeful sustainable strategies in anticipation of the inevitability of involuntary resettlement.

As in most involuntary resettlement policies, the basic objective is to restore communities to pre-displacement status, in this case pre-disaster status. This can be done by considering key land use and resettlement planning principles. Table 07 illustrates that resettlement plans are required once losses in housing, community structures, and services are incurred, even with a minimum of 200 people.

The Asia Development Bank's Handbook on Resettlement (1998, p. 18) lists key planning concepts to be taken into consideration when developing a resettlement plan:
• The policy framework – does it already exist or are new policies needed?
• Defining entitlements and eligibility – who will receive compensation and rehabilitation and how will these measures be structured?
• Gender planning – are the needs of women taken into consideration?
• Social preparation – will the needs of indigenous peoples and vulnerable groups be met?
• Budget – how will land acquisition and resettlement be financed?
• Timeline – how will land acquisition and resettlement fit into the overall development project schedule?

Notably, the application of land use planning to resettlement sites has been omitted. More often, if it is mentioned at all in resettlement planning, it is applied only peripherally to illustrate pre-disaster conditions or to describe economic outputs, such as in rural China.

From a draft of the Thanh Hoa Resettlement Plan for Central Region Water Resources Project of the Asia Development Bank, Table 08 presents an example of how land use is used to describe pre-displacement of affected persons and total affected land area, but not to derive a detailed land use resettlement plan.

A second example looks at resettlement policies in rural China, where village units and production groups assign land uses to community members as a form of long-term agreement towards grain and tax quotas set by the township government. Land uses, in this case, serve as contracts to intensify production and outputs. In cases where agricultural productivity is low, the affected people are assigned non-farm jobs or non-agricultural or urban residences. Specific activities, in this instance, are assigned to members regardless of land use capability or compatibility as long as production outputs are targeted.

But land use as applied to the planning of resettlement areas needs to consider many things. In the case of those displaced by climate change-induced phenomenon, resettlement is more permanent. Land use planning for such resettlement sites should integrate pre-disaster conditions, particularly livelihood and civic uses in the appropriation of land and designation of activities. An example of how resettlement programs incorporating land use can more effectively capture the needs of displaced communities is shown in Table 09.

Innovation in resettlement design can also replicate to some extent pre-damage livelihood, such as that from farming, fishing, and tourism. A growing body of organisations are developing and delivering innovative design solutions for post-disaster reconstruction and the rebuilding of resettlement communities, as well as for humanitarian and community projects throughout the world.

| Severity | Number of affected persons | Requirements |
|---|---|---|
| Loss of productive and other assets (including land), incomes, and livelihoods | 200 plus | Compensation at replacement costs, transfer and income substitution for down time, income restoration measures |
| Installation of web-based, weather-station-automated irrigation controllers with a drip irrigation system | 200 plus | Compensation at replacement rates, transfer assistance and relocation plans, measures to restore living standards |

TABLE 07

Examples of resettlement planning for selected severities (Asian Development Bank 1998, p. 13)

| Commune | Temporary Land Loss (square metres) | | | | | Permanent Land Loss (square metres) | | | | |
|---|---|---|---|---|---|---|---|---|---|---|
| | Total households | Residential | Agricultural | Forest | Total | Total households | Residential | Agricultural | Forest | Total |
| Thanh Van | 6 | | 1,318 | | 1,318 | 3 | | 504 | | 504 |
| Thanh Tam | | | | | 0 | 26 | 385 | 4,200 | 48,790 | 53,375 |
| Thach Binh | 19 | | 4,441 | 10,000 | 14,441 | 36 | 200 | 15,805 | | 16,005 |
| Thach Cam | | | | | 0 | 33 | 755 | 4,096 | | 4,851 |
| Thach Quang | | | | | 0 | 15 | 650 | 2,634 | | 3,284 |
| Thach Long | | | | | 0 | 2 | 300 | 2,400 | | 2,700 |
| Thach Dinh | 65 | | 2,339 | | 2,339 | 66 | | 3,506 | | 3,506 |
| Thach Son | | | | | 0 | 89 | 3,175 | 13,538 | | 16,713 |
| Thach Cam | 73 | | 6,812 | | 6,812 | 252 | | 22,916 | | 22,916 |
| Thach Quang | 18 | 600 | 2,000 | | 2,600 | 133 | 1,850 | 14,815 | | 16,665 |
| Thanh Truc | | | | | 0 | 257 | 20 | 29,145 | | 29,165 |
| Thanh Vinh | 388 | 400 | 18,716 | | 19,116 | 434 | 54 | 21,383 | | 21,437 |
| Thanh My | | | | | 0 | 51 | 65 | 2,234 | | 2,298 |
| Total | 569 | 1,000 | 35,626 | 10,000 | 46,626 | 1,397 | 7,453 | 137,176 | 48,790 | 193.419 |

**TABLE 08**
Loss of land (Asian Development Bank 2005)
Draft/not yet Board approved document

| Land use | Population | Livelihood population | Land area | FAR |
|---|---|---|---|---|
| Residential | 1,000 | 200 | 100,000 | 2 |
|     Rural | 500 | 100 | | |
|     Non-farm | 500 | 100 | | |
| Agriculture | | 80 | 250,000 | 2 |
|     Farming | | 60 | | |
|     Livestock | | 20 | | |
|     Fishing | | 0 | | |
| Agro-industry | | 10 | 20,000 | 1 |
| Non-farm | | 50 | 5,000 | 1 |
|     Cottage industry | | 30 | | |
|     Trading | | 20 | | |
| Tourism | | 20 | 20,000 | 2 |
| Hotel | | 5 | 1,500 | 3 |
| Retail | | 15 | 5,000 | 2 |
|     Wet and dry market | | 15 | | |
| Civic facilities | | 200 | 5,000 | 2 |
|     Schools | | | | |
|     Religious facilities | | | | |
|     Health centre | | | | |
| Total | 1,000 | 400 | 406,500 | 15 |

TABLE 09
Sample resettlement land use

# Climate: designing a new future

# The era of the ecological metropolis

## Stephen Engblom, Claire Bonham-Carter

The most important issue that faces all landscape architects, environmental planners and designers in the 21st century will be precisely the integration, perhaps by shotgun, of current economic and political thinking with ecological reality. (Garrett Eckbo 1960)

How did we get here? The climate crisis facing us in the twenty-first century is a direct result of nineteenth century industrialisation and the land planning and urban design solutions of the twentieth century. Suburban utopia was promised; the desire to separate living from working drove everyday decisions. Advances in technology and industry allowed us to move ourselves, our needs, and our wastes across great distances. Cultural obsession with the automobile and separated housing districts further drove this phenomenon. The infrastructure and policy developments required for this shift from the previous urban centre model surrounded by open space and agrarian areas were enormous. Unprecedented migrations from rural living to suburban and urban living and economic development resulted; yet, today, it can be argued that we stand at the endpoint of that twentieth century post-industrial trajectory—diminishing returns are now evident.

We have strained the equilibrium between humans and nature to the breaking point. By using the next generation of city building as an opportunity to restore this equilibrium, we can avert further climatic and ecological disaster while reaching new heights of economic and cultural vibrancy. We are now on the eve of a new era of climatic-responsive urban design: the era of the ecological metropolis.

The climate crisis facing us in the twenty-first century is a direct result of nineteenth century industrialisation and the land planning and urban design solutions of the twentieth century.

### Whose future are we living?

In 1939, the New York City World's Fair provided the perfect opportunity to showcase the suburban model. Visited by 44 million people (the equivalent of one third of the continental United States population which was 131 million at the time), the fair provided visitors with a fully synthesised, three-dimensional image of the future. The General Motors pavilion demonstrated a journey through increasingly lifelike scales of suburban living, where smiling families drove cars across the landscape and around cloverleaves for the first time to suburban houses in the countryside. The Chrysler pavilion was the first public building with air conditioning. These fantastic visions struck a chord; visitors left the fair with buttons that read, *I have seen the future*, believing in and desiring to live the vision they had seen. Then, between 1941 and 1945, the United States engaged in the Second World War, after which followed a perfect storm of forces that would realise the 1939 vision of suburban utopia; a vision so compelling it continues to be replicated across continents today.

- **Lifestyle:** seeking an escape from the congestion and cost of the city, consumers embraced the suburban model of cheap land and green acres.

- **Economies:** seeking maximum profit, developers fulfilled the market's demand by providing production housing and affordable cars and products on an unprecedented scale.

- **Politics:** seeking economic growth for their jurisdictions, local policy-makers approved road building programs and suburban mortgage lending policies, thus eradicating the previous paradigm of a regional core within an ecological hinterland.

At a moment when everyone seemed to be benefitting, no one reckoned the long-term costs of single-use land development or automobile dependency: loss of open space and biological diversity and scarcity of water, clean air, and oil. The new ecological metropolis with its climatic-responsive urban design seeks to plan and design a more sustainable future.

It is a plan to offer consumers what the suburbs never could: urban vibrancy and convenience paired with a sustainable lifestyle and an authentic experience of nature.

## The city of the future – integrated systems

What will a sustainable future look like? The answer emerging in the work of forward-thinking planners and designers lies in the integration of technologically-advanced human civilisation with nature. Not simply a plan to avert disaster, it is a plan to achieve new heights of urban civilisation. It is a plan to offer consumers what the suburbs never could: urban vibrancy and convenience paired with a sustainable lifestyle and an authentic experience of nature.

In this century, even as we become more urban, we must understand ecology as our primary context and commit our society to true cooperation with natural processes. From now on, dramatically shifting populations, environmental awareness, rapidly developing technologies, and dynamic new economic models will shape consumer demands and policymaker and private sector discussions about city making.

*Integrating ecological and human made systems*
Major greenways frame the urban boundary, carrying natural systems and processes throughout the city, allowing human society to participate in the natural order. Humans and nature must be considered simultaneously. By mimicking ecological functionality, integrated land use patterns can provide abundant areas for clustered human settlements that synergise with natural systems to realise new functionally and celebrate new urban identities, the likes of which have not been seen on such a scale.

*Providing a new generation*
*of economic development*
In the past, the balance sheets neglected to calculate the cost of the land use implications of car culture – road building and parking lots as well as the ecological impacts, such as loss of biological habitat and degraded air and water resources due to disconnected land use planning. We must encourage a new culture of accountancy that recognises the true cost-benefit analysis of urban form decisions. New real estate speculation will engender new ways of supplying buildings with more sustainable forms of energy.

*Providing self-sustaining infrastructure*
New urban design solutions must integrate humans and nature: mobility, biodiversity, energy, and water must be fundamental provisions in all of our cities, both new and old. We must also update our economic model for these new urban design solutions.

*Responding to demographics*
*and inspiring new migrations*
Booming populations and an escalating urbanisation of humanity provide an unprecedented opportunity to design living environments. Evolving consumer desires coupled with ingenious design and holistic policy that transcends local boundaries and politics can have a profound impact on how people want to live.

The adjacent matrix compares twentieth and twenty-first century urban design decisions and their impacts on the climate.

| | Twentieth century | Twenty-first century |
|---|---|---|
| Water resources | Engineered solutions were developed to deliver, manufacture, process, and dispose of water resources. | Scarcity of water resources and increasing unpredictability of storm events will force us to reimagine how we use and reuse water, thus demanding new water sensitive urban design form. |
| Habitat restoration | Disconnected land uses and human made infrastructure encroached on biological habitats. | Nodes and corridors of human settlement will co-exist with ecological corridors of restored and enhanced biological habitat. |
| Energy sufficiency | Centralised fossil fuel burning plants with inefficient grid delivery systems provided a non-renewable, inefficient energy source. | Local generation of energy from renewable and low-carbon sources will deliver heat, cooling, and power on a district-by-district, building-by-building basis. |
| Economic prosperity | Automobile-oriented urban design policy and land planning spurred a synergistic acceleration of real estate, automobile industry, and infrastructure engineering | New economies and technologies will provide the impetus for new land use planning using efficient renewable energy and mobility. New economic models will invent new ways for speculative real estate entrepreneurs to create smart nodes of development. |
| Social equity | Suburban development in many developed economies stratified populations into sub-economic and racial groupings. | New population demographics and migrations will drive a new pattern wherein diversity is the greatest socio-economic asset. |
| Mobility | The automobile and airplane had the largest impacts on how we moved globally, regionally, and locally and contribute the largest amount of greenhouse gas emissions. | Concern for our carbon footprint and scarcity of oil drive new technologies (and reinvent old technologies, such as high speed rail) that will radically alter local, regional, and global movement patterns. Proactive policy to encourage these systems and redesign our urban environments to accommodate them will transform our lifestyle. |
| Built form | Singular use, large footprint, isolated standalone buildings celebrated a profligate use of energy and an automotive lifestyle | Mixed use, self-sustaining eco-block development, with integrated smart energy and water saving systems will become desired. |

**TABLE 01**
Comparing twentieth and twenty-first century urban design decisions and their impacts on the climate.

**Ecologically engineering a new future**
The History Channel's City of the Future competition challenges teams to deliver a vision of our cities in 100 years.

*Atlanta 2108*
In 2008, the greatest challenge facing Atlanta is the cost associated with replacing its twentieth century water and wastewater systems. Estimated at nearly a US$4 billion expense, the over 100-year old system must be replaced to provide the city with adequate water and wastewater and flood control. Rather than taking a twentieth century approach of a singular engineering solution to replacing the sewer systems, the team took an integrated approach to studying the inextricable impacts of land planning and engineering challenges inherent in this issue.

The design solution envisions vibrant urban corridors along transit routes on the ridges while allowing stormwater to be naturally collected and processed in restored creeks and wetlands in the lower ground, providing the city with an ample water supply and reducing the need for the extensive infrastructure currently used to rid the city of its stormwater. The residual impact of this planning is that the city would enjoy new open space frameworks that would generate biodiversity and economic regeneration—a priceless benefit for future generations of environmentalists and entrepreneurs alike.

*Los Angeles 2106*

Over the past 100 years, Los Angeles has transformed from a unique plain caught between the mountains and the ocean with an amazing array of biodiversity to one of the world's greatest economic engines and a melting pot of human culture and ingenuity. Standing as perhaps the greatest realisation of the 1939 car-oriented version of utopia, the Los Angeles basin today is a series of 81 towns and cities interconnected by human made infrastructure and disconnected from the natural environment that was its compelling *raison d'être*. Ecologically engineering the valley to update the infrastructure, while reconnecting the urban fabric to its local ecology, will allow Los Angeles to regenerate its economy and ecology for the next 100 years.

Four big moves are proposed.

- **Restored watershed:** By reconnecting the mountains to the ocean through the natural watershed, the Los Angeles basin could restore some of its greatest assets. The centrepiece of this program is the restoration of the Los Angeles River as the namesake of the city.

- **New coastline:** Over the next 100 years, we will encounter a certain degree of sea level change. For Los Angeles, this sea level change would inundate many of the low-lying areas traditionally associated with the port and oil refinery activities. With innovative economic incentives that transfer these property rights to new development areas, these zones could be envisioned as areas for new coastal-focused development and open space reserves.

- **Smart corridors:** The sprawling highway corridors of Los Angeles are at once the greatest landholdings of the city and the centre of the lowest land values, thus offering an unprecedented urban regeneration opportunity. By imagining new transportation solutions and stylish new clusters of urban living, Los Angeles could create a compelling new urban pattern for the twenty-first century. New advances in building technologies and water sensitive urban design would allow this new generation of buildings to be self sufficient and net exporters of energy.

- **Eco-grid:** By transferring development into the new smart corridors, 25 per cent of low-grade twentieth century development would be transformed into open space corridors and parks that

These 100-year plans inspired by mass media challenge design teams to consider the past as a way to inform the future. Incremental decisions supporting the car-oriented city are made decade by decade. In the same way, as we begin to steer design in a new direction, step-by-step, ecologically-based decisions that will transform the design of our cities in response to climate change are critical. Incremental changes are occurring all around the world. And we can already note the cities and the projects that are beginning to implement the new ecological metropolis.

## Ecological policy begins today

In New York, Mayor Bloomberg announced PlaNYC 2030 on Earth Day 2007, putting forth a holistic set of 127 initiatives that aim to address five key areas of sustainability for the city in the next 25 years: land, air, water, energy, and transportation. One of these is the reforestation initiative, which aims to increase the city's tree canopy from 24 to 30 per cent by planting forest on 2,000 acres of city parkland. This increase is planned to mitigate the environmental effects of a predicted population rise. It will also offset the effects of climate change within the city, as tree plantings will improve air quality, manage stormwater, provide wildlife habitat, mitigate heat island effect, offer recreational opportunities, and help with carbon sequestration.

While this ecological restoration is underway, the city is also reconsidering some of its transit environments with work on the 2nd Avenue Subway. The goal is to create transit that is not only environmentally sustainable but offers the consumer a more appealing experience, so mass transit can be considered a preferred option. Ultimately, sustainable choices must be holistically preferable, not only for their environmental benefits but because they are convenient and culturally favoured.

The goal is to create transit that is not only environmentally sustainable but offers the consumer a more appealing experience, so mass transit can be considered a preferred option.

In the United Kingdom, where sustainable development has been strongly mandated by government, work on future-oriented communities is occurring at all levels. Upton provides an exemplar for a mixed-use town. As an extension to the village of Northampton, Upton incorporates a sustainable urban drainage system, solar panels, green roofs, heat recovery ventilation, ground source heat pumps, communal biomass boilers, and low-flow plumbing; measures that have exceeded the scores necessary to achieve the United Kingdom's BREEAM Excellent Rating. Open space has also been heavily favoured in the development. This is in addition to an overall masterplan and hierarchy of design types that promote pedestrian mobility and encourage social cohesion.

At the larger scale, London is using the 2012 Olympics to restore one of its poorest areas, the Lower Lea Valley. In addition to dramatic socioeconomic improvement, the project will restore degraded and polluted waterways and green space, providing the largest urban park built in Europe in the past 150 years. A network of cycle and pedestrian paths will encourage healthy, zero-emission transportation and increase connections among communities.

In China, where urbanisation races ahead, steps are being taken to preserve ecology before it is completely paved over. Shenzhen has grown from a fishing village of 68,000 people to a city of 12 million in three decades. The city is now preserving its remaining 300 kilometres of undeveloped coastline. As developed cities seek to restore their urban ecologies, developing cities must limit their development to conserve their natural environments before they disappear completely.

In Tokyo, the largest metropolitan area in the world, land is at a premium, and the notion of leaving it undeveloped is a difficult sell. Thus, the developer of Tokyo Midtown was making a bold and forward-thinking decision in setting aside half of its 10 hectares for open space. In the city of the future, the liveability of dense urban corridors will be critical, and this project achieves exactly that. Landscaped spaces and purely open spaces form the connective tissue to a vibrant commercial district, inviting the public and offering respite amidst one the world's busiest places.

In Abu Dhabi, where a new urban quarter is emerging on an empty desert island, the opportunity exists to start anew, albeit in difficult geographic circumstances. Saadiyat Island is envisioned to catalyse a post-oil economy of cultural tourism in the context of a sustainable development. High urban densities, integrated mass transit, a pedestrian-oriented urban core, and ecological restoration will make this development a tangible example of smart growth in a region that needs it urgently. The MASDAR carbon-neutral city is perhaps the most advanced economic model for realising a new city, building a multi-billion dollar photovoltaic plant for the generation of solar energy coupled with the primacy of public over private transportation is proposed to create a net carbon-positive city.

While these projects represent exemplary work in forward-thinking design and planning, they are but the first steps toward what must be a fully committed global effort. It is however one that cannot be mandated by a single governing body. It must be led by innovative projects such as those described above.

## The path ahead

The achievement of sustainable development on a scale that can offset climate change will depend upon planning and design that begins at the regional context. Thousands of hectares must be considered at once to build ecological frameworks into which cities can be integrated. Appreciating the myriad values of the natural environment, we must fundamentally revise the ratio between developed and undeveloped land. With the global population increasing and cities projected to grow, we must look to the creation of super-regions and smart-cities that weave together new models for economic, social, and cultural vitality with thriving, integrated ecologies.

We stand at the turning point in global urbanisation and land development. Consumers have evolved from cheap and disposable to sustainable and authentic; policy discussions are mandating that environmental impacts be included in the costs and benefits of development, and the private sector is rapidly evolving new technologies and lifestyles that will drive the new paradigm. This book is about design's ultimate effect on the global climate. How design embraces nature directly determines our impacts on the climate. The task is an urgent one, and the work has begun: designers and planners must produce the model that replaces that seen at the 1939 World's Fair. What will the new model be that addresses ecological realities, is concretely feasible, and that captures the hearts and the minds of the consumer?

Landscaped spaces and purely open spaces form the connective tissue to a vibrant commercial district, inviting the public and offering respite amidst one the world's busiest places.

Twentieth century

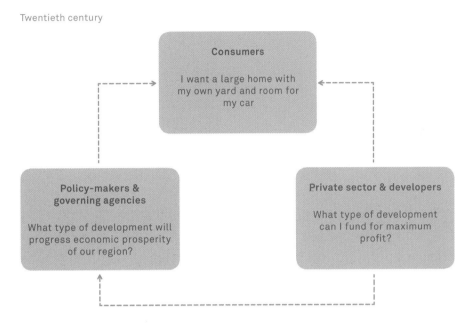

Twenty-first century

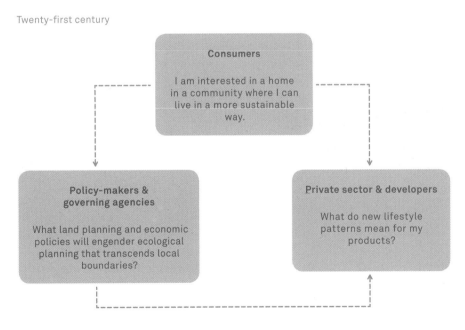

**FIGURE 01**

Land use and development – who decides?

Afterword

# Working on the future now

## Jason Prior

### Our role

Climate change is a reality and its impacts are being widely felt. Every day we see evidence of changes affecting the way we work, and we know too that these impacts will have the most profound effect on design and planning and other professions for decades.

We are in a strong position to tackle the many challenges. The traditional role of design has been largely about the application of technology—we operate at the point where science meets culture. And we have the skills and experience to make sure complex solutions can be made easily accessible. In the case of climate change, this very often means a key part of our job is about encouraging people to feel positive about adapting their lifestyles and making it easier to live in a more sustainable way through better neighbourhood design, reliable public transport systems, accessible cycle routes and pathways, energy-efficient homes, and easy-to-use recycling systems.

### What have we learned?

From our experience of working with climate change, one valuable lesson we have learned is that there is no one-size-fits-all solution. As ever, it is important to understand the context in which we work. That way we know different communities and cultures will have different priorities, whether they may be food, water, energy, citymaking, or transport. For example, while nuclear power is readily accepted as the answer to clean energy production in countries like France, there are plenty of places in the world where the suggestion of building a nuclear plant would be rejected outright. So we must learn from our experiences and work not just to provide the best solutions, but to make sure they are appropriate too.

### Future projects

AECOM's Design + Planning practice is in a unique position when it comes to being well equipped to design for climate change. We are already working with the natural and urban systems most prone to change and we have a tremendous bank of knowledge in areas such as water management, improving the natural landscape, biodiversity, energy production, urban design and planning, architecture, and more. With our focus on environmental, economic, and social sustainability, we understand the need for mitigating the effects of climate change through the careful use of resources and good planning. It is important to remember the possible adverse impacts of changes we make: in imposing solutions and adaptations we must take care to look at all those affected, because too often it is the poor and vulnerable who bear the brunt of change.

Work in the future will involve further embedding the philosophy of joined-up thinking and joined-up working. The solutions for coping with the effects of climate change will not be the sole preserve of a single profession; in fact a narrow professional approach to these issues is very likely to be counterproductive. More than ever, the challenges will require a collaborative and multidisciplinary response. There is little advantage in specifying low-energy light bulbs for a badly insulated house served by electricity produced in an inefficient, dirty, coal-fired power station 300 miles away. Always take care to look at the whole picture.

And along with the integration of different professions, projects should also be able to anticipate change, building in flexibility, extra capacity, and adaptability. For example, in anticipation of rising temperatures in the United Kingdom, new landscape schemes should be specifying tree species able to thrive in more arid conditions. But also remember that hotter summers are likely to be accompanied by more storm and flood events, so again, understanding the bigger picture is crucial to making successful and long-lasting schemes.

Finally, the most important factor of all is to approach future work as an opportunity. For example, in designing urban communities to be resilient to climate change, we can rethink cities to be water sensitive places, where ecosystem services are integrated to optimise and conserve water resources and protect aquatic environments. In tackling the negative effects of urban heat islands, we can provide a positive solution, combining the planting of new trees, roof gardens, and open rills to carry water through the streets. The response to climate change can be a delight, providing more opportunities for growing food in the city, increasing biodiversity, improving air quality, reducing carbon footprints, managing and conserving water resources, reducing flood risk, making better places to live, and bringing us closer to nature.

There are clear opportunities to develop a new aesthetic too. This is the moment to reappraise the ways we have been working, question them, and find the most appropriate and beautiful solutions. While most of the evidence suggests we are just at the start of this phase of change, there is no time to waste on ignoring the science. The best way of dealing with climate change is to embrace the facts and start working on the future now.

Contributors
and sources

# Contributors

**Jasmin Abad** is an economist, architect, and urban and regional planner based in AECOM's Design + Planning studio in Hong Kong. Jasmin advises on industrial and new city developments throughout Asia and provides feasibility studies, market research, and regional comparative studies.

**Curtis Alling** is an environmental planner and principal of AECOM's Design + Planning practice. Based in Sacramento, he leads the firm's environmental and ecological planning practice in the western areas of the United States. Curtis is a recognised authority on US environmental legislation and regulations and an experienced manager of complex environmental impact assessment, climate change policy, and conservation planning programs. He also teaches courses for the Association of Environmental Professionals, the American Planning Association, and the University of California.

**Karen Appell** is a senior ecological engineer based in AECOM's Design + Planning studio in New York. Karen's technical expertise lies in ecological restoration, specifically wetland and stream ecosystems. She manages various large-scale environmental projects for federal and state clients, focusing on the integration of engineering, ecological, and economic aspects of planning, design, and construction.

**Stephane Asselin** is a water resources and coastal engineer and a principal of AECOM's Design + Planning practice. Based in Hong Kong, he also leads the firm's global environmental and ecological planning practice. He has been involved with the planning, design, and construction of several high profile wetland restoration and flood protection projects throughout the United States, Europe, and Asia. He co-edited EDAW AECOM's *Wetland Restoration Handbook*, a guide for conservation and recovery of China's wetlands, released in 2007 and written in collaboration with China's State Forestry Administration.

**Christopher Benosky** is based in AECOM's Design + Planning studio in New York and leads the firm's water and environmental practice in the central and eastern areas of the United States. His expertise lies in wetland and stream restoration, hydrologic and hydraulic analyses, stormwater management, dam and geotechnical engineering, and construction management. Over the years, Christopher has been involved in the restoration of more than 10,000 acres of wetlands throughout the Atlantic coast of North America.

**David Blau** is an environmental planner and landscape architect and a senior principal of AECOM's Design + Planning studio in San Francisco. He specialises in water resource planning, land resource management, and the integration of design thinking with ecological restoration principles. David is driving the firm's current efforts to integrate future water supply planning with global climate change implications. He is also a leader of the wider AECOM global water practice.

**Claire Bonham-Carter** is a principal of AECOM's Design + Planning studio in San Francisco and a leader of AECOM's wider sustainable development efforts, ensuring sustainability is an integral part of all practices. Claire has extensive experience in sustainable design and construction. She is working on climate action plans for northern Californian cities and sustainability design guidelines for plans ranging in scale from a downtown area in San Francisco to large, new communities in Saskatoon, Canada and Santiago, Chile.

**Isaac Brown** is an urban planner, ecological designer, and natural resource manager based in AECOM's Design + Planning studio in Irvine. His innovative work emphasises the role of landscape, open space, and urban form in reducing greenhouse gases and adapting built and natural systems to climate change.

**Joe Brown** is a landscape architect and urban designer and CEO of AECOM's Design + Planning practice. He directs many of the firm's high-profile projects and is particularly focused on new community planning, urban planning and redevelopment, community revitalisation, historic and cultural design, and issues confronting rapid-growth areas.

**Cathryn Chatburn** is a landscape architect and urban designer, based in AECOM's Design + Planning studio in Brisbane. She actively pursues her interest in the emerging sustainability agenda, heading a number of internal 'think tanks' and ensuring, in her project work, the delivery of exemplar sustainable design within the context of large-scale masterplanning and regeneration.

**Heather Cheesbrough** is a town planner and landscape architect, based in AECOM's Design + Planning studio in London. A specialist in urban regeneration, masterplanning, and spatial planning, Heather's particular interest lies in embedding sustainability principles within design and planning solutions at all scales.

**Christopher Choa** is an architect and urban designer and a principal of AECOM's Design + Planning studios in London and Abu Dhabi. In his work he focuses on realising social, economic, and environmental sustainability in urban development in the United Kingdom, the Middle East, and China.

**Roger Courtenay** is a landscape architect and principal of AECOM's Design + Planning studios in Alexandria and Charlottesville. His project experience throughout North America has made for innumerable lessons of place-making, urban design, and landscape architecture that serve people, habitat, and environment. Underpinning his work is an abiding love of the American cultural landscape, and of the environmentally-sustainable principles that make healthy, worthwhile, and memorable places.

**Professor Peter Droege** is an authority on renewable energy, urban design, development, and infrastructure. He serves as Expert Commissioner on Cities and Climate Change to the World Future Council and as a Steering Committee Member of the Urban Climate Change Research Network, and he is Asia Pacific Chair of the World Council for Renewable Energy. Professor Droege is author of *The Renewable City, Urban Energy Transition*, and *100% Renewable – Energy Autonomy in Action*. For more information see www.solarcity.org.

**Stephen Engblom** is an architect and urban designer and a principal of AECOM's Design + Planning studio in San Francisco. Leader of the firm's global master planning practice, Stephen heads many high-density urban revitalisation, new town planning, and campus planning projects and has practiced in Asia, Mexico, Europe, the Middle East, and throughout the United States.

**Dr David Gallacher** is a senior environmental planner and ecologist, based in AECOM's Design + Planning studio in Hong Kong. Throughout his professional and academic career, he has worked on numerous environmental planning, ecological monitoring, impact assessment, habitat design studies, and habitat compensation and creation projects in the Middle East, Hong Kong, China, and South East Asia.

**Gary Grant** is a chartered environmentalist and ecologist, based in AECOM's Design + Planning studio in London, and an authority on green infrastructure, ecological restoration, the integration of biodiversity into the built environment, and water sensitive urban design. He is a leading expert on living roofs and walls, having published a book on the subject for BRE Press and contributed to the technical report supporting the Mayor's London Plan Policy on Living Roofs and Walls.

**Dr Courtney Henderson** is an ecologist, based in AECOM's Design + Planning studio in Sydney. His expertise lies in vegetation ecology, soil science, and water chemistry and he advises on wetland and biofilter design and ecosystem assessment, rehabilitation, and management.

**Richard W. John** is Head of Sustainability for AECOM Europe, based in London. He has worked in the sustainability area for more than 25 years and has advised the British Government on climate change policy, particularly how to include sustainability and energy efficiency in planning requirements, building regulations, and environmental labelling. Richard has also acted as an advocate on carbon reduction with more than 30 major corporate firms, making the business case for companies to tackle climate risk.

**Steve Kellenberg** is an urban designer and a principal of AECOM's Design + Planning studio in Irvine. An experienced leader of large-scale master planning and new town planning projects, Steve heads the firm's global green communities initiative, directing new community plans that integrate green building practices.

**Vivian Lee** is a specialist in water and coastal resource planning, based in AECOM's Design + Planning studio in Hong Kong. With expertise in hydrologic, hydraulic, water quality, coastal, and sediment transport modelling systems, Vivian leads the firm's environmental and ecological practice in Asia. She heads environmental studies in Asia, the United States, and the Middle East, enhancing stormwater and flood management, water quality, and wetland systems in these places.

**José Mantilla** is a principal environmental engineer at AECOM in Melbourne, where he assesses strategies to reduce transportation energy consumption and greenhouse gas emissions, and implements sustainable mobility initiatives for urban development projects in Australia, the Middle East, and China.

**Celeste Morgan** is a specialist in the application of sustainable design in the development of places and landscapes, based in AECOM's Design + Planning studio in London. Her background in environmental engineering has informed her understanding of technical design behind resource use and she is able to apply this practical knowledge to masterplanning and urban design to give a creative yet deliverable vision for the design and planning of communities.

**Ann-Marie Mulligan** is a transport planner and engineer at AECOM in Sydney. Combining a passion for sustainability with best practice transport planning principles, she has developed sustainable transport solutions for new developments and existing urban areas in Australia, New Zealand, and the United Kingdom.

**Ellen Nuñez** is an economist based in AECOM's Design + Planning studio in Shenzhen. Along with her expertise in retail and banking, she has undertaken research into poverty in the Philippines.

**Lester Partridge** is a qualified building services engineer and a technical director of AECOM's Buildings practice. Based in Sydney, he is also national director of AECOM's Applied Research and Sustainability group. His expertise lies in sustainable building design and modelling for passive ventilation and daylighting, along with building energy simulation and comfort analysis modelling. Lester has worked in Australia, Singapore, Hong Kong, China, New Zealand, the United Kingdom, and the United States.

**Damien Pericles** is a designer and landscape architect, based in AECOM's Design + Planning studio in Perth. From detailed urban sites to large-scale community or strategic landscape planning projects, he is passionate about infusing art, ecology, and community into his work.

**Eli N. Pincus** is an economic analyst, based in AECOM's Design + Planning studio in Hong Kong, and advises on economic development, urban regeneration and revitalisation, public policy, tourism planning, community development, and financial feasibility on projects throughout Asia.

**Jason Prior** is President of AECOM's Design + Planning practice, based in London, and specialises in the design and implementation of complex landscape, urban design, and regeneration projects. Jason was one of the key consultants responsible for the development framework, detailed masterplan, and public realm strategy for Manchester city centre following the 1996 IRA bombing. He also led the team which developed the Lower Lea Valley Regeneration Framework and the Olympic and Legacy Masterplans, which formed part of London's bid for the 2012 Games.

**James Rosenwax** is a landscape architect and a principal of AECOM's Design + Planning studio in Sydney and he leads the firm's environmental and ecological practice in Australia. Throughout his professional career, he has fused design and environmental processes and his project portfolio includes innovative solutions to stormwater management and habitat creation.

**Jon Shinkfield** is a landscape architect and urban designer and a principal of AECOM's Design + Planning studio in Melbourne. His 25 years of practice range from intimate, site-specific landscape to strategically-based urban design. Design frameworks for energy generation, consumption reduction, waste minimisation, and the integration of production-based gardens in an urban context are increasing concerns for Jon.

**Jason Veale** holds a degree in architecture and is a principal sustainability specialist with AECOM in Sydney. His experience lies in building thermal design, sustainability ratings tools, carbon modelling, and government sustainability policy. Jason is a contributing author to the Australian Council of Built Environment Design Professions' Environmental Design Guide, to the software for the New South Wales Government's award-winning Building Sustainability Index (BASIX), and to Section J of the Building Code of Australia on energy efficiency measures for non-residential buildings.

Honey Walters is an air quality and climate change specialist, based in AECOM's Design + Planning studio in Sacramento. Her greenhouse gas analyses have been published by the US Environmental Protection Agency and the Intergovernmental Panel on Climate Change, to name just two bodies. She has also contributed to the greenhouse gas analytical methods and mitigation strategies which underpin the California Environmental Quality Act & Climate Change resource guide, released in January 2008.

Nathalie Ward has strived to create sustainable and meaningful places in her work in Australia, Hong Kong, and the United Kingdom. A principal of AECOM's Design + Planning studio in Brisbane, Nathalie's expertise lies in the realms of high-density residential design, park design, urban design, infrastructure, site rehabilitation, and visual impact assessment.

Richard Weller is Professor of Landscape Architecture at the University of Western Australia, where he is renowned for combining teaching, research, and practice in a dynamic student-centred environment. In 2009, Professor Weller delivered the book *Boomtown 2050*, which explores the extreme economic and environmental pressures the city of Perth faces today and in the future and presents a model for other cities experiencing rapid growth.

Ichsani Wheeler is an environmental scientist specialising in water sensitive urban design and sustainable management of soil and water within the landscape. Her expertise lies in microbial ecology, soil science, environmental physics and chemistry, fluvial and groundwater geomorphology, rural and urban water management, sustainable agriculture, and ecologically-sustainable development. Ichsani is undertaking her PhD in soil carbon accounting at the University of Sydney.

Tony Wong is a principal of AECOM's Design + Planning studio in Melbourne and an Honorary Professorial Fellow of Monash University. A respected authority on integrated urban water cycle management and water sensitive urban design, Professor Wong was engaged as a consultant by the Public Utilities Board of Singapore to develop the framework for institutionalising water sensitive urban design in Singapore.

Vivien Wu is a graduate of Harvard University, where she specialised in environmental science and public policy. As part of her studies, she undertook a three-month internship at AECOM's Design + Planning studio in Hong Kong, which informed her thesis on sustainable design and environmental policy.

Fan Yang is an architect and urban designer and a graduate of Harvard University's Masters of Design program, where she specialised in real estate and project management. As part of her studies, she undertook a three-month internship at AECOM's Design + Planning studio in Hong Kong.

Chris Yoshii is a principal of AECOM's Design + Planning studio in Hong Kong and leads the firm's economics practice in Asia. His expertise has ensured the economic feasibility of projects in the realms of new town planning, destination resort development, urban regeneration, and tourism planning throughout Asia, the Middle East, and the United States.

Jessie Zhang is an economist based in AECOM's Design + Planning studio in Singapore and a specialist in urban planning, regional economics, and environmental economics. Her indepth understanding of urban and economic development issues has been garnered through her work in China and Canada.

# Photography and references

## Foreword

**Design and planning for the age of climate change: context and assumptions**

Peter Droege

**Photography**

Pages 4, 6, Dixi Carrillo

**References**

BP 2004, *BP Statistical Review of World Energy*, British Petroleum, London, United Kingdom.

Droege, P. 2006, *The Renewable City*, John Wiley and Sons Ltd, United Kingdom.

Droege, P. (ed.) 2009, *100% Renewable – Energy Autonomy in Action*, Earthscan, United Kingdom.

Fell, H.J. 2009, 'The Renewable Imperative – providing climate protection and energy security', in Droege, P. (ed.) 2009, *100% Renewable – Energy Autonomy in Action*, Earthscan, United Kingdom.

Gleick, P.H. 1994, 'Water and Energy', *Annual Review of Energy and Environment,* vol. 19, pp. 267-299.

Hansen, J., Sato, M., Kharecha, P., Beerling, D., Berner, R., Masson-Delmotte, V., Pagani, M., Raymo, M., Royer, D.L. & Zachos, J.C. 2008, 'Target atmospheric $CO_2$: Where should humanity aim?', *Open Atmospheric Science Journal*, vol. 2, pp. 217-231, viewed 5 February 2009, http://arxiv.org/abs/0804.1126.

Lenzen M., Wood R. & Foran B. 2008, 'Direct versus embodied energy – the need for urban lifestyle transitions' in Droege P., *Urban Energy Transition*, pp. 91-120, Elsevier, United Kingdom.

Lenzen, M., Dey, C. & Hamilton, C. 2003, 'Climate Change' in Hensher, D.A. & Button, K.J. (eds), *Handbook of Transport and the Environment*, Elsevier, United Kingdom.

Lohman, L. (ed.) 2007, *Carbon Trading - a critical conversation on climate change, privatisation and power*, Dag Hammarskjøld Foundation, Sweden.

Schindler J. & Zittel W. 2008, *Crude Oil – The Supply Outlook*, Energy Watch Group, Germany, viewed 20 November 2009, http://www.energywatchgroup.org/fileadmin/global/pdf/2008-02_EWG_Oil_Report_updated.pdf.

## The emerging direction

**Photography**

Page 10, David Lloyd

Page 27, Simon Kenny

Page 28, Jan Ayalin

# Productive places

## Photography

Page 34, courtesy of Gold Coast City Council

Page 36, Shannon McGrath

Page 43, Gary Grant

Page 44, both by David Lloyd

Page 48, draft concept images courtesy of TDIC

Page 51, Maryanne Natarajan

Page 53, Maryanne Natarajan

Page 55, Josh Segal

Page 56, Narendra Veeranna

Page 58, Dixi Carrillo

Page 60, Dixi Carrillo

## References

### The story of apples and fish: designing for urban productivity

Ichsani Wheeler

Mazoyer, M., & Roudart, L., 2006, *A history of world agriculture – from the Neolithic age to the current crisis*, translated by Membrez, J., Earthscan, London.

Mollison, B., 1988, *Permaculture – a designers manual*, Tagari Publishing, Australia.

Russel, M., 2000, 'Food and the Environment', in F. Magdoff, J. Foster & F. Buttel (eds), *Hungry for Profit: The Agribusiness Threat to Farmers*, pp. 203-213, Monthly Review Press, New York.

Trivedi, B., 2008, 'Dinners Dirty Secret', *New Scientist*, vol. 199, no. 2673.

Tudge, C., 2007, *Feeding People is Easy*, Pari Publishing, Italy.

Volk. T., 1997, *Gaia's Body – Toward a Physiology of Earth,* 1st edn, Copernicus/ Springer-Verlag, New York.

Walker, B. & Salt, D., 2006, *Resilience Thinking: Sustaining Ecosystems and People in a Changing World*, Island Press, USA.

### Energy: creating an energy efficient landscape with green roofs

Gary Grant

City of Chicago n.d., *Monitoring the Rooftop Garden's Benefits*, viewed 13 August 2008, http://egov.cityofchicago.org/city/webportal/portalContentItemAction.do?BV_SessionID=@@@@0813497735.1231293192@@@@&BV_EngineID=cccfadegefgjkhjcefecelldffhdfho.0&contentOID=536908579&contenTypeName=COC_EDITORIAL&topChannelName=Dept&blockName=Environment%2FCity+Hall+Rooftop+Garden%2FI+Want+To&context=dept&channelId=0&programId=0&entityName=Environment&deptMainCategoryOID=-536887205.

Liu,K. 2002, 'Going green – A National Research Council Canada study evaluates green roof systems' thermal performances', *Professional Roofing Magazine*, September 2002, viewed 13 August 2008, http://www.professionalroofing.net/search.aspx?query=Energy+Efficiency+of+and+Environmental+Benefits+of+a+roof+top+garden&si=proroof.

Rosenzweig, C., Gaffin, S., and Parshall, L. (eds.) 2006, *Green Roofs in the New York Metropolitan Region: Research Report*, Columbia University Center for Climate Systems Research and NASA Goddard Institute for Space Studies, New York, viewed 13 August 2008, http://ccsr.columbia.edu/cig/greenroofs/index.html.

Roth-Kleyer, S. 2009, *Green Roofs as a Module of Urban Water Management*, Proceedings International Green Roof Congress, Nurtingen, Germany, viewed 16 June 2009, http://www.greenroofworld.com/EN/congress.html

Ryerson University 2004, *The Environmental Benefits and Costs of Green Roof Technology*, viewed 13 August 2008, http://www.toronto.ca/greenroofs/findings.htm.

Slosberg, R., Rosenzweig, C. & Solecki, W. 2007, *New York City Regional Heat Island Initiative: Mitigating New York City's Heat Island with Urban Forestry, Living Roofs, and Light Surfaces*, New York State Energy Research and Development Authority, viewed 13 August 2008, www.nyserda.org/programs/environment/emep/project/6681_25/6681_25_project_update.pdf.

### Food: integrating agriculture into landscapes

Gary Grant, with a case study by Isaac Brown

Diamond, J. 2005, *Collapse: How Societies Choose to Fail or Succeed*, Viking Press, United States.

Hodges, C., Thompson, T., Riley, J. & Glenn, E., 1993, 'Reversing the Flow: Water and Nutrients from the Sea to the Land', *Ambio Journal of the Human Environment*, vol. XXII, no. 7, pp. 483-490, viewed 13 August 2008, http://www.seawaterfoundation.org/pdf_archives/Attachment%2005%20-%20Ambio%20Reversing%20the%20Flow.pdf.

King, F. 1911, *Farmers of Forty Centuries, Or, Permanent Agriculture in China*, Korea and Japan, Mrs. F.H. King, United States.

## Water: urban landscapes and water management
Stephane Asselin

Asselin, S., Demgen, F. & Johnson, R. 2005, 'Alameda Creek Flood Control and Wetland Restoration Project', *World Water and Environmental Resources Congress*, Anchorage, Alaska, 15-19 May 2005.

Colombo, A. & Karney, B. 2003, 'The labyrinth of water distribution systems: Demand, energy, and climate change', in Cabrera & Cabrera Jr (eds), *Pumps, Electromechanical Devices and Systems Applied to Urban Water Management* 2003, Swets & Zeitlinger, Lisse, pp.239-246.

Intergovernmental Panel on Climate Change 2007, *Climate Change 2007: Synthesis Report*, viewed 27 July 2008, http://www.ipcc.ch/pdf/assessment-report/ar4/syr/ar4_syr.pdf.

International Scientific Congress on Climate Change in Copenhagen 2009, *Rising sea levels set to have major impacts around the world*, viewed 18 June 2009, http://climatecongress.ku.dk/newsroom/rising_sealevels/

Kadlec, R. & Knight, R. 1995, *Treatment Wetlands: Theory and Implementation*, CRC Press, United States.

Lawrence Berkeley National Laboratory Water Energy Technology Team 2008, *Wastewater Treatment and Water Reclamation*, viewed 29 July 2008, http://water-energy.lbl.gov/node/16.

Ramsar Convention on Wetlands 1971, *Climate Change Mitigation,* viewed 30 July 2008, http://www.ramsar.org/info/values_climate_e.htm.

United Nations Population Fund 2005, *Urbanization: A Majority in Cities,* viewed 30 July 2008, http://www.unfpa.org/pds/urbanization.htm.

# Applications

## Photography

Page 62, David Lloyd

Page 65, Brenda Curtis

Page 66, Karen Esslemont

Page 70, Elven Tang

Page 72, Ben Palmer

Page 74, Yan Mei

Page 85, Amy Pang

Page 89, David Lloyd

Page 90, Dixi Carrillo

Page 94, Dixi Carrillo

Page 98, Michael Clarkson

Page 103, Mark Fuller (sketch)

Page 104, Dixi Carrillo

Page 106, David Lloyd

Page 108, David Lloyd

Page 110, David Lloyd

Page 112, David Lloyd

Page 116, David Lloyd

Page 118, Cathryn Chatburn

Page 127, (top to bottom) Richard Glover, The GPT Group, John Gollings

Page 142, David Lloyd

Page 144, Shannon McGrath

Page 149, Brett Boardman

Page 153, Alex de Dios

Page 154, David Lloyd

Page 160, Christopher Frederick Jones

Page 162, David Garzon

Page 178, Jan Ayalin

Page 180, Desmond Ong

## References

### Design and natural systems: design with nature
James Rosenwax, Celeste Morgan, Dr Courtney Henderson

Clark, C. W.1973, 'The Economics of Overexploitation. Severe depletion of renewable resources may result from high discount rates used by private exploiters', *Science*, vol. 181:630-634.

Daily, G.C. 2000, 'Management objectives for the protection of ecosystem services', *Environmental Science & Policy*, vol. 3:333-339.

Millennium Ecosystem Assessment 2005, *Ecosystems and Human Well-Being: Synthesis*, Island Press, Washington.

Odum, E. P.1969, 'The Strategy of Ecosystem Development. An understanding of ecological succession provides a basis for resolving man's conflict with nature', *Science*, vol. 164:262-270.

Walker, B., Holling, C.S., Carpenter, S. R. & Kinzig, A. 2004, 'Resilience, Adaptability and Transformability in Social–ecological Systems', *Ecology and Society*, vol. 9(2):5.

### Design and urban systems: the low-carbon commune
Christopher Choa

Brown, M., Southworth F., & Sarzynski, A. 2008, 'Shrinking the Carbon Footprint of Metropolitan America', The Brookings Institution, viewed on 15 August 2008, http://www.brookings.edu/reports/2008/~/media/Files/rc/reports/2008/05_carbon_footprint_sarzynski/carbonfootprint_report.pdf.

Energy Information Administration 2009, *State Energy Profiles: New York*, viewed 15 August 2008, http://tonto.eia.doe.gov/state/state_energy_profiles.cfm?sid=NY.

Energy Information Administration 2009, *State Energy Profiles: New York*, viewed 15 August 2008, http://tonto.eia.doe.gov/state/state_energy_profiles.cfm?sid=NY.

Ginsberg, M. 2003, *New York City – A Case Study in Density After 9/11*, Boston Society of Architects, viewed 25 August 2009, http://www.architects.org/emplibrary/C6_b.pdf.

Jun, L. 2007, 'Why building energy efficiency matters', *China Dialogue*, viewed on 15 August 2008, http://www.chinadialogue.net/article/show/single/en/1425-Why-building-energy-efficiency-matters.

New York City Department of City Planning 2006, 'New York City Pedestrian Level of Service Study – Phase I', p.4, Official New York City Web Site, viewed 10 August 2008, http://home2.nyc.gov/html/dcp/pdf/transportation/td_fullpedlosb.pdf.

Tokyo Metropolitan Government 2006, Tokyo Metropolitan Government Environmental White Paper 2006, Tokyo Metropolitan Government, viewed 20 August 2008, http://www2.kankyo. metro.tokyo.jp/kouhou/env/eng_2006/ chapter2_3.html.

Vaughan, A. 2009, *City dwellers have smaller carbon footprints*, The Guardian, viewed 23 March 2009, http://www.guardian.co.uk/ environment/2009/mar/23/city-dwellers-smaller-carbon-footprints.

World Resources Institute 2008, 'Energy and Resources — Energy Consumption: Total energy consumption per capita', World Resource Institute, *EarthTrends: The Environmental Information Portal*, viewed on 12 August 2008, http://earthtrends.wri.org/text/ energy-resources/variable-351.html.

World Resources Institute 2008, 'Energy and Resources, Country Profile – United States', World Resource Institute, *EarthTrends: The Environmental Information Portal*, viewed on 12 August 2008, http://earthtrends.wri.org/text/ energy-resources/country-profile-190.html.

## Land: climate change and terrestrial environment
Isaac Brown

Braun, L. 1950, *Deciduous forests of Eastern North America*, Hafner Publishing Company, New York, NY.

Crowley, T. 1996, 'Pliocene climates: the nature of the problem', *Marine Micropaleontology*, vol. 27, pp. 3-12.

Ecological Society of America 2008, 'Climate Change and Species Distributions', *Science Daily*, viewed 4 August 2008, http://www.sciencedaily.com/ releases/2008/08/080804100143.htm.

Grivet, D., Sork, V., Westfall, R. & Davis, F. 2007, 'Conserving the evolutionary potential of California valley oak (*Quercus lobata* Nee): a multivariate genetic approach to conservation planning', *Molecular Ecology*, vol. 17, pp. 139-156.

Hannah, L., Midgley, G. & Millar, D. 2002, 'Climate change-integrated conservation strategies', *Global Ecology and Biogeography*, vol. 11, pp. 485-495.

Hansen J., Sato M., Ruedy R., Lo K., Lea D, & Medina-Elizade M. 2006, 'Global temperature change', *Proceedings of the National Academy of Sciences of the United States of America*, **vol.** 103 (39), 14288–93.

Hoegh-Guldberg, O., Hughes, L., McIntyre, S., Lindenmayer, D., Parmesan, C., Possingham, H. & Thomas, C. 2008, 'Moving with the times: assisted colonization and rapid climate change', *Science Daily*, viewed 18 July 2008, http://www.sciencedaily.com/ releases/2008/07/080717140445.htm.

Joyce, L., Blate, G., Littell, J., McNulty, S., Millar, C., Moser, S., Neilson, R., O'Halloran, K. & Peterson, D. 2008, 'National Forests', in Julius, S., West, J. (eds), Baron, J., Griffith, B., Joyce, L., Kareiva, P., Keller, B., Palmer, M., Peterson, C. & Scott, J., *Preliminary review of adaptation options for climate-sensitive ecosystems and resources*, U.S. Climate Change Science Program and the Subcommittee on Global Change Research, U.S. Environmental Protection Agency, Washington, D.C., pp. 3:1 to 3:127.

Julius, S., West, J., Blate, G., Baron, J., Griffith, B., Joyce, L., Kareiva, P., Keller, P., Palmer, M., Peterson, C. & Scott, J. 2008, 'Executive Summary', *Preliminary review of adaptation options for climate-sensitive ecosystems and resources*, U.S. Climate Change Science Program and the Subcommittee on Global Change Research, U.S. Environmental Protection Agency, Washington, D.C., pp. 1-1 to 1-6.

Kaplan, S. 1995, 'The restorative benefits of nature: Toward an integrated framework', *Journal of Environmental Psychology*, vol. 15, pp. 169-182.

Kellert, S. 2005, *Building for life: Designing and understanding the human-nature connection*, Island Press, Washington, D. C.

Millar, C. & Woolfenden, W. 1999, 'The role of climate change in interpreting historical variability', *Ecological Applications*, vol. 9(4), pp. 1207-1216.

Millennium Ecosystem Assessment 2005, *Ecosystems and Human Well-being: Biodiversity synthesis*, World Resources Institute, Washington D.C., viewed on 15 July 2008, http://www.scribd.com/ doc/5250332/MILLENNIUM-ECOSYSTEM-ASSESSMENT-2005.

United States Environmental Protection Agency 2008, *Heat Island Effect,* viewed 9 September 2008, http://www.epa.gov/ heatisland/index.htm.

University of Wisconsin-Madison 2007, 'Global Warming Forecasts Creation, Loss of Climate Zones', *Science Daily*, viewed 19 September 2008, http://www.sciencedaily.com/ releases/2007/03/070326181452.htm

## Changing climates and the world's rivers and wetlands
Karen Appell, Christopher Benosky, Dr David Gallacher

Barnett, T., Adam, J. & Lettenmaier, D. 2005, 'Potential Impacts of a Warming Climate on Water Availability in Snow-Dominated Regions, *Nature*, no. 438, pp. 303-309.

BBC 2007, *Flood defence money 'falls short'*, BBC, United Kingdom, viewed 10 October 2007, http://news.bbc.co.uk/2/hi/uk_ news/7036904.stm.

Bergkamp, G. & Orlando, B. 1999, *Wetlands and Climate Change: Exploring collaboration between the Convention on Wetlands (Ramsar, Iran, 1971) and the UN Framework Convention on Climate Change*, Ramsar, Switzerland, viewed 2 August 2008, http://www.ramsar.org/ key_unfccc_bkgd.htm.

Campbell, C. & Ogden, M. 1999, *Constructed Wetlands in the Sustainable Landscape*, John Wiley and Sons Inc., New York, NY.

Costanza, R., d'Arge, R., de Groot, R., Farber, S., Grasso, M., Hannon, B., Naeem, S., Limburg, K., Paruelo, J., O'Neill, R., Raskin, R., Sutton, P. & van den Belt, M. 1997, 'The value of the world's ecosystem services and natural capital', *Nature*, no. 387, pp. 253-260.

Elsner, J. 2006, 'Evidence in Support of the Climate Change – Atlantic Hurricane Hypothesis', *Geophysical Research Letters*, Vol. 33, L16705.

Farris, G., Smith, G., Crane, M., Demas, C., Robbins, L., and Lavoie, D. (eds) 2007, 'Science and the Storms – the USGS Response to the Hurricanes of 2005', *U.S. Geological Survey Circular*, no. 1306, p. 283.

Hooijer, A., Wösten, H., Silvius, M. & Page, S. 2008, *Peat CO_2: Assessment of CO_2 emissions from drained peatlands in South-east Asia*, Wetlands International, Netherlands, viewed 5 July 2008, http://www.wetlands.org/WatchRead/tabid/56/mod/1570/articleType/ArticleView/articleId/1491/Peat-CO2.aspx.

Intergovernmental Panel on Climate Change 1990, *Working Group I – Scientific Assessment of Climate Change*, Cambridge University Press, UK.

Intergovernmental Panel on Climate Change 2001, *Climate Change 2001: Working Group II: Impacts, Adaptation and Vulnerability, Impacts on Wetland Services*, Intergovernmental Panel on Climate Change, Switzerland, viewed 1 July 2008, http://www.ipcc.ch/ipccreports/tar/wg2/273.htm.

Intergovernmental Panel on Climate Change 2007, *Climate Change 2007: Synthesis Report, Summary for Policymakers*, Intergovernmental Panel on Climate Change, Switzerland, viewed 1 July 2008, http://www.ipcc.ch/pdf/assessment-report/ar4/syr/ar4_syr_spm.pdf.

Kadlec, R. & Knight R. 1996, *Treatment Wetlands*, Lewis Publishers, Boca Raton, FL.

Kusler, J. 1999, 'Climate Change in Wetland Areas Part II: Carbon Cycle Implications', *Acclimations*, Newsletter of the US National Assessment of the Potential Consequences of Climate Variability and Change, July-August 1999, viewed 15 July 2008, http://www.usgcrp.gov/usgcrp/Library/nationalassessment/newsletter/1999.08/Wet.html.

Ministry of Water Resources, P.R. China 2006, *2004-2005 Annual Report*, viewed 1 July 2008, http://www.mwr.gov.cn/english1/20060404/69725.asp.

Mitsch, W. & Gosselink, J. 2000, *Wetlands*, 3rd edn, Wiley, New York.

Palmer, M., Reidy Liermann, C., Nilsson, C., Flörke, M., Alcamo, J., Lake, P. & Bond, N. 2008, 'Climate Change and the World's River Basins: Anticipating Management Options', *Frontiers in Ecology and the Environment*, vol. 6, iss. 2, March 2008.

Parliamentary Office of Science and Technology 2002, 'Access to Water in Developing Countries', *POSTnote*, no.178, May 2002.

Pfeffer, W., Harper, J., O'Neel, S. 2008, 'Kinematic Constraints on Glacier Contributions to 21st Century Sea-Level Rise', *Science,* vol. 321, no. 5894, pp. 1340-1343.

Ramsar Convention Bureau 1996, 'Wetlands and biological diversity', distributed at the *Third Meeting of the Conference of the Parties to the Convention on Biological Diversity*, Buenos Aires, Argentina, 4-15 November 1996, viewed 5 July 2008, http://www.ramsar.org/about/about_biodiversity.htm.

Ramsar 2000, 'Reservoirs of Biodiversity', *Wetland Values and Functions*, viewed 12 June 2008, http://www.ramsar.org/info/values_biodiversity_e.htm.

Ramsar 2007, *Ramsar Information Paper no. 1*, viewed 18 June 2008, http://www.ramsar.org/about/info2007-01-e.pdf.

Revenga, C., Murray, S., Abramovitz, J. & Hammond, A. 1998, *Watersheds of the World: Ecological Value and Vulnerability*, World Resources Institute, Washington, DC, viewed 25 June 2008, http://pubs.wri.org/pubs_description.cfm?PubID=2900.

Scientific and Technical Review Panel of the Ramsar Convention on Wetlands 2002, 'Climate Change and Wetlands: Impacts, Adaptation and Mitigation', distributed at the *Eighth Meeting of the Conference of the Contracting Parties to the Convention on Wetlands (Ramsar, Iran, 1971)*, Valencia, Spain, 18-26 November 2002, viewed 19 July 2008, http://www.ramsar.org/cop8/cop8_doc_11_e.htm.

Scholz, M. 2006, *Wetland Systems to Control Urban Runoff*, Elsevier Science & Technology Books, London.

Talling, J. & Lamoalle, J. 1998, *Ecological Dynamics of Tropical Inland Waters*, Cambridge University Press, Cambridge.

Tranvik, L., Jansson, M.; Reply; Evans C., Freeman C., Monteith, D., Reynolds, B. & Fenner, N. 2002, 'Climate Change (Communication Arising): Terrestrial Export of Organic Carbon', *Nature*, vol. 415, iss. 6874, pp. 861-862.

Trulio, L., Callaway, J. & Crooks, S. 2007, *White Paper on Carbon Sequestration and Tidal Salt Marsh Restoration*, South Bay Salt Pond Restoration Project, San Francisco, viewed 25 June 2008, http://www.southbayrestoration.org/pdf_files/Carbon%20Sequestration%20Dec%2020%202007.pdf.

United States Environmental Protection Agency 2006, *Wetlands: Protecting Life and Property from Flooding*, viewed 7 July 2008, http://www.epa.gov/owow/wetlands/pdf/Flooding.pdf.

Warren, R. & Niering, N. 1993, 'Vegetation change on a Northeast Tidal Marsh: Interaction of Sea level Rise and Marsh Accretion', *Ecology*, 74, pp. 96-103.

Watson, R., Zinyowera, M. & Moss, R. (eds) 1996, *Climate Change 1995: Impacts, Adaptations and Mitigation of Climate Change – Scientific-Technical Analysis*, Cambridge University Press, UK.

World Wildlife Federation 2008, *Threats to Wetlands*, viewed 21 July 2008, http://www.panda.org/about_wwf/what_we_do/freshwater/about_freshwater/intro/threats/index.cfm.

## Coastal design and planning: areas of transition

Vivian Lee

Burkett, V., Slovinsky, P., Powell, J., & VanLuven, D. 2008, *Wetlands and Climate Change*, Hazardous Waste Clean-Up Information, United States, viewed 17 August 2008, http://www.clu-in.org/conf/tio/owwcc_051308/.

Chmura, G., Anisfeld, S., Cahoon, D., & Lynch, J. 2003, Global carbon sequestration in tidal, saline wetland soils', *Global Biogeochemical Cycles*, vol. 17, no. 4, viewed 16 August 2008, http://felix.geog.mcgill.ca/faculty/chmura/GlobalCforGBCrev2fordistrib.pdf.

Choi, Y. & Wang, Y. 2004, 'Dynamics of carbon sequestration in a coastal wetland using radiocarbon measurements', *Global Biogeochemical Cycles*, vol.18, no. 4, viewed 18 August 2008, http://www.gly.fsu.edu/~ywang/pdf/Paper3.pdf.

Dilley, M., Chen, R., Deichmann, U., Lerner-Lam, A., & Arno, M. 2005, *Natural Disaster Hotspots: A Global Risk Analysis*, Socioeconomic Data and Applications Center, United States, viewed 19 August 2008, http://sedac.ciesin.columbia.edu/hazards/hotspots/synthesisreport.pdf.

Food and Agriculture Organisation of the United Nations 1998, *Integrated coastal area management and agriculture, forestry, and fisheries*, viewed 15 August 2008, http://www.fao.org/docrep/W8440e/W8440e02.htm#P5_148.

Harakunararak, A., & Aksornkoae, S. 2005, *Life-Saving Belts: Post-Tsunami Reassessment of Mangrove Ecosystem Values and Management in Thailand*, Thailand Environment Institute, viewed 19 August 2008, http://www.tei.or.th/eehrdc/pdf/Life_Saving_Belts.pdf

Intergovernmental Panel on Climate Change 2008, *Technical Paper VI Climate Change and Water*. Intergovernmental Panel on Climate Change, Switzerland, viewed 15 August 2008, http://www.ipcc.ch/pdf/technical-papers/ccw/chapter5.pdf.

Intergovernmental Panel on Climate Change Working Group II 2001, *Climate Change 2001: Impacts, Adaptation, and Vulnerability, Chapter 6.6.2: Resilience and Vulnerability,* GRID-Arendal, viewed 17 August 2008, http://www.grida.no/climate/ipcc_tar/wg2/301.htm.

Kay, R., & Alder, J. 2005, *Coastal Planning and Management*, 2nd ed, Taylor & Francis, London, viewed 18 August 2008, http://books.google.com.hk/books?id=EQA4sGMPVRwC&pg=PA47&lpg=PA47&dq=coastal+planning,+climate+change&source=web&ots=YrItoQP5ab&sig=dJ-j_65flnk2kDLF0bGgnEs9nv0&hl=en&sa=X&oi=book_result&resnum=1&ct=result#PPA48,M1.

Kusler J. 1999, 'Climate Change in Wetland Areas Part II: Carbon Cycle Implications', *Acclimations,* Newsletter of the US National Assessment of the Potential Consequences of Climate Variability and Change, viewed 30 September 2008, http://www.usgcrp.gov/usgcrp/Library/nationalassessment/newsletter/1999.08/Wet.html.

Lauretta B., Bryant, D., McManus, J. & Spalding, M. 1998, *Reefs at Risk: A map-based indicator of potential threats to the world's coral reefs*, World Resources Institute, Washington, D.C., viewed 18 August 2008, http://archive.wri.org/item_detail.cfm?id=2922&section=archive&page=pubs_content_text&z.

McGranahan, G., Balk, D., & Anderson, B. 2007, 'The rising tide: assessing the risks of climate change and human settlements in low elevation coastal zones', *Environment & Urbanization*, vol 19(1), pp. 17-37, viewed 19 August 2008, http://eau.sagepub.com/cgi/content/abstract/19/1/17.

National Oceanic and Atmospheric Administration 2007, *Ocean and Coastal Resource Management*, National Oceanic and Atmospheric Administration, United States, viewed 15 August 2005, http://coastalmanagement.noaa.gov/impacts.html.

Nicholls, R., Hanson, S., Heweijer, C., Patmore, N., Muir-Woods, R., Hallegatte, S., Corfee-Morlot, J., & Chateau, J. 2007, *Ranking of the World's Cities Most Exposed to Coastal Flooding Today and In The Future*, Organisation for Economic Co-operation and Development, France, viewed 14 August 2008, http://www.oecd.org/dataoecd/16/10/39721444.pdf.

Nicholls, R., Hoozemans, F., & Marchand, M. 1999, Increasing flood risk and wetland losses due to global sea-level rise: regional and global analyses. *Global Environmental Change*, vol. 9(1), pp. S69-S87, viewed 19 August 2008, http://www.sciencedirect.com/science?_ob=ArticleURL&_udi=B6VFV-3XR2V33-6&_user=10&_coverDate=10%2F31%2F1999&_rdoc=6&_fmt=high&_orig=browse&_srch=doc-info(%23toc%236020%231999%23999909999.8998%23137271%23FLA%23display%23Volume)&_cdi=6020&_sort=d&_docanchor=&view=c&_ct=7&_version=1&_urlVersion=0&_userid=10&md5=0428268561409bac2f9af8a84312cf37.

UK Biodiversity Group 1999, *Habitat Action Plan – Mudflats*, UK Biodiversity Action Plan, United Kingdom, viewed 17 August 2008, http://www.ukbap.org.uk/UKPlans.aspx?ID=34.

United Nations Population Fund 2007, *State of the World Population 2007*, United Nations Population Fund, New York, viewed 19 August 2008, http://www.unfpa.org/swp/2007/english/notes/notes_for_indicators5.html

United States Environmental Protection Agency 2008, *About Estuaries*, United States Environmental Protection Agency, United States, viewed 17 August 2008, http://www.epa.gov/nep/about1.htm.

## Urban regeneration and climate change

Heather Cheesbrough

Department for Communities and Local Government 2007, *Planning and Climate Change Supplement to Planning Policy Statement 1*, London.

Department for Communities and Local Government 2007, *Planning Bill 2007-2008*, London.

Department for Communities and Local Government 2005, *Planning Policy Statement 1 Delivering Sustainable Development*, London.

Department for Communities and Local Government 2004, *Planning Policy Statement 22 Renewable Energy*, London.

Department for Communities and Local Government 2006, *Planning Policy Statement 25 Development and Flood Risk*, London.

Department for Communities and Local Government 2008, *PPS 12 Local Spatial Planning*, London.


**Creating environments that engage**
Cathryn Chatburn
Brundtland Commission 1987, *Our Common Future: Report of the World Commission on Environment and Development*, United Nations, viewed 8 July 2009, http://www.un-documents. net/wced-ocf.htm.

The Urban Task Force 1999, *Towards an Urban Renaissance*, Routledge, United Kingdom.


**Urban form and low-carbon buildings**
Lester Partridge, Jason Veale
Architecture 2030 2009, *The Building Sector: A Hidden Culprit*, Architecture 2030, viewed 1 July 2009, http://www.architecture2030.org/ current_situation/building_sector.html.

Australian Greenhouse Office 1999, *Australian Commercial Building Sector Greenhouse Gas Emissions 1990–2010,* Australian Government Department of the Environment, Water, Heritage and the Arts, viewed online 3 July 2009, http://www.environment.gov.au/ settlements/energyefficiency/buildings/ publications/pubs/commbuild.pdf.

Centre for International Economics 2007, *Capitalising on the building sector's potential to lessen the costs of a broad based GHG emissions cut*, Australian Sustainable Built Environment Council, viewed 2 July 2009, http://www.asbec.asn.au/files/Building-sector-potential_Sept13.pdf.

City of Sydney 2008, *Sustainable Sydney 2030 Vision*, City of Sydney, viewed 1 July 2009, http://www.cityofsydney.nsw.gov.au/2030/.

Department of Climate Change 2009, *National Greenhouse Gas Inventory: accounting for the KYOTO target*, Australian Government Department of Climate Change, viewed 1 July 2009, http://www.climatechange.gov.au/ inventory/2007/pubs/nggi_2007.pdf.

Levine, M., Ürge-Vorsatz, D., Blok, K., Geng, L., Harvey, D., Lang, S., Levermore, G., Mongameli Mehlwana, A., Mirasgedis, S., Novikova, A., Rilling, J., & Yoshino, H. 2007, 'Residential and commercial buildings', in Metz, B., Davidson, O.R., Bosch, P.R., Dave, R., & Meyer, L.A. (eds), *Climate Change 2007: Mitigation*, Contribution of Working Group III to the Fourth Assessment Report of the Intergovernmental Panel on Climate Change, Intergovernmental Panel on Climate Change, viewed 1 July 2009, http:// www.ipcc.ch/pdf/assessment-report/ar4/wg3/ ar4-wg3-chapter6.pdf.

McKinsey & Company 2008, *An Australian Cost Curve for Greenhouse Gas Reduction*, McKinsey & Company, Australia.

Myors, P., O'Leary, R. & Helstroom, R. 2005, *Multi Unit Residential Buildings Energy & Peak Demand Study, NSW Government BASIX,* viewed 3 July 2009, http://www.basix.nsw.gov. au/docs/multi/Multi_Unit_Energy_and_Peak_ Demand_Study.pdf.

Newman, P. 2006, *Transport Greenhouse Gases and Australian Suburbs: What Planners Can Do*, Garnaut Climate Change Review, viewed 3 July 2009, http://www. garnautreview.org.au/CA25734E0016A131/ WebObj/D0820912ResponsetoIssuePaper5-PeterNewman-TransportGreenhouseGasandA ustralianSuburbsPeterNewman/$File/D08%20 20912%20Response%20to%20Issue%20 Paper%205%20-%20Peter%20Newman%20 -%20Transport%20Greenhouse%20 Gas%20and%20Australian%20Suburbs%20 Peter%20Newman.pdf.

Nicol, F. & Pagliano, L. 2007, *Allowing for thermal comfort in free-running buildings in the new standard prEN15251*, Australian Energy Agency, viewed 3 July 2009, http://www.eva. ac.at/publ/pdf/keepcool_epic2.pdf.


**Measuring carbon performance and climate stable practice**
Steven Kellenberg, Honey Walters
Intergovernmental Panel on Climate Change 2007, *Climate Change 2007: Synthesis Report, Contribution of Working Groups I, II and III to the Fourth Assessment Report of the Intergovernmental Panel on Climate Change*, IPCC, Geneva, Switzerland.


**Water sensitive cities: a road map for cities' adaptation to climate and population pressures on urban water**
Professor Tony Wong
Brown, R. 2004, 'Local Institutional Development and Organisational Change for Advancing Sustainable Urban Water Futures', *Proceedings of the 3rd International Conference on Water Sensitive Urban Design: Cities as Catchments*, 21-25 November 2004, Adelaide, Australia.

Brown, R. and Clarke, J. 2007, *Transition to Water Sensitive Urban Design: The story of Melbourne*, report no. 07/1, Facility for Advancing Water Biofiltration, Monash University, Melbourne.

Clarke, J. and Brown, R. 2006, 'Understanding the factors that influence domestic water consumption within Melbourne', *Australian Journal of Water Resources*, vol. 10 (3), pp. 261-268.

## Transit-oriented development: land use and transportation planning in the context of climate change

José G. Mantilla, with a case study by Damien Pericles and Ann-Marie Mulligan

*José G. Mantilla wishes to thank Robert Armstrong for thoughtful comments on earlier drafts of this essay. He also thanks Professor John Whitelegg for insights on the interrelationship between transportation, environmental, and social systems.*

Abbot, C. 2002, 'Planning a Sustainable City: The Promise and Performance of Portland's Urban Growth Boundary', in Squires, G., *Urban Sprawl*, The Urban Land Institute, pp. 207-235.

Akerman, J. & Hojer, M. 2006, 'How Much Transport Can the Climate Stand? – Sweden on a Sustainable Path in 2050', *Energy Policy* vol. 34, pp. 1944-1957.

Arrington, G. & Cervero, R. 2008, 'Effects of TOD on Housing, Parking, and Travel', *Transit Cooperative Research Program Report 128*, Transportation Research Board, Washington, D.C., pp. 1-58, viewed 28 November 2008, http://onlinepubs.trb.org/onlinepubs/tcrp/tcrp_rpt_128.pdf.

Australian Green House Office 2003, *Australia's National Greenhouse Gas Inventory 1990, 1995 and 1999, End Use Allocation of Emissions,* Department of Climate Change, viewed 20 August 2008, http://www.climatechange.gov.au/inventory/enduse/index.html.

Australian Greenhouse Office 2006, *Global Warming: Cool It*, Department of the Environment and Heritage, Australian Government, Canberra.

Badland, H. & Schofield, G. 2005, 'Transport, urban design, and physical activity: an evidence-based update', *Transportation Research: Part D-Transport and Environment*, vol. 10(3), pp. 177-196, viewed 29 January 2009, http://cat.inist.fr/?aModele=afficheN&cpsidt=16849955.

Bartholomew, K. 2007, 'Land Use-Transportation Scenario Planning: Promise and Reality', *Transport*, vol. 34 (4), pp. 397-412, viewed 28 November 2008, *www.arch.utah.edu/bartholomew/fulltext.pdf.*

Bauman, A., Rissel, C., Garrard, J., Ker, I., Speidel, R., and Fishman, E. 2008, *Cycling: Getting Australia Moving: Barriers, facilitators and interventions to get more Australians physically active through cycling*, Cycling Promotion Fund, Melbourne.

Bureau of Transport and Regional Economics 2005, *Health impacts of transport emissions in Australia: Economic costs*, Working paper 63, Bureau of Transport and Regional Economics, Canberra, viewed 29 January 2009, http://www.bitre.gov.au/publications/94/Files/wp63.pdf.

Bureau of Transport and Regional Economics 2007, *Estimating urban traffic and congestion cost trends for Australian cities*, Working paper 71, Bureau of Transport and Regional Economics, Canberra, viewed 29 January 2009, http://www.bitre.gov.au/publications/49/Files/wp71.pdf

Cameron, I., Lyons, T. & Kenworthy J. 2004, 'Trends in Vehicle Kilometres of Travel in World Cities 1960-1990: Underlying Drives and Policy Responses', *Transport Policy*, vol. 11, pp. 287-298, viewed 28 November 2008, http://www.sutp.org/index.php?option=com_docman&task=doc_details&gid=289&Itemid=54&lang=uk.

Cervero, R. & Kockelman, K. 1997, 'Travel Demand and the 3Ds: Density, Diversity, and Design', *Transportation Research*, vol. 2 (D), pp. 199-219.

Cervero, R. 1998, *The Transit Metropolis*, Island Press, Washington, D.C.

Cervero, R., Murphy, S., Ferrell, C., Goguts, N., Tsai, Y., Arrington, G., Boroski, J., Smith-Heimer, J., Golem, R., Peninger, P., Nakajima, E., Chui, E., Dunphy, R., Myers, M., McKay, S. & Witenstein, N. 2004, 'Transit-Oriented Development in the United States: Experiences, Challenges, and Prospects', *Transit Cooperative Research Program Report 102*, Transportation Research Board, Washington, D.C. pp. 1-481, viewed 28 November 2008, http://onlinepubs.trb.org/onlinepubs/tcrp/tcrp_rpt_102.pdf.

Cervero, R. 2005a, *Accessible Cities and Regions: A Framework for Sustainable Transport and Urbanism in the 21st Century*, pp. 1-44, University of California Berkeley Center for Future Urban Transport, United States, viewed 28 November 2008, http://www.its.berkeley.edu/volvocenter/mobilityandaccessibility.html.

Cervero, R. 2005b, 'Progressive Transport and the Poor: Bogotá's Bold Steps Forward', *Access*, no. 27, pp. 24-30, viewed 15 January 2009, www.uctc.net/access/27/Access%2027%20-%2005%20-%20Progressive%20Transport%20and%20the%20Poor.pdf.

Cervero, R. 2007, 'Transit-Oriented Development's Ridership Bonus: A Product of Self-Selection and Public Policies', *Environment and Planning A,* vol. 39 (9), pp. 2068-2085, University of California Berkeley Center for Future Urban Transport, United States, viewed 28 November 2008, http://www.its.berkeley.edu/volvocenter/mobilityandaccessibility.html.

Cervero, R. and Day, J. 2008, *Residential Relocation and Commuting Behaviour in Shanghai, China: The Case for Transit Oriented Development*, pp. 1-31. UC Berkeley Center for Future Urban Transport, viewed 28 November 2008, http://www.its.berkeley.edu/volvocenter/mobilityandaccessibility.html.

City Mayors 2009, 'The Largest Cities in the World by Land Area, Population and Density', *City Mayors Statistics*, viewed 25 January 2009, http://www.citymayors.com/statistics/largest-cities-density-125.html.

Costello, D., Mendelsohn, R., Canby, A. &
Bender, J. 2003, *The Returning City: Historic
Preservation and Transit in the Age of Civic
Revival*, Federal Transit Administration,
National Trust for Historic Preservation,
Washington, D.C, viewed 28 November
2008, www.preservationnation.org/issues/
transportation/additional-resources/returning-
city-1.pdf.

Cullinane, C., 2002, 'The Relationship between
Car Ownership and Public Transport Provision:
A Case Study of Hong Kong', *Transport Policy*,
vol. 9, pp. 29-39.

Davis, S., Diegel, S. & Boundy, R. 2009,
*Transportation Energy Data Book: Edition
28,* Center for Transportation Analysis, Oak
Ridge National Laboratory, United States
Department of Energy, viewed 3 July 2009,
http://cta.ornl.gov/data/download28.shtml.

Davis, S., Diegel, S. & Boundy, R. 2008,
*Transportation Energy Data Book: Edition
27,* Center for Transportation Analysis, Oak
Ridge National Laboratory, United States
Department of Energy, viewed 28 November
2008, http://cta.ornl.gov/data/download27.
shtml.

Department for Environment, Food and Rural
Affairs 2008, *Guidelines to DEFRA's Greenhouse
Gas Conversion Factors for Company Reporting,*
Department for Environment, Food and Rural
Affairs, United Kingdom, viewed 27 November
2008, http://www.defra.gov.uk/environment/
business/envrp/conversion-factors.htm.

Dierkers, G. 2005, 'Land Use: Transit and Travel
Demand Management', *CCAP Transportation
Emissions Guide-Book*, Center for Clean Air
Policy, Washington D.C, viewed 28 November
2008, http://www.ccap.org/safe/guidebook/
guide_complete.html.

Energy Information Administration 2009,
*International Energy Outlook 2009*, Energy
Information Administration, United States,
viewed 3 July 2009, http://www.eia.doe.gov/
oiaf/ieo/index.html.

Energy Information Administration 2008,
*International Energy Outlook 2008*, Energy
Information Administration, United States,
viewed 26 November 2008, http://www.eia.
doe.gov/oiaf/ieo/index.html.

Estupiñán, N. & Rodríguez, D. 2008, 'The
Relationship between Urban Form and Station
Boardings for Bogotá's BRT', *Transportation
Research*, part A, vol. 42, pp. 296-306.

Ewing, R. and Cervero, R. 2001, 'Travel and the
Built Environment: A Synthesis', *Transportation
Research Record*, vol. 1780, pp. 87-114, viewed
28 November 2008, www.ce.berkeley.edu/~yuli/
ce259/reader/Ewing%20and%20Cervero%20
TOD.pdf.

Ewing, R., Pendall, R. & Chen, D. 2003,
'Measuring Sprawl and its Transportation
Impacts', *Journal of the Transportation
Research Board,* vol. 1832, pp. 175-183, viewed
28 November 2008, www.smartgrowthamerica.
org/sprawlindex/MeasuringSprawl.PDF.

Ewing, R., Bartholomew, K., Winkelman, J. &
Chen, D. 2008, *Growing Cooler. The Evidence
on Urban Development and Climate Change*,
The Urban Land Institute Washington D.C. pp.
1-170.

Feigon, S., Hoyt, D., McNally, L., Mooney-
Bullock, R., Campbell, S. & Leach, D. 2003,
'Travel Matters: Mitigating Climate Change
with Sustainable Surface Transportation',
*Transit Cooperative Research Program Report
93*, pp. 17-37, Transport Research Board,
Washington D.C, viewed 28 November 2008,
www.trb.org/publications/tcrp/tcrp_rpt_93.pdf.

Gilat, M. and Sussman J. 2003, 'Coordinated
Transportation and Land Use Planning in
the Developing World: Case of Mexico City',
*Transportation Research*, vol. 1859, pp. 102-
109.

Gilbert, A. 2008, 'Bus Rapid Transit: Is
TransMilenio a Miracle Cure?', *Transport
Reviews*, vol. 28, no. 4, pp. 439–467.

Goodwin, P. 1999, 'Transformation of Transport
Policy in Great Britain', *Transportation
Research*, vol. 33 (7/8), pp. 655-669.

Greene, D. & Schafer, A. 2003, *Reducing
Greenhouse Gas Emissions from United States
Transportation*, Pew Center on Global Climate
Change, United States, viewed *28 November
2008,* www.pewclimate.org/docUploads/
ustransp.pdf.

Gwilliam, K., Kojima, K. & Johnson, T. 2004,
*Reducing Air Pollution from Urban Transport*,
The World Bank, Clean Air Initiative, United
States, viewed 28 November 2008, www.
cleanairnet.org/cai/1403/articles-56396_
entire_handbook.pdf.

Holtzclaw, J. 2000, *Does A Mile In A Car Equal
A Mile On A Train? Exploring Public Transit's
Effectiveness In Reducing Driving*, Sierra
Club, United States, viewed 27 November
2008, www.sierraclub.org/sprawl/articles/
reducedriving.asp

Hook, W. 2003, 'Preserving and Expanding the
Role of Non-Motorised Transport', *Sustainable
Transport: A Sourcebook for Policy-makers in
Developing Cities*, GTZ, Eschborn, Germany,
viewed 10 January 2009, www.itdp.org/
documents/NMTmodule.pdf.

Hook, W. 2006, 'Urban Transportation and
the Millennium Development Goals', *Global
Urban Development*, vol. 2, issue 1, viewed 10
January 2009, http://www.globalurban.org/
GUDMag06Vol2Iss1/Hook.htm.

International Energy Agency 2008, *World
Energy Outlook,* International Energy Agency,
United States, viewed 26 November 2008,
http://www.worldenergyoutlook.org/2008.asp

Intergovernmental Panel on Climate Change
2007, *Transport and its Infrastructure
in Climate Change 2007: Mitigation of
Climate Change*, Working Group III Report,
Intergovernmental Panel on Climate Change,
Switzerland, viewed 26 November 2008, http://
www.ipcc.ch/ipccreports/ar4-wg3.htm.

Lundqvist, L. 2003, 'Multifunctional land Use
and Mobility', in Nijkamp, C., Rodenburg, A. &
Vreeker, R. *The Economics of Multifunctional
Land Use*, Vrije Universiteit, Amsterdam and
Habiforum, pp. 37-40.

Marshall, J. 2008, 'Energy-Efficient Urban Form. Reducing Urban Sprawl Could Play an Important Role in Addressing Climate Change', *Environmental Science & Technology*, May 1, American Chemical Society, pp. 3133-3137.

Mathers, C., Vost, T., & Stephenson, C. 1999, *The burden of disease and injury in Australia*, Australian Institute of Health and Welfare, Canberra, viewed 15 January 2008, http://www.aihw.gov.au/publications/health/bdia/bdia.pdf.

Metrovivienda 2009, viewed 27 January 2009, http://www.metrovivienda.gov.co.

Nelson, A. 2006, 'Leadership in a New Era', *Journal of the American Planning Association*, vol. 72 (4), pp. 393-407.

Newman, P. & Kenworthy, J. 1999, *Sustainability and Cities: Overcoming Automobile Dependence*, Island Press, Washington, D.C., pp. 442.

Norman, J., MacLean, H. & Kennedy, C. 2006, 'Comparing High and Low Residential Density: Life-Cycle Analysis of Energy Use and Greenhouse Gas Emissions', *Journal of Urban Planning and Development*, vol. 132, no. 1, March 2006, pp. 10-20.

NSW Premier's Council for Active Living 2007, *Why Active Living Statement*, Premier's Council for Active Living, New South Wales, viewed 20 January 2009, http://www.pcal.nsw.gov.au/__data/assets/file/0007/27646/active_living_statement.pdf

Rodríguez, D. & Targa, F. 2004, 'Value of Accessibility to Bogotá's Bus Rapid Transit System', *Transport Reviews*, vol. 24, no. 5, pp. 587-610.

Rodríguez, D. & Mojica, C. 2008, 'Land Value Impacts of Bus Rapid Transit: The Case of Bogotá's TransMilenio', *Land Lines*, April 2008, pp. 2-24, viewed 27 January 2009, www.planning.unc.edu/files/Land%20lines%20final.pdf.

Schafer, A. 2000, 'Regularities in Travel Demand: An International Perspective', *Journal of Transportation and Statistics*, vol. 3 (3), pp. 1-31, viewed 28 November 2008, http://ntl.bts.gov/lib/10000/10900/10907/1schafer.pdf.

Sperling, D. & Salon, D. 2002, *Transportation in Developing Countries: An Overview of Greenhouse Gas Reduction Strategies*, pp. 40, Pew Center on Global Climate Change, United States, viewed 28 November 2008 http://pubs.its.ucdavis.edu/download_pdf.php?id=327.

Stone, B., Mednick, A., Holloway, T. & Spak, S. 2007, 'Is Compact Growth Good for Air Quality?', *Journal of the American Planning Association*, vol. 73, pp. 404–418, viewed 26 November 2008, www.informaworld.com/ampp/siteindex?request=%2Findex%2F785038105.pdf.

TransMilenio 2009, viewed 27 January 2009, http://www.transmilenio.gov.co/WebSite/Default.aspx.

Turcotte, M. 2008, 'Life in Metropolitan Areas: Dependence on Cars in Urban Neighbourhoods', *Canadian Social Trends*, vol. 11, pp. 20-30.

United States Environmental Protection Agency 2006, *Air Emissions Summary through 2005*, United States Environmental Protection Agency, United States, viewed 26 November 2006, www.epa.gov/airtrends/2006/emissions_summary_2005.html.

United Nations 2008, *World Urbanisation Prospects: The 2007 Revision Population Database*, United Nations Department of Economic and Social Affairs, New York, viewed 26 November 2006, http://esa.un.org/unup/.

Vigar, G. 2002, *The Politics of Mobility: Transport, the Environment and Public Policy*, Routledge, United States.

Washington Metropolitan Area Transit Authority 2009, viewed 27 January 2009, http://www.wmata.com.

Willoughby, C. 2001, 'Singapore's Motorisation Policies: 1960-2000', *Transport Policy*, vol. 8, pp. 125-139.

World Business Council for Sustainable Development 2004, *Mobility 2030: Meeting the Challenges to Sustainability*, World Business Council for Sustainable Development, Switzerland, viewed 26 November 2008, http://www.wbcsd.ch.

## Economic and planning responses to climate change

Jasmin Abad, Ellen Nunez, Eli N. Pincus, Vivien Wu, Yang Fan, Chris Yoshii, and Jessie Zhang

Andrews, K. 2008, *Svalbard Global Seed Vault Opens in Norway*, Inhabitat, United States, viewed 6 March 2008, http://www.inhabitat.com/2008/03/06/svalbard-global-seed-vault-opens/.

Asian Development Bank 1998, *Handbook on Resettlement: Guide to Good Practice*, Asia Development, Philippines.

Asian Development Bank 2005, *Summary of Thanh Hoa Resettlement Plan for Central Region Water Resources Project (Not a Board Approved Document)*, Asian Development Bank, Philippines.

Atelier SOA 2006, 'Can you build a 100-acre farm in the middle of the metropolis?' *Buildings (ULI Info Pack)*, November 2006.

Bibby, D. 2008, *Climate Change Is Changing Where and How We Build*, Multi-Housing News, United States, viewed 14 August 2008, http://www.multihousingnews.com/multihousing/search/article_display.jsp?vnu_content_id=1003820479.

Broughton, J. 2008, 'Cost, Savings and Value: Construction Costs and Operating Savings of Green Buildings', *ULI Packet No. 3033: Costs and Benefits of Green/Sustainable Developments*, Urban Land Institute, United States.

Buildings 2008, www.buildings.com, Stamats Business Media, United States.

Cassidy, R. 2007, 'Editorial: Modest Proposal for Combating Climate Change', *Building, Design + Construction*, November 2007.

Chen, O. 2008, *Prefab Friday: Recycled Shipping Container Harbinger House, Lawrence Group's SG Block Container House*, Inhabitat, United States, viewed 26 September 2008, http://www.inhabitat.com/2008/26/09/Prefab-friday-recycled-shipping-container-harbinger-house.

Churchill, G. 2008, *Case Study: The Dalles Middle School*, Oregon Office of Energy, United States, viewed 15 August 2008, http://www.oregon.gov/ENERGY/CONS/school/docs/thedalles.pdf.

Cohen, R. 2008, *For Disaster IDPs: An Institutional Gap – Natural Disasters, Internal Displacement, Migration, Human Rights, Foreign Policy*, The Brookings Institution, Washington, D.C., viewed 4 August 2008, http://www.brookings.edu/opinions/2008/0808_natural_disasters_cohen.aspx.

Collins, A. & Watts, S. 2008, '*Pencilling Out Sustainability*', *Urban Land*, July 2008, pp. 96-100.

Cymbalsky, J. 1998, *The Importance of Location and Housing Type with Respect to Future Residential Sector Energy Use*, Energy Information Administration, United States, viewed 19 July 2008, http://www.eia.doe.gov/oiaf/archive/issues98/house.html.

Delaware Valley Green Building Council 2008, *The Plaza at PPL Center*, Delaware Valley Green Building Council, United States, viewed 10 August 2008, http://www.dvgbc.org/green_resources/case_studies/ppl/ppl_alt.html.

Despommier, D. 2008, 'The Vertical Farm: Skyfarming', *Urban Land* (July 2008), pp. 101-104.

Drummer, R. 2008, *REITs Buying into 'Green Premium'*, *ULI Packet No. 3033: Costs and Benefits of Green/Sustainable Developments*, Urban Land Institute, United States.

Eichholtz, P., Kok, N. & Quigley, J. 2008, *Doing Well By Doing Good? Green Office Buildings*, Program on Housing and Urban Policy, Working Paper Series, University of California, Berkeley.

Energy Information Administration 2004, 'Residential Energy Use – Energy Used in Households', *2001 Residential Energy Consumption Survey*, Energy Information Administration, United States, viewed 15 July 2008, http://www.eia.doe.gov/kids/energyfacts/uses/residence.html.

Energy Information Administration 2003, 'Commercial Energy Use', *2003 Commercial Buildings Energy Consumption Survey*, Energy Information Administration, United States, viewed 15 July 2008, http://www.eia.doe.gov/kids/energyfacts/uses/commercial.html.

Fahey, M. 2007, 'The Chicago Climate Exchange: Precursor of What's To Come?', *Urban Land*, September 2007, pp. 149-154.

Ferris, E. 2007, 'Making Sense of Climate Change Natural Disasters and Displacement: A Work In Progress', *5th Annual Winter Course on Forced Migration*, Kolkata, India, 1 December-15 December 2007

Finoki, B. 2008, *Prefab 4th of July Housing Beyond Borders*, Inhabitat, United States, viewed 7 April 2008, http://www.inhabitat.com/2008/07/04/happy-4th-prefab-friday-housing-beyond-borders/.

Frank, L., Kavage, S. & Appleyard B 2007, 'The Urban Form and Climate Change Gamble: How transportation and land development affect greenhouse gas emissions', *Planning*, August/September 2007.

Golan, M. 2008, 'Going Green Pays Off for Two Leading Businesses', *ULI Packet No. 3033: Costs and Benefits of Green/Sustainable Developments*, Urban Land Institute, United States.

Grubbs & Ellis 2007, 'Meeting the Carbon Challenge: The Role of Commercial Real Estate Owners, Users and Managers', *Insight Carbon Footprint*, April 2007, pp. 149-154.

Harvey, D. 2007, 'The New Urbanism and The Communitarian Trap', *Harvard Design Magazine*, Winter/Spring 1997.

Heggelund, G. 2006, 'Resettlement Programs and Environmental Capacity in the Three Gorges Dam Project', *Development and Change*, vol. 37(1), pp. 179-199.

Hirschborn, J. & Souza, P., *New Community Design to the Rescue: Fulfilling Another American Dream*, National Governors Association, Washington, D.C. viewed 5 August 2008, http://www.nga.org/Files/pdf/072001NCDFULL.pdf

Internal Displacement Monitoring Center 2007, *Internal Displacement: Global Overview of Trends and Developments in 2006*, Internal Displacement Monitoring Center, Switzerland, viewed 1 August 2008, http://www.internal-displacement.org/8025708F004BE3B1/(httpInfoFiles)/9251510E3E5B6FC3C12572BF0029C267/$file/Global_Overview_2006.pdf.

Jeffries, A. 2008, *Travelodge Hotel Made From Shipping Containers*, Inhabitat, United States, viewed 22 August 2008, http://www.inhabitat.com/2008/08/22/travelodge-shipping-container-hotel/.

Kalin, W. 2008, *The Climate Change Displacement Nexus*, Brookings Bern Project on Internal Displacement, Relief Web, New York, viewed on 5 August 2008, http://www.reliefweb.int/rw/rwb.nsf/db900SID/SKAI-7GNQV9?OpenDocument.

Kats, G. 2003, *The Costs and Financial Benefits of Green Buildings*, University of California, Berkeley, viewed 15 August 2008, http://www.usgbc.org/Docs/News/News477.pdf.

Kellenberg, S. & Schweitzer, J. 2007, *The Costs and Benefits of Sustainable Development, Developing Sustainable Planned Communities*, Urban Land Institute, Washington.

Lockwood, C. 2007, 'Regulating Sprawl', *Urban Land*, October.

Matthiessen, L. 2006, *Cost of Green Study 2006*, Davis, Langdon and Seah International, London.

McIlwain, J. 2008, 'Workforce Housing and Climate Change', *Urban Land*, February 2008.

McMahon, E. 2008, 'Climate Change and the Built Environment', *Urban Land*, June 2007.

Perrine, J. 2007, *Perrinepod*, Inhabitat, United States, viewed 10 August 2007, http://www.inhabitat.com/2007/08/10/prefab-friday-perrinepod/

Pew Center On Global Climate Change 2008, www.pewclimate.org.

Pilloton, E. 2007, *Shigeru Ban Paper Church*, Inhabitat, United States, viewed 30 July 2007, http://www.inhabitat.com/2007/08/10/prefab-friday-perrinepod/.

Pyke, C. 2008, *Green Buildings and Climate Change, Best Practice to Demonstrate Performance*, CTG Energetic Inc., viewed on 15 July 2008, http://www.ctg-net.com/content/upload/publications/2/pyke_usgbc_fed_summit_presentation_05-19-08.pdf.

Royal Institute of Chartered Surveyors 2008, *Green Value*, Royal Institute of Chartered Surveyors, United Kingdom, viewed 22 August 2008, http://www.rics.org/NR/rdonlyres/93B20864-E89E-4641-AB11-028387737058/0/GreenValueReport.pdf.

Srinivasan, R. 2008, *Operational Policy 4.12 Involuntary Resettlement*, The World Bank ECSSD, viewed 22 August 2008, http://siteresources.worldbank.org/INTECASAF/Resources/InvoluntaryResettlement.ppt#286,3,IMPACTSTHATTRIGGEROP4.12.

Steffen, B. 2008, *Living Walls Provide Local Produce*, Inhabitat, United States, viewed 20 August 2008, http://www.inhabitat.com/2008/08/20/green-living-technologies-green-walls-produce/.

Tarnay, S. & McMahon, E. 2005, 'Toward Green Urbanism' *Urban Land*, June.

The Climate Group 2008, *Case Studies*, The Climate Group, viewed 20 July 2008, http://www.theclimategroup.org/index.php/reducing_emissions/case-studies/.

The Observer 2006, 'Shanghai Plans Eco-Metropolis on its Mudflats', *The Observer*, 8 January 2008, The Guardian, United Kingdom, viewed 15 July 2008, http://www.guardian.co.uk/business/2006/jan/08/china.theobserver.

Thomson Reuters 2008, *Abu Dhabi's Masdar Initiative Breaks Ground on Carbon-Neutral City of The Future*, Thomson Reuters, New York, viewed 17 July 2008, http://www.reuters.com/article/pressRelease/idUS55436+09-Feb-2008+PRN20080209.

Urban Land Institute 2008, 'Climate Change and Real Estate, Selected References', *ULI Info Packet No. 3032*, April 2008, Urban Land Institute, Washington D.C.

Urban Land Institute 2008, 'Cost and Benefits of Green/Sustainable Development, Selected References', *ULI Info Packet, No. 3033*, April 2008, Urban Land Institute Washington D.C.

US Department of Housing & Urban Development and US Census Bureau 2006, *American Housing Survey for the United States 2005*, US Department of Housing and Urban Development and the US Census Bureau, United States, viewed 5 August 2008, http://www.census.gov/prod/2006pubs/h150-05.pdf.

US Green Building Council 2008, *Green Building Research*, US Green Building Council, United States, viewed 18 July 2008, http://www.usgbc.org/DisplayPage.aspx?CMSPageID=1718.

US Green Building Council 2008, *LEED for Neighbourhood Development*, US Green Building Council, viewed 18 July 2008, http://www.usgbc.org/DisplayPage.aspx?CMSPageID=148.

US Green Building Council 2008, *Seattle Justice Center*, US Green Building Council, viewed 18 July 2008, http://leedcasestudies.usgbc.org/overview.cfm?ProjectID=225.

Wiedmann, T. & Minx, J. 2007, *A Definition of Carbon Footprint*, Centre for Sustainability Accounting, United Kingdom, viewed 18 July 2008, http://www.isa-research.co.uk/docs/ISA-UK_Report_07-01_carbon_footprint.pdf.

World Resources Institute 2008, www.wri.org.

# Climate: designing a new future

### The era of the ecological metropolis
Stephen Engblom, Claire Bonham-Carter

**Photography**
Page 184, Aubrey Hake
Page 186, Dixi Carrillo
Page 188, Dixi Carrillo

## Afterword

### Working on the future now
Jason Prior

**Photography**
Page 198, David Lloyd
Page 200, Dixi Carrillo

## Contributors and sources

**Photography**
Page 202, Simon Kenny

## Index

**Photography**
Page 220, David Lloyd

# Index

# Index

ORO *editions*
Publishers of Architecture, Art, and Design
Gordon Goff – Publisher
USA: PO Box 998, Pt Reyes Station, CA 94956 USA
Asia: Block 8, Lorong Bakar Batu #02-04 Singapore 348743
www.oroeditions.com
info@oroeditions.com

Copyright © 2010 by ORO *editions*

ISBN: 978-0-9820607-1-1

AECOM
Project Directors: James Rosenwax, Stephane Asselin
Content Editor: Professor Peter Droege
Project Manager and Copy Editor: Kim Murphy
Editorial Team: Stephane Asselin, Daniel Elsea, Dr David Gallacher, Natasha Mavlian,
Kim Murphy, James Rosenwax
Production: Kim Murphy, Nicole Phillips
Graphic Designers: Nicole Phillips, with Nic Drummond, Peter Rudledge, Catherine Smith
Reviewers: Curtis Alling, David Blau, Mark Fuller, Fran Hegeler, Jacinta McCann

ORO *editions*
Graphic Designers: Sally Roydhouse and Davina Tjandra
Production: Joanne Tan
Color Separation and Printing: ORO *group* Ltd

ORO *editions* has made every effort to minimize the overall carbon footprint of this project.
As part of this goal, ORO *editions*, in association with Global ReLeaf, have arranged to plant
two trees for each and every tree used in the manufacturing of the paper produced for this
book. Global ReLeaf is an international campaign run by American Forests, the nation's
oldest nonprofit conservation organization. Global ReLeaf is American Forests' education
and action program that helps individuals, organizations, agencies, and corporations
improve the local and global environment by planting and caring for trees.

North American and International Distribution:
Publishers Group West
1700 Fourth Street
Berkeley, CA 94710
USA
www.pgw.com